Feminist Perspectives on Politics

FEMINIST PERSPECTIVES SERIES

Series Editors:

Professor Pamela Abbott, University of Teesside
Professor Claire Wallace, University of Derby and Institute for
Advanced Studies, Vienna

Published Titles:

Feminist perspectives on the body
Barbara Brook

Feminist perspectives on language
Margaret Gibbon

Feminist perspectives on ethics
Elizabeth Porter

Forthcoming Titles:

Feminist perspectives on postcolonialism
Maryanne Dever and Denise Cuthbert

Feminist perspectives on disability
Barbara Fawcett

Feminist perspectives on domestic violence
Laura Goldsack and Jill Radford

Feminist perspectives on environment and society
Beate Littig and Barbara Hegenbart

FEMINIST PERSPECTIVES SERIES

Feminist Perspectives on Politics

Chris Corrin

LONGMAN
London and New York

Pearson Education Limited
Edinburgh Gate
Harlow
Essex CM20 2JE
England
and Associated Companies throughout the world

Published in the United States of America
by Pearson Education Inc., New York

Visit us on the World Wide Web at:
http://www.awl-he.com

First published 1999

ISBN 0 582 35638 5

British Library Cataloguing-in-Publication Data

A catalogue record for this book is available from the British Library

Typeset by 35 in 10/12pt New Baskerville
Printed in Malaysia, PP

For Margaret, with love and thanks

Contents

Series Editors' Preface

The aim of the Feminist Perspectives series is to provide a concise introduction to different topics from a feminist perspective. The topics were chosen as being of interest for students on a range of different degree courses and in a range of different disciplines. They reflect the current interest in feminist issues and in women's studies in a wide range of fields. The series aims to provide a guide through the burgeoning and sometimes rather arcane literatures which have grown around various feminist topics. The texts are written by experienced teachers and academics providing lively and interesting accounts of topics of current interest. They include examples and case studies or statistical information where relevant in order to make the material more accessible and stimulating.

The texts contain chapter outlines and summaries for convenient, quick access. There are also suggestions for further reading.

We are especially pleased to have a text on Politics in the Feminist Perspectives series. Politics has been an area of special concern for feminists – indeed feminism is itself political. As Chris Corrin's text makes explicit, feminists have been concerned to demonstrate that the subordination of women by men is a political act. Furthermore they have demonstrated that not only has women's mainstream political activity been ignored in male-stream analysis but that much political activity by women has been seen as a concern with ethical or personal issues rather than political ones. Women have been portrayed as less concerned with politics than men and less able to be political. The outcome is that issues that are of concern to women are defined as not political and women are then said to be less interested in politics, less knowledgeable about politics and less adept at politics than men, and that issues which are of concern to women are seen as unimportant or trivial, or as moral rather than political.

Claire Wallace and Pamela Abbott

Preface

At the outset I decided I would write this book for my students, especially those taking Ordinary Politics, the first year course at Glasgow University. At the conclusion I realise I have written this book for myself, to better understand the connections I wish to make in studying and teaching politics from a feminist perspective. I am very grateful for the insights given from students over the years particularly those who have undertaken my courses on Feminist Thought and Political Theory and our Women's Studies courses.

In trying to achieve a wholeness within this book I realise that my understanding of politics, as actively trying to change injustice, centrally involves my feelings and thinking about politics. If there had been more space within this short book I would have been pleased to include some of the wonderful political poetry that feminists have written to support, sustain and 'sister' women. As Audre Lorde pointed out over 20 years ago:

> For women, then, poetry is not a luxury. It is a vital necessity of our existence. It forms the quality of the light within which we predicate our hopes and dreams toward survival and change, first made into language, then into idea, then into more tangible action. . . . As they become known to and accepted by us, our feelings and the honest exploration of them become sanctuaries and spawning grounds for the most radical and daring of ideas. They become a safe-house for that difference so necessary to change and the conceptualization of any meaningful action.
> (Lorde 1996: 96)

As is often the case, Audre manages to capture my thoughts, in the potential for change, which is the cornerstone of our actions.

Several friends and colleagues helped with this project in their willingness to read draft chapters, generally at short notice. I thank Chris Berry, Cordelia Ditton, Anita Franklin, Eleanor Gordon, Barbara Littlewood, Neeraj Malhotra, Julie Matthews and Susan Stewart. My thanks also go to Jeanette Berrie for her help in getting the typescript into a readable order. I would be very pleased to hear from anyone who wants to write any comments on this book.

Acknowledgements

We are grateful to the following copyright holders for permission to reproduce copyright material.

Table 1.1 reproduced with permission of Macmillan Press Ltd. from Hague, R., Harrop, M. and Breslin, S. (1992) *Comparative Government and Politics: An Introduction* Basingstoke: Macmillan, Table 7.1

Figure 4.1 reproduced with permission of New Internationalist © New Internationalist (1985) *Women: A World Report* London: Methuen, Fig. 1: Paid and Unpaid Work of Husbands and Wives

Table 8.1 reproduced with permission of the Inter-Parliamentary Union from Inter-Parliamentary Union (1997) *Men and Women in Politics: Democracy Still in the Making, A World Comparative Study* Geneva: IPU

Tables 8.2 and 8.3 reproduced with permission of the Inter-Parliamentary Union from IPU (1997) and http://www.ipu.org/wmn-e/world.htm

Figure 8.1 reproduced with permission of the authors from Gustafsson, G., Eduards, M. and Ronnblom, M. (1997) *Towards a New Democratic Order? Women's Organising in Sweden in the 1990s* Stockholm: Publica

Appendix 1 reproduced with permission of the Inter-Parliamentary Union from IPU (1997) and http://www.ipu.org/wmn-e/suffrage.htm

The Publisher has made every attempt to obtain permission to reproduce material in this book from the appropriate source. If there are any errors or omissions please contact the publisher who will make suitable acknowledgement in the reprint.

Chris Corrin
Politics Department,
Glasgow University.

Chapter 1

Feminist perspectives on politics

Chapter outline

This chapter aims to introduce the reader to some of the main aspects of feminist thinking about politics, raising key issues which are explored throughout the book. The plurality of **feminisms** is highlighted throughout, recognising that there can be no unitary 'feminism' but rather feminist perspectives which aim to unify ways of thinking and actions towards social change:

- feminist perspectives consider how different ways of thinking can affect what we see, what we 'know' and how we consider ideas about social and political change;
- ideas about **difference** are discussed, with relations between difference and **identity** seen as significant in raising questions about what women share in common;
- terms such as *social* **construction, essentialism** and **gender** are considered in relation to notions of femininity and masculinity;
- feminist examinations of political analyses and **activism** raise questions about **oppression** and **resistance** within relations of power, and recognition is given to overcoming binary divisions;

Introduction

Acknowledging the old adage that 'knowledge is **power**' this book is an attempt to add to existing work on feminist thinking and politics. It is recognised that: 'If knowledge and power go hand in hand, it is the responsibility of feminism both to acquire knowledge and to transform it' (Cameron and Frazer 1992). I am aware of the breadth of subjects considered within this book and view this as one part of a larger process, rather than a completed project. This work does not aim to answer all questions regarding feminisms and politics, but considers how different ways of thinking can affect what we see and how we view ideas about social and political change. The ideas I discuss are not new but their incorporation within the frame of feminist perspectives on politics aims to make some useful connections. Audre Lorde long ago pointed out that: 'there are no new ideas, just new ways of giving those ideas we cherish breath and power in our living' ('Sister Outsider' [1984] in Lorde 1996: 181). In this vein, bringing together feminist perspectives on politics in a holistic manner, I attempt to overcome some of the divisions between theory and practice that seem to endure strongly within much work on politics.

I believe passionately in the importance of learning – not just within formalised institutional education – but within our lives. Since much feminist thinking focuses on the consciousness, of how our experience can be used as a basis for theorising, it asks questions concerning the construction of knowledge. This in turn raises questions about how such knowledge can be built upon in creating social and political change. There is not a strong focus within this book on Women's Studies (WS). This is not because I do not consider WS an important area of feminist activism but because it is currently something of a 'growth industry' in terms of feminist publishing. As there are many comprehensive collections and anthologies on feminist perspectives in WS, I signal these, where relevant, in the text. As will be seen, feminisms challenge academic disciplines widely within an interdisciplinary context.

Considering feminist uses of the term *difference*, attention is paid to which groups are deemed to be different – who decides and why. It is necessary to be clear about which women are being considered, by whom and at which levels of political participation and activism. Obviously there are many differences among women in terms of age, **class**, non-disabled/**disabled**, **ethnicity**, **race**, **sexuality**, wealth and opportunity. Political analysts and policy-makers often do not make differentiations between women, so generalities in politics and policy literature have been challenged. Within academic thinking, understanding the relations between differences and identity has been significant in raising questions about what women share in common. This applies also to feminist theories, as some of the partial analyses of early feminist thinking labelled certain women as *other*, thereby centralising particular, essentialist notions of 'women'. In deconstructing such partial thinking, recognition is given in feminisms to the range of oppressions faced by **Black**, lesbian, disabled women, and 'Third World' women (the uses of these terms are explained in the Glossary and later chapters). Questions have also been tied in with feminist ideas about *belonging*, to groups, communities, 'sisterhoods', in coalitions and in collective resistance. In the varying responses and reflections, feminist strategies for resistance are elaborated.

Subordination of women

It is clear that images of women have been, and still are, very important in the development of feminist political thinking. Mary Wollstonecraft pointed out how stereotypical images, of women as weak and dependent, actively prejudiced women's life chances. The madonna/whore images of Victorian times presented working-class women, when not viewed as weak or dependent, as having 'unwomanly' sexual appetites. Angela Davis, and other critics, argue that Black women were not viewed as women at all and were treated more like animals than property, were not theorised about as people or as citizens (Davis 1982; Collins 1990; hooks 1989; Guy-Sheftall 1995). In colonial situations, images of White women in need of 'protection' against constructed threats from 'native' men were put forward to uphold **colonial** power structures (Stoler 1997). In all, the construct 'woman' is seen to change over time and in different situations. Considering constructs such as *woman*, **gender** and **race**, it is important to remember that these are also *lived experiences* so are not abstract terms. These issues are explored in many ways throughout the book.

The term *social construction of woman* refers to the feminist belief that women are not oppressed by being female (biologically) but by the social and cultural powers which generate notions of femininity. As we see, ideas and **ideologies** about *women* have been manufactured by male theorists in support of supposedly 'neutral' arguments about why women should remain subservient and not become full **citizens** exercising power. In Chapter 2 we find women barred from voting for all sorts of 'reasons', ranging from their lack of intelligence, to the 'fact' that politics is a male preserve and to the belief that *women are too good* for politics. Many of these arguments can be termed **essentialist**, in that they categorise women on the basis of biological assumptions. The actions and arguments of suffragists and other feminists have challenged these notions of women as less than men.

Feminist thinking highlights the whys and wherefores of how women come to be subordinated. Anne Phillips notes that subordination identifies *the agents in the process* of forces that combine to oppress women: 'Women don't just happen to have less than men; they are actively subordinated by the holders of power' (1987: 1). Feminisms considers the cultural, economic, social and political processes through which women's subordination is established and reproduced. The relations of subordination and oppression have been given different emphases in debates over time as Stevi Jackson argues:

> Certainly within Western societies, feminists have addressed three key questions: How is male dominance sustained? How are gender differences constituted? How do we make sense of the diversity of women's experiences arising from differences of class, race or sexuality amongst us? These interrelated issues of dominance, difference and diversity have been the subject of considerable debate.
>
> (Jackson 1993: 3)

Although much discussion has ensued in feminist circles regarding the term *gender* I use it to refer broadly to the social 'roles' that are overlaid on to biological attributes of men and women. One example is that while only women can bear and suckle children, men and women can care for children. However, women have generally been viewed as being childcarers, and the terms *mother* and *father* have different inscriptions of care, duty and responsibility. The stereotypes of 'man the breadwinner' and 'woman the carer' have proved very difficult to remove from much social and political thinking and policy-making. The legacies of such thinking can still structure many women's opportunities today (see Chapters 8 and 9).

In considering feminist perspectives of women's experiences and how such experiences have been constructed and reflected upon, recognising structural links between oppressions is significant. The term feminisms is also significant. As a plural term it shows that feminist thinking is not one body of thought. In the many strands of expression which make up feminisms lie much of the strength of the arguments. As Dale Spender recognises:

> Feminists, therefore, have had to break with the conventions in which they were reared, and come to terms with the possibility that *there is more than one truth.* . . . it is one of the reasons why there are not – and cannot be – any 'official' explanations for feminism . . . Instead there is a multiplicity of interpretations . . . an acceptance – in varying degrees – of the coexistence of diverse and even contradictory explanations. A feminist framework which took women's experience of the world as central could hardly go any other way.
>
> (Spender 1985: 25–26)

Some feminists have argued against theory and rationality altogether, viewing them as masculine mechanisms used to oppress women (Daly 1978). Others propose that we need different tools and methodologies to deconstruct masculinist thought (Lorde 1996 [1984]). For some feminist thinkers, theory is viewed as unnecessary in mediating experience and knowledge, as women's experience constitutes the most suitable basis for generated knowledge (Stanley and Wise 1983). Much feminist thinking has been constantly challenged by major debates between liberal, radical and socialist thinkers, between Black and 'Third World' women and White feminists, lesbians and non-lesbians as well as by discussions between disabled and non-disabled feminists. These debates are explored throughout the book.

Feminist criticism

In aiming to provide an introduction to relationships between political thinking and social and political change, the emphasis is on how feminist considerations have criticised, and continued to develop, *political writing* and *practices.* From the early liberal and radical thinkers of the eighteenth and nineteenth century, examples of resistance to oppressive ways of thinking can be seen. It is within this context that aspects of conventional political debates are considered. In challenging the terms of debate, feminist critiques have broadened considerations of politics and political participation (Coole 1994 [1988]; Eisenstein 1984; hooks 1984; Hull *et al.* 1982; Pateman 1988; Phillips 1987; Randall 1987). Feminist thinking and women's political activities generate new perspectives on politics. By uniting feminist criticism of politics with instances of the practical involvement in groups, movements and societies, feminist analysts actively intervene to create change. Just as for Karl Marx: 'Philosophers so far have only interpreted the world, the point is to change it' (Tucker 1978), for feminists, **praxis**, the belief in uniting theory and practice through action, has significance. Kum-Kum Bhavnani defines politics as: 'the means by which human beings regulate, attempt to regulate and challenge, with a view to changing unequal power relationships' (Bhavnani 1993). Inevitably feminism involves thinking about women's oppression and subordination and ways of creating change – individually, collectively and specifically.

In assessing the depth of men's need to ensure their **privileged** position, it has been realised that some feminist analyses have only partially reflected upon the ways in which feminist thinking shared elements of privilege retention. In this way recognition of power imbalances in feminist thinking about who was naming whom as 'different' became evident. One consequence of partiality and prejudice within education can be that the 'perceived problems' are considered in such a way that they become 'other' and outside general academic **discourse**. The interdisciplinary impact of feminisms on the academic world is apparent in that 'feminist enquiries into gendered power structures cannot be contained within any one traditional aspect of learning' (Frazer *et al.* 1992: 3). In this connection Rossi (1974: 620) argues that one feature of the 1920–1960 period in the USA was the vast expansion of higher education and the professions in which: 'a particular set of values was held among scholars and intellectuals. It was a period of academic specialization of knowledge . . . the underlying assumption in scholarship was one of value neutrality.' It is precisely the assumed 'neutrality' and 'objectivity' of such values that feminist thinking critiques. Humm concludes that modern feminism: 'dramatically reconceptualises knowledge itself, which academic feminism reflects in new institutional practices (women's studies). Altered understanding about gender have emerged in a number of disciplines' (1992: 56).

Viewing the politics of domination and resistance through the lens of feminist analysis widens the examination of political analysis and activism. By thinking through various relations of power, binary oppositions are recognised and contextualised within the systems of power which oppress individuals and groups. These binaries range from issues of male/female sexism, White/Black racism, straight/gay heterosexism to non-disabled/disabled prejudice and beyond. Such divisions are questioned by feminist analyses and the power politics within them are exposed. This has not been a linear progression as will be seen. Power is an important concept in politics. Our experiences of power can be positive and negative, individual and systematic. It is useful to make distinctions between uses of power – to control others or to extend power and 'empower' people. Given the aims of feminisms in wishing to prevent particular misuses/uses of power and to end certain unbalanced power relations, concern with issues of how power is understood are central. In this context Anna Yeatman considers the ambiguous relationship of feminism to concepts of power and distils three strands: 'power as coercion; power as protection; and power as capacity' (Shanley and Narayan 1997: 145). These aspects of power run through many streams of feminist thinking and recur throughout this book.

One major use of coercive power in societies has been to 'normalise' or legitimise women's subordination. In recognising the use and abuse of coercive power, as part of our daily lives, various feminist theories have been developed to attempt strategic interventions within politics. These cover a range of feminist arguments, such as: unless society is radically restructured then working within existing structures is hopeless (Hartsock 1981); until the realities of Black people's historical experience is recognised racism cannot be challenged (Davis 1982); laws must be changed to 'outlaw' the power of sexual violence such as pornography (MacKinnon 1982); and arguing for a recognition of the power of the erotic (*Sister Outsider* (1984) in Lorde 1996). In a recent rethinking of her work on power Nancy Hartsock quotes Lorde's 'important advice' on issues of 'difference' so that 'intersecting axes of domination' can be further considered (Hirschmann and Di Stefano 1996: 44–45). This self-reflection and revisioning are key aspects of feminist analysis.

For Bhavnani (1993) the word feminism 'retains a vision of *all* women challenging sexualised, gendered, racialised and economic control over our lives through ideology and politics'. By analysing interlocking aspects of oppression and resistance and attempting to disentangle historical complexities, Black feminist thought, lesbian theorising and writings by disabled feminists encompass a range of women's histories and perspectives on politics in assessing holistic and inclusive ways of working towards political change. This manner of reflection moves debates forward to encompass *alternative* ways of thinking and to highlight various ways of creating change. Some feminist networks and campaigns act to build upon this knowledge to develop political change which is positive for all oppressed groups. It is important to recognise that positive change for marginalised groups can detract from the privileges and powers of other individuals and groups (women and men). In practice, resistance to feminist change is apparent across many political systems as it generally undermines a 'status quo', from which many men (and some women) benefit.

Patriarchy and power relations

In terms of its usefulness in analysing the systematic organisation of women's oppression, the term **patriarchy** has been much debated. Originally this term was associated with 'the rule of the father' but feminists broadened its use to cover other aspects of male domination. It was certainly significant in feminist theorising from the 1960s, encouraging various theoretical shifts and innovations in ways of thinking about women's oppression. For Marxist feminists the recognition that patriarchy and capitalism were twin motors of women's oppression allowed extensive revisions and new constructions in conflict analysis. For radical feminists the breach with existing theorising was revolutionary in their belief that all previous theory was patriarchal and therefore not redeemable. In considering the politics of how patriarchal relations of power differ within and across societies, Adrienne Rich notes that patriarchy is:

> a familial–social, ideological, political system in which men by force, direct pressure, or through ritual, tradition, law, and language, customs, etiquette, education, and the division of labor, determine what part women shall or shall not play and in which the female is everywhere subsumed under the male.
>
> (Rich 1977: 57)

In her work Rich emphasises the difficult reality of male control under patriarchy, as it permeates everything, including how we speak and think of our selves. Such systems of control are not inevitable and cannot be defended. Analyses of patriarchy have shown the potent destabilising force that feminism can become when challenges are made to the core of our personal lives as political. In challenging politics as *relations of power* within our lives, feminist critiques caused people to consider all forms of relationships as political and therefore able to be criticised and changed. The phrase 'the personal is political' is used in such contexts to emphasise the breadth of political realities and how these can be analysed and changed. For Zillah Eisenstein the public/private split is vital in this regard:

> The division of public and private life as one that differentiates the woman (private) from the man (public) is the overarching ideological tool of patriarchy . . . Patriarchy is ultimately the politics of transforming females and males (biological sex) into women and men (politicized gender), while differentiating the woman from the man by privileging the man.
>
> (Eisenstein 1984: 16–17)

Here we see the divisions of public/private and sex/gender challenged within an analysis of power and privilege. The ways in which feminists have analysed women's oppression under *capitalist patriachy* is further considered in Chapter 4.

Defining 'the political'

In conventional definitions of *politics* and *political science* in the UK and the USA the conceptual framework of empiricism became dominant during the 1950s. This meant a preference for 'objectivity' and a confirmation of the nature of politics as concerned with specific *structures* and *external events* rather than everyday life. In attempting to understand why political science has been so male-dominated, feminist writers outline how such definitions are themselves political (Bryson 1992; Coole 1994 [1988]; Lovenduski and Hills 1981; Mohanty et al. 1991; Randall 1987). The focus of political thinking on conventional political behaviour clearly reflected the views of those who held them.

With feminist political criticism a shift can be seen from traditional thinking about politics as concerned solely with structures, functions and activities to feminist views of politics as the working out of **power relations**. Vicky Randall outlines two main and contrasting views (1987: 10):

1 **traditional** – politics as an *activity*. It is the conscious, deliberate participation in the process by which resources are allocated amongst citizens;

Feminity view s 'the Alternat'

2 **alternative** – politics as a process of *articulation,* a working out of relationships within an already-given power structure.

In this way it is not just the business of government – political parties, elections, voters and government policies – that is political, it is also the politics of people's lives – family, ethnicity, gender, disability, sexuality, upbringing, class and so on.

Feminist analysts do focus on women's **participation** in public politics and the impact of policy-making on women to explain how women influence and are affected by the social allocation of resources. It is the arena of this focus, broadened to include sexual politics (issues of resistance to male violence against women, the politics of reproductive health and sexuality) that becomes the focal point of analysis. In challenging structured power frameworks some feminists highlight sexual difference, while others view politics as 'above sex'. Arguing from both perspectives Anne Phillips notes: 'I regard the emphasis on sexual differentiation as necessary, but transitional, for I do not want a world in which women have to speak continuously as women – or men are left to speak as men' (Phillips 1991: 7). More specifically, in the context of **citizenship**, the expectation is participation of people as equals deciding common goals.

Political participation

One definition of political participation is: 'Those legal activities by private citizens which are more or less directly aimed at influencing the selection of government personnel and/or the actions they take' (Nie and Verba 1972). The emphasis here on legal and independent activity makes this definition too narrow. Various wider questions as to the nature of participation need to be asked. In assessing participation in terms of electoral turnout, what knowledge is gained of party and group membership and participation in community activities? Do women's ways of participation 'fit' into such conventional definitions of political participation? How does this view account for participation within new social movements? Are conceptions of citizenship gendered? In short, the above definition is inadequate because it excludes attitudes towards, and beliefs about, politics and the ways in which people negotiate aspects of civic activity generally.

The 'private' citizen in such a definition exemplifies the traditionalist view that excludes sexual politics and familial activities (Jaggar 1983; Lorde 1996 [1984]; Phillips 1987; Pateman 1988; Collins 1990; Nye 1988). Such narrow definitions are too limited for analysts who accept the modern definitions of politics, which feminisms have pioneered, as affecting not only the actions and decisions of governments, state forces and elected representatives, but also political interactions in societies, communities and our homes. There are tensions within democratic theories concerning a number of political principles and practices traditionally viewed as being concerned with participation – voting, electoral representation and political equality. In conventional views of political participation, distinctions have been made between voluntary participation, regimented participation and personal manipulation (Hague *et al.* 1992: 156–7). Feminist studies have pointed out the various misunderstandings of women's participation contained within much conventional literature (Norris 1986; Githens *et al.* 1994).

'New' politics

From the 1960s, in the wake of the questioning of 'old' style politics, the scope of political participation was greatly extended. A 'new' politics was to emerge with activism in the Black Civil Rights movements in the USA extending into Black Power politics. With these activities and developments in youth politics and involvement in anti-war demonstrations there emerged a flowering of a radicalism which broke with conventional political participation. Table 1.1 attempts to illustrate some of the major differences between 'new' and 'old' style politics.

Key differences between traditional citizen's rights groups and the new social movements concerned not only the political aims of each, but the ways in which politics is practised. One example of this was the move from the citizens' rights demands of the early Black civil rights groups to the Black Power arguments arising in the 1960s which challenged racist stereotyping and exploitation and supported positive **Black** identities. In this way the latter group moved beyond civil rights as defined by dominant ideas and extended their politics to include issues of ethical values, culture and identity.

Table 1.1 Old and new politics

	Old politics	New politics
Attitude to political system	Supportive	Critical
Vehicle of participation	Parties	Single-issue groups
Style of participation	Orthodox	Unconventional
Concerns	Interests	Values
Motives	Instrumental	Expressive
Typical age	Middle-aged	Younger
Gender balance	Male-dominated	Balanced

Source: Hague *et al.* 1992: 161 (gender balance added by author).
Reproduced courtesy of Macmillan Press Ltd.

In the newer social movements stress is on grass-roots involvement against elitist, hierarchical, bureaucratic ways of working. Issues developed within new social movements tended to be interconnected – such as the linking of the proliferation of nuclear weapons/power with environmental degradation. Different ways of 'doing' politics were also apparent in the small non-hierarchical groups which rotated tasks and chose consensus over voting and collective working over centralised leadership. Strong moral and ethical convictions underlay the 'new' political demands and goals, and debate was extended beyond Cold War ideological distinctions of left and right, stressing universal principles and consequences (Offe 1985; Melucci 1988; Tatur 1992; Hall 1995). These 'expressive values' noted above can be seen in contrast to the 'instrumental interests' of orthodox politics. The moral imperatives in political life were very much apparent in oppositional writings in Central and Eastern Europe in the 1980s (Havel *et al.* 1985; Konrad 1984; Keane 1988).

Feminist challenges

With this resurgence of new forms of activism in many contexts, including feminism, during the 1960s, it became apparent that feminist criticism could pierce the core of conventional readings of political science. Yet, feminist interpretations have become accepted into 'malestream' thinking (O'Brien 1981) unevenly and with much disagreement and debate. That there are contradictions between various feminist interpretations is inevitable and enriching.

Before the development of feminist criticism, women's activities were included within a male 'norm' of politics. In viewing politics as involving a dynamic process of articulation (see discussion on Randall above, pp. 9–10) feminists challenged the idea of boundaries which separated politics from social life generally. This meant that the politics of the family or the politics of reproduction could be studied in the same way as the politics of elections (Corea 1985; Millett 1970; Malos 1980; Rich 1977). As nothing constituted a separated politics from everday life, arguments concerning public and private spheres took on added significance. Aspects of these critical ideas were apparent in the arguments of Mary Wollstone-craft (A *Vindication on the Rights of Woman* 1992 [1792]) and of John Stuart Mill (*On The Subjection of Women* 1983 [1869]). Each of these thinkers argued that women should not be confined to a private world without access to public, civic life. Yet each, and particularly Mill, clung to the liberal belief in the need for separation.

What is feminist theorising?

Before the 1960s, issues of women's individual and collective social and political interests, and women's self-determination were discussed by feminists within the conventional limits of 'the political'. When these traditional constraints were seriously challenged a much more comprehensive debate on the politics of women's lives became possible. In particular, the various tensions between liberal views on public/private distinctions and between notions of equality and of difference came to the surface. Since the second half of the twentieth century, feminists across the globe have been challenging aspects of political 'knowledge' and practice, using feminist methods and drawing upon the strength of their own experience. For many feminists these arguments are concerned with solidarities from feminist standpoints together with the celebration of identities which include women's various strengths, and opportunities to form coalitions (Brah 1996; Lorde 1996; Reagon 1983).

To describe how feminist knowledge can be constructed we can state that feminist theorising:

1 is based upon women's experiences
2 considers how such experiences have been constructed
3 reflects upon the power relations present

4 builds upon the knowledge gained in order to consider changes in ways of thinking and to challenge collectively social and political injustice

The above is by no means an exhaustive outline of feminist theorising but I use it in what follows as a basis to separate out various strands for analysis, which in reality are very much interrelated. Each of these elements are apparent in various guises within feminist critiques of conventional political theory and participation. In considering these various aspects the interrelations become apparent.

Theorising from experience

Basing theory upon experience was not discovered with feminism, yet within feminist analysis the recognition that 'the personal is political' takes on very different perspectives for various reasons. In privileging women's experience feminisms emphasise how our life experiences inform our politics and are informed by politics. This does not mean that 'experience' is the only means of analysis, but it does recognise women as *subjects* and as *agents of change*. In breaking down public/private distinctions and extending the political in our lives, the complexity of attempting to understand relations between politics and aspects of women's lives becomes more apparent.

Construction of experience – power relations

Twentieth-century feminist analyses focus upon *difference* and *equality* in various ways. In Chapters 2 and 3 many of the arguments proposed by feminist thinkers are concerned with proving women's *equality* with men. As we see, in women's liberation politics, issues of power are considered in terms of women's difference from men and of differences between women. The use of the key theoretical tool of patriarchy made conceptualising women's difference from men easier as it enabled feminist thinkers to focus on women's specific exploitation. One example is that while capitalism oppressed men and women it did not oppress them in the same way. Women were exploited in workplace relations and within the home. Patriarchal *relations of power* could be looked to for ways to analyse women's specific exploitation. In considering *differences among women* it is recognised that early White feminisms were constructing their theories within a White, middle-class, heterosexual framework in which 'other' women, who differed from this norm, were considered to be 'different'. In challenging this, Black feminists reintroduced issues of power and domination. 'Black' and 'White' cannot be seen as just 'different' because the latter are in *structural* relation of domination over the former. That is, Black people historically have been oppressed by the dominant White systems of power. Such oppression continues today in various forms and is discussed in subsequent chapters.

Within this questioning, issues of power relations remain central in challenging oppression through such (often interlocking) systems of power relations embedded in racism, heterosexism and ablism. Important in this context is the recognition that feminist analyses are not merely concerned with reflecting upon women's experience as recounted, but considering how these experiences have been *constructed*. A good example of a social construction of 'woman' is given by a former slave Sojourner Truth in asking 'Aren't I a Woman?' in Chapter 5.

Questions of power relations are embedded in considerations of oppression. In considering people's experience of oppression Audre Lorde points out that there can be no order of dominance. For example, in various situations, for some women their experience of racism cannot easily be separated from their experiences of sexism, heterosexism or ablism.

> I have learned that sexism (a belief in the inherent superiority of one sex over all others and thereby the right to dominance) and heterosexism (a belief in the inherent superiority of one pattern of loving over all others and thereby its right to dominance) both arise from the same source as racism – a belief in the inherent superiority of one race over all others and thereby its rights to dominance.
>
> (Lorde 1993: 17)

None of these experiences can be seen as more important than others. They are indicators of oppressive power relations and how patterns of dominance shift over time and in various situations.

Building upon feminist knowledge

Following from considerations of how women's experiences are constructed and within what systems of power relations, feminist thinkers continue to analyse their role in the process of building knowledge from their own and other women's experiences. This involves critically examining the ideas and beliefs on which theories and particularly Western 'traditions' have been founded. An example from Zillah Eisenstein considers the liberal roots of North American feminism explaining that:

> Until a conscious differentiation is made between a theory of individuality that recognizes the importance of the individual within the social collectivity and the ideology of individualism that assumes a competitive view of the individual, there will not be a full accounting of what a feminist theory of liberation must look like in our Western society.
>
> (Eisenstein 1984: 5)

Another example, that Elizabeth Spelman discusses, is in terms of the formulation of much Western feminist thought: 'we should be sceptical about any claim that theories constructed by and for one group of women will automatically enlighten (rather than deeply mislead) us about all women's lives' (Spelman 1988: 9). So, whilst considerations of how to speak collectively about certain issues and needs are fundamental to much feminist activism, recognising specific contexts and unique identities highlights the complexities and contradictions apparent in such undertakings. Sensitivity, respect and stamina are key ingredients of all collective endeavours.

Theory and practice

Feminisms are concerned with social and political change as well as developing analyses of politics and society. The term *praxis* is often used to denote the combination of theory and practice through action. By thinking through why women are oppressed, feminists work to change the conditions which give rise to that oppression, reflect upon any changes that are made and begin again to consider any new relations which are developed. This can be seen as a form of dialectic with the *thesis* proposed that women for example deserve to be able to vote in government elections. After examining the reasons put forward by conservative thinkers, feminists proposed an *antithesis*, showing that this reasoning was poor and was not valid. They agitated in many, varied ways to protest about this injustice. Eventually women gained the right to vote and then feminists began to reflect upon this *synthesis*, as to what gains this gave them. In turn, it was proposed that gaining the vote was only a *very first step* towards women's liberation so the *synthesis* in turn becomes another *thesis*. The thesis of what was needed for women's full liberation has taken much exploration.

Feminist thinking generally attempts to overcome the crude divisions between theory and practice, viewing them as parts of a whole. This does not mean that feminists do not consider theorising important, but their critiques are generally of the ways in which this is carried out, on what premises and for what purposes. Theories based on partial aspects of our lives can cause misunderstanding and generate misleading 'knowledge'. In the context of understanding the need for connection, Audre Lorde maintains that:

> my fullest concentration of energy is available to me only when
> I integrate all the parts of who I am, openly, allowing power
> from particular sources of my living to flow back and forth freely
> through all my different selves, without the restriction of externally
> imposed definition.
>
> (*Sister Outsider* [1984] in Lorde 1996: 120–121)

Here Lorde is highlighting the powerful impact of the holistic aspects of feminist thinking in being able to acknowledge our selves without compartmentalising 'bits' of experience. We are then able to turn our attention to whatever it is we wish to consider.

It is the reconceptualisation through feminisms of political ideas and actions that informs this book. As noted I use the term 'feminisms' because there can be no unitary 'feminism'. Feminist analysis is not a monolithic unity, but rather it attempts to unify ways of thinking and action towards social change. In analysing certain thinkers, and the movements with which their ideas were involved, consideration is given largely to UK and US sources. This is mainly because of my decision to limit discussion to English language sources. Within this is a recognition that before the twentieth century only very few individuals and groups left 'source' evidence because they had access to preserving their work through publication and/or public discussion. Many feminist political figures over the centuries have had neither the access nor the social positioning to enable their arguments to be widely received or seriously considered. As a former slave speaking out, Sojourner Truth was treated by some as a 'curiosity', but at least her words were preserved (Guy-Sheftall 1995; hooks 1984). Many politically active women did not have access to an education or 'free' time that would provide them with opportunities to enable them to reflect on the implications of the connections between their oppression and their resistance. In cases when political women did attempt to speak their truths the climate of oppression was often such that they were not given the chance to be heard.

Summary

• Feminist thinking criticises traditional definitions of politics and shifts the focus from politics as concerned with external events to considerations of relations of power in our everyday lives.

• With extended feminist interpretations including sexual politics and an emphasis on 'the personal as political' we see different assessments of women's political participation.

• Feminist analysis questions how knowledge is constructed. This raises questions about how knowledge can be built upon to create social and political change.

• The relationship between knowledge and power is a crucial feminist issue and feminist analyses have critiqued 'malestream' constructions of knowlege, challenging many areas of thinking across social sciences, arts and sciences.

• Feminist ideas about politics consider how and where women can engage on behalf of women's rights and women's liberation.

• Issues concerning relations between identity and difference are significant in questioning what it is that women share in common.

Further reading

Ang-Lygate, M., Corrin, C. and Henry, M. (eds) (1997) *Desperately Seeking Sisterhood: Still Challenging and Building* London: Taylor and Francis

Humm, M. (1992) *Feminisms: A Reader* Hemel Hempstead: Harvester Wheatsheaf

Lorde, A. (1996) *The Audre Lorde Compendium* introduced by Alice Walker, London: Pandora

Randall, V. (1987) *Women and Politics: An International Perspective* Basingstoke: Macmillan, 2nd edn 1994

Chapter 2

Liberal feminist debates and activism

What is now called the nature of women is an eminently arti-ficial thing – the result of forced repression in some directions, unnatural stimulation in others.
J.S. Mill *On the Subjection of Women* 1983 [1869]

Hopelessly ignorant of politics, credulous to the last degree and flickering with gusts of sentiment like candles in the wind.
Asquith's view of women 1920 (Banks 1981: 125)

Chapter outline

In this chapter consideration is given to the development of liberal debates regarding women's place in society and women's rights – to education, to equality in politics, for the vote – and to women's politics aimed at achieving these and other various goals. In considering Wollstonecraft's writing, women's self-images are important, in that they are seen not as subjects but as objects or functionaries. Primary themes arise regarding:

- the nature of citizenship – in what ways was it gendered? How do facts of gender affect the meaning of such ethical concepts as rights, justice, duty, virtue, pleasure, guilt and shame?
- beliefs about 'public man' and 'private woman' in the construction of knowlege and political life;
- questions of morality, particularly with regard to the importance of women's sexual reputation;
- issues of slavery and colonial politics within debates regarding equality, **liberalism**, suffrage and citizenship.

Introduction

Here, and in Chapter 3, I consider the liberal and socialist political traditions – their debates, campaigns and the social and political changes arising from these. The histories of these two streams of thinking and means of mobilisation are intertwined throughout the nineteenth and twentieth centuries. The developments in political structures and social movements of nineteenth-century Europe, North America and Australasia have been characterised as the era of 'bourgeois liberalism' (Evans 1977); with the later part of the nineteenth century the era of 'high' imperialism (Midgley 1998; Waylen 1996). The nineteenth century was very much a time of political ferment with a groundswell of conflicting ideas competing in an arena of increasing political activism, not least on the part of women. Liberal feminist debates and campaigns are important in the development of feminisms in various guises into the twentieth century and I discuss them mainly in a British context within a comparative frame. Imperial feminism in Britain is considered, with its ongoing impact and challenges regarding racism forming themes throughout the book. Some of the impacts of imperialist developments in colonised countries are assessed in their gendered context. In this way it is possible to see how the eclipse of Western women's emancipation movements after the Second World War prepared the ground for some of the more nuanced debates on politics, feminism and women's liberation in the second half of the twentieth century. The most important aspects of such debates have hinged precisely on the necessity to include both specificity and difference in analyses of politics and gender. Different aims, expectations and opportunities have arisen for different groups of women over time. In focusing mainly on nineteenth- and early twentieth-century liberal projects in which there was much overlap with revolutionary developments (considered in Chapter 3), the dual aspect of arguing for women's equality with, and women's difference from, men is apparent. The limitations of liberal arguments as a basis for feminist ideas in creating radical social and political change are also emphasised. Key writers such as Wollstonecraft, Mill and Taylor are considered alongside the various movements which used their writings (and that of others) as cornerstones for campaigns. Changing conceptions of women's equality and difference become apparent throughout these debates and campaigns, forming the basis of multiple legacies bequeathed to feminist thinking and campaigns in the later twentieth century.

Background

Ideas concerning women and citizenship have been around since Plato and Aristotle were considering the ideal city-state (polis) in the fourth century BC (Coole 1994 [1988]). Western philosophy since then has generally viewed women as less than men, as imperfect or incomplete versions of the real (male) citizen. Feminist arguments reject ideas of male superiority arguing that the basis of such theorising is faulty. The dualistic nature of Western thought has accepted various binary oppositions and Diana Coole notes that these structured the horizons of debates:

> mind–body; subject–object; reason–passion (or appetite); form–content; culture–nature; order–chaos; and so on. Correlating to them is a further polarity: male–female. Indeed this is often treated as the primary dualism and used to illustrate, or give meaning to, the rest.
>
> (Coole 1994 [1988]: 1)

These pairs are generally conceived in terms of good/bad, superior/inferior so that the first mentioned (man) becomes a standard or norm, identified by what it is not (woman).

The public expression of political theorising which bears upon feminist thinking is apparent within a 'European' context from the fourteenth century (for discussion of the term 'European' see Corrin 1996). An early French theorist Christine de Pisan (1364–1430) has been described as 'the first woman to write about the rights and duties of her sex' (Bryson 1992: 11). Whilst such writing did not analyse gendered power relations in a recognisably feminist manner, it did highlight women's roles in society as a fitting focus for political theory. Given that six centuries later there are still debates about the gendered nature of political theorising this was a significant step in political studies.

Engendering liberal debates

The divided pairings on which liberal thinking on women's interests concentrated its challenges were those of man/woman and public/private. The arguments made in these areas were not smoothly developed nor have they become accepted without much disagreement and debate. In her overview Dale Spender identifies Aphra Behn, Mary Astell, 'Sophia', Catherine Macaulay, Olympia de Gouges and Helen Maria Williams (alongside Mary Wollstonecraft) as pioneers on behalf of their sex. Yet their works went unrecognised:

> It is because such knowledge of women of the past – and there have been hundreds of them – is empowering for women that every effort has been made to make it disappear in a patriarchal society where power is perceived as the prerogative of men.
>
> (Spender 1983: 50)

One of the more influential of the writers on women's situation was Mary Wollstonecraft whose work *A Vindication of the Rights of Woman* (1992 [1792]) has been considered and discussed over a period of 200 years. Issues of public/private were more apparent with work being removed from the home as factories replaced cottage industries and small holdings. The writings of John Locke, Jean-Jacques Rousseau and the Protestant Dissenters (of which she was a member) all influenced Wollstonecraft's work. Locke's theory of natural rights rejected the divine right of kings in favour of government based on contract, arguing against arbitrary rule over any being who possessed reason. For Wollstonecraft, denial of women's rights because of their environment and lack of education was clearly wrong. Here she shares the outlook of the Enlightenment. Although Wollstonecraft espoused many of Rousseau's republican values she reacted strongly against his belief in the need for a private sphere, believing the public sphere to be an aggregate of the private (foretelling some radical feminist arguments of the next century). Those activities which Rousseau deemed private and women's province, Wollstonecraft argued influence the social good. For example, she argued that child-rearing is the training of future citizens and those doing this must be informed and educated to understand the implications of their actions.

The influence of the Rationalist group of liberals *The Dissenters*, particularly Tom Paine in *Common Sense* (1776) was significant in Wollstonecraft's thinking. Paine argued vigorously for the supremacy of 'reason' over primogeniture, hereditary power and Monarchy against reactionaries like Edmund Burke, whose *Reflections* (1790) argued for hereditary rights with political knowledge embodied in social and political mores and customs. By the time of publication in 1792, Paine had escaped his death sentence by fleeing to France. Wollstonecraft's words also inspired passionate hostility:

Her own contemporaries called her a shameless wanton, a 'hyena in petticoats', a 'philosophizing serpent', or wrote jibing epigrams in the *Anti-Jacobin Review*, like 'For Mary verily would wear the breeches, God help poor silly men from such usurping b . . . s.

(Miriam Brody's Introduction to *Vindication*
Wollstonecraft 1992 [1792]: 1)

In the above we see something of how, like many women before (and after) her, Wollstonecraft was neatly fitted into the inferior slot of 'other/woman' whose writings were not worthy of consideration by serious men. Two hundred years after the publication of *Vindication* much scholarship has been devoted to analysing this work and its place within the political canon (see Wollstonecraft 1992).

Men's knowledge, women's inferiority

It was on the grounds of such presumptions of female inferiority with regard to culture, spirit and reason that Mary Wollstonecraft attacked the apparent bias in thinking about politics. Commenting on the linkages made between the actual and the abstract, Coole notes the symbolic associations to which the sexual dualism gives rise: 'Then the female principle, and all it represents – nature, flesh, appetite – is to be subordinated to that of the male, signifying culture, spirit and reason' (Coole 1994 [1988]: 2). Wollstonecraft points out the difference between the 'genderless citizen' of political writing and the realities that women experienced. Political thinking often considers the differences between reality and utopia – the ideal. Early liberal 'feminist' thinkers were questioning what is the 'ideal' for women. The term 'feminism' was used first in English in the 1890s but can be traced back to at least the eighteenth century. Women were constantly pictured and appraised *not* as subjects but as objects or functionaries – wife, daughter, mother, sister, housekeeper, nursemaid. Here we see the basic divide between orthodox views of politics with traditional ideas about functions, and alternative, feminist, views in which political interaction is about relations of power.

It is important to recognise *Vindication* as a polemical work not designed solely to advise women to take up reading or breast-feeding, but to convince *men in power* to grant women political rights and education. To convince men to share power required that the arguments be recognisably in their interests, so that proposing radical changes in the division of labour had no useful place whereas attempting to make women better wives and mothers was very useful in this context. In arguing for the adoption of 'manly values' Wollstonecraft has been criticised, yet such values are neither male nor female but were deemed masculine simply because they were valued highly. In its eighteenth-century context the stereotype on manliness was one of *courage* so Wollstonecraft is also undermining the 'ideal' of woman as weak, timorous, dependent and requiring protection. *Vindication* is also criticised for its lack of utopian elements, its acceptance of economic inequalities and different provision of education for different social classes. In *Vindication* there are critiques of economic inequalities, and Wollstonecraft's ideas do show more radical elements than simply a claim for the negative freedom of the English political tradition. To make society virtuous would require a 'politicising' of the whole of society, not just the public sphere.

Wollstonecraft argued against the double standards embodied in men's domestic tyranny over women. This theme is returned to by Engels (see Chapter 3). The social construction of femininity in the Western world made sexual reputation all important for women – with the images of madonna/whore in people's consciousness. In this way, morality, honour and virtue were all seen as purely **sexual** matters for women. Whilst men could excel in public virtue, women's lives were regulated by their sexuality. Being dependent upon men – from fathers to husbands – for their economic and social existence women were encouraged to develop servile habits to please men. These habits were then assumed to be women's 'natural' characteristics and women were then devalued because of them. Basically Wollstonecraft was applying **Enlightenment** ideas to the situation of women, arguing that as men and women were equally rational so they deserved the same rights and opportunities, particularly in politics and education. In considering the history of feminist thinking Susan Parsons notes the links with certain types of moral thinking:

> From the early days during the Enlightenment through to the development of utilitarian thinking in the nineteenth century, feminists have made use of this understanding of rational moral behaviour in order to plead the case for women's rights.
>
> (Parsons 1992: 386)

In this way, feminists argued that physical and psychological differences did not exclude women from politics.

Wollstonecraft's radicalism can be seen in her critique of domestic tyranny. Her opening letter in *Vindication* to the French minister Tallyrand questions the denial of rights of *citoyennes* – assessing domestic tyranny of men as being destructive in the same way as the royal tyranny of kings or slavery (Wollstonecraft 1992 [1792]: 87–88). Domestic tyranny denied women political rights, education and equal work for financial independence; indeed marriage could be viewed as 'legal prostitution' and a form of slavery. Whilst politicians respected in their public duties could indulge in private debauchery without criticism, the loss of women's sexual reputation – through male violence, poverty or abuse – meant their 'fall'. The choice between the 'Angel of the House' and the 'fallen woman' was no choice at all. Despite Wollstonecraft's (unlike Rousseau's) radical arguments that women be educated in the same terms as men, she saw household work and caring for children as something women would probably wish to do. Such work should not be devalued as rearing children was itself an important civic duty. Given that childcare and rearing is always going to be an issue for women (and men) the solutions Wollstonecraft offers are not radical and show her ties both to the time and her need to persuade those in power (see Brody in Wollstonecraft 1992 [1792]; Coole 1994 [1988]).

Early struggles for political recognition

Throughout the world women have been politically active within their societies in a variety of different ways; much of this activity has not been fully documented or accurately recorded and much is only now being 'uncovered'. Spender notes that: 'In the last few decades of the eighteenth century, women in the old world and the new were beginning systematically to question sexual inequality and to take a variety of steps towards bringing about change' (Spender 1983: 116). In the USA, women had been active in the revolutionary events leading to the American Revolution (1776) by signing petitions, organising societies such as 'Daughters of Liberty' and proposing that new law codes framed by the revolutionary state should take account of women's interests and rights. Abigail Adams was one such activist and her now famous letter to her husband (and future President, John Adams) is evidence of discussion amongst women about claims for justice for women and recognition that claims by men for individual liberty could apply equally to women (see Rossi 1974). Before the Revolution women had been able to vote for a time in Virginia and in New Jersey but after the Revolution had been won 'for America', these concessions were forgotten and state and national constitutions were designed without mention of the rights of women (see Tyler in Welter 1973: 77).

In Britain, women were recognised as actively taking part in social protests in the so-called food riots – when shortage occurred food prices rose sharply. Threats faced by many households went beyond food supply as families were facing enclosures or land clearances which could dispossess them of their homes. Regulations based on the Poor Law imposed the possibilities of splitting families, although this did not become an urgent issue until the New Poor Law of 1834. Riots occurred in 1795–1796; 1800–1801; 1810–1813 and 1816–1818 and evolved to become a movement which 'politicised' women. (Thomis and Grimmett 1982: 28). Some middle-class women in Britain were active in the anti-slavery movement from the 1830s (Hall 1992; Midgley 1998).

Women in France participated in the political unrest of the 1790s – women in Paris and other French cities began to organise themselves, forming political clubs and exerting pressure on the men's political clubs which were equivalent to political parties. Olympia de Gouges drafted a *Declaration of the Rights of Woman* (1790) modelled on the basic document of the Revolution – *French Declaration of Man and Citizen* (1789). Yet feminism in France was short lived with Olympia de Gouges executed as a Royalist in 1793 and: 'the women's clubs were dissolved by the Convention, at the instigation of the Jacobins, in 1793, after the most prominent of them, the *Citoyennes Republicaines Revolutionaires* had moved to the far left and involved itself with the ultra radical Jacques Roux and the *enrages'* (Evans 1977: 16). As in the USA, feminists in France were a marginal part of the Revolution, with no political backing. The major figures of the Revolution were not concerned with women's rights. In Britain when war with France was declared in 1793, all attempts at reform of Parliament smacked of revolution and the backlash against treason and 'seditious meetings' meant that reform moves were repressed until the Reform Bill of 1832.

It is significant to note that whilst the Western liberal writings of Mary Astell ('A Serious Proposal to the Ladies for the Advancement of their True and Greatest Labour' 1694), Wollstonecraft and others were being discussed in terms of ideas of freedom and equality, women's lives in other parts of the world were in the midst of quite different revolutionary struggles. In writing of events of 1791 in the Caribbean, Patricia Mohammed notes C.L.R. James' description of the Haitian Revolution as the only successful slave revolt in history (Mohammed 1998: 12). In terms of feminist critiques, Mohammed shows that:

> the class of women who would and could question the ideology of male dominance with the pen was limited . . . At the same time, we should not conclude that women, black, white or brown, were indifferent or lacking in consciousness of gender, however defined in the Caribbean . . . The peculiarity of women's situation is that they are at the same time inside and outside of politics.
>
> (Mohammed 1998: 12)

In considering White women's situation at that time Mohammed makes it clear that while White women were governed by English law, with the advantage of being part of the elite by virtue of their whiteness, the shortage of White women was no advantage in coupling, as concubinage of Black and Brown women was deeply entrenched. Marriage, being a form of 'coverture' did not grant White women independence. Nevertheless, White women's existence in Jamaica did ensure certain status symbols of ruling class privilege over the middle and lower classes (Mathurin 1974: 248). The politics of racialised and gendered sexuality, using arguments concerning White women's 'protection', was played out to the full in varying colonial situations (see Chapter 5).

Debates on suffrage in Britain

Western societies developed various 'social contracts' between their citizens and the state structures. Traditional standard texts speak of citizens' two-fold identity – as participants in public political action and as heads of private households. Feminist analysts have pointed out that there was no reason of abstract principle why these models should not be applied to both sexes indifferently – political life could be viewed as part of the social whole, not a specialist public activity of men. This was seen to be true in the extreme for those involved in the various activities of the suffragettes: marches, pickets, imprisonment and hunger strikes. For many women and men it was a uniquely new phenomenon to have women publicly demanding their right to vote. This public, challenging activity on the part of women had various phases and consequences, not least to initiate debates around the conflicting loyalties of class and gender and to raise issues of racism.

Before the Reform Act of 1832 which extended the electorate but excluded women (by default) for the first time, a minimal proportion of the British population could vote. The focus was the extent of the Parliamentary franchise and many sections of society, including women and working-class men, began to campaign for universal male suffrage. However, this did not mean a common front. Chartists and other groups feared that in gaining votes for women they would jeopardise their claims for wider male franchise. Reported public opinion at the time appeared to view women as lacking the necessary qualities for citizenship, yet Owenite socialism of the 1830s and 1840s viewed the extension of the franchise to women as essential for sexual and social equality. The general consensus among socialists and working-class political organisations from the nineteenth century through to the early twentieth century was that the franchise need not be extended to women. There were of course exceptions, such as the Owenites and the Independent Labour Party (ILP). Many socialist supporters clashed over granting the franchise to only middle-class women who were judged as enhancing their own cause. These issues remained hotly debated into the twentieth century.

In the liberal traditions the most forceful proponents of women's rights combined arguments from several traditions. Of the three important elements in the development and inspiration of feminism, Evans (1977) notes the social ideology of liberal Protestantism alongside ideas from the Enlightenment and the French Revolution. The coming together of Enlightenment rationalism and the moral dynamics of Protestantism was most apparent in the creed of liberalism. The most forceful proponents of this creed with regard to women's rights were John Stuart Mill and Harriet Taylor. Mill's work is generally taken as advancing views for women's emancipation within his own frame of reference. Diana Coole notes Mill's interest in women within the context of political economy, in how women's emancipation fitted with his utilitarian and liberal vision. In *On Liberty* (Mill 1869) he notes that interfering with another's liberty can only be warranted for self-protection, yet intervention in the way husbands abuse their domestic power and in the case of educating children are two areas that he does propose. Mill accepts the male as breadwinner and Malthusian views on reproduction.

These interventions show Mill's interest to be as much an economic one as a concern for women's and children's liberation. What makes Mill a prominent agent in terms of the liberation debates is that he was well-known and was involved in a practical capacity as an MP (for a short time) as well as in writing on marriage, employment and the vote (all subjects for emerging women's movements). The 1867 Reform Bill gave the vote to most of the urban male working class but Mill's amendment to enfranchise single women on the same basis failed. He gave evidence on the Contagious Diseases Act which he saw as an offence to principles of liberty, and spoke for women's education. Mill's advocacy of sexual equality in *On the Subjection of Women* (1869) fits his general pursuit of social utility and was given a priority by him at the time.

The pro-feminist aspects of Mill's work have been undervalued and overlooked by many later scholars and the writing and influence of Harriet Taylor has similarly been marginalised. Taylor wrote *The Enfranchisement of Women* (in Mill 1983 [1851]) although it was often attributed to Mill. Taylor also played a large role, before her death, (in Mill's admission – see Spender 1983: 188) in early collaboration on *Subjection*. This latter work was first published in Britain, North America, Australia and New Zealand and in translation in France, Germany, Austria, Sweden and Denmark and by 1870 appeared in Polish and Italian. Evans notes that this work was influential: 'because it summed up the feminist case in a way that linked it firmly to the political theory of liberal individualism and tied it to the assumptions about society and politics held by its audience'. Yet it was very 'Victorian': 'Its power derived precisely from the fact that it was in many ways a summary of the prejudices and preconceptions of the age. Its rhetoric is redolent of the optimism and arrogance of mid-Victorian liberalism' (Evans 1977: 19). Certainly Mill's arguments, founded on the belief in the English model of political constitutionalism and social and economic *laissez-faire* appealed to liberal thinkers elsewhere. It builds upon legacies from the French Revolution in appealing to principles of equality before the law, recognition of merit and talents, representative government and the sanctity of property. In this context, although Mill broke with his father (James Mill) in his call for British women's self-representation, he adhered to his father's belief that India, at that time, could only be governed by enlightened British despotism, without any Indian input.

It is to Taylor's work that later feminists have looked to see the recognition that men define the world in relation to themselves

ie basis of their experience, acknowledging no reality not
consistent with such experience. This, of course, denies the broad
range of women's understandings and forms of operating in the
world (see Rossi 1974: 101). Taylor writes that women as 'subjects'
have come to acquire the qualities agreeable to the 'rulers' and
the male rulers have succeeded in making their subjects consider
such qualities agreeable. Men discouraged every form of growth
and development in women to channel them into marriage, maternity and maids for men. Arguing against the reform position (held
by Mill) Taylor asserts that educating women to be suitable com-
panions rather than slaves actually exposes the double standards
that exist with regard to men and women. Her work foretells much
of the later twentieth-century feminist writing especially with regard
to men's experience not being the whole of human experience.
Her clear arguments, again influential on Mill's work, against the
'natural' aspects of marriage, mothering and servitude for women
question why so many barriers are erected for women wishing
other options, if the former are indeed what nature intended. While
Mill's attitude to marriage was conventional with traditional roles
for men (breadwinner) and women (dependent homemaker) Taylor
argued that women should gain economic independence from
men. Her critique in the *Westminster Review* appeared shortly after
her marriage to Mill. Their marriage was not a conventional one.
For Taylor the only obstacles to women realising full political rights
lay with the men who held power.

Political cross-currents

Significant aspects of cross-currents within the women's movements
around the suffrage question were the conflicts of loyalty experienced by women suffragists campaigning for sexual equality in the
very period when working-class movements began to organise for
the independent representation of their interests in Parliament.
Party politics in Britain during the latter half of the nineteenth
century and early years of the twentieth century were very much
in flux. The Liberal Party was involved in negotiating an extensive
programme of social reform yet was seriously divided on the issue
of votes, being led by one of its most emphatic antisuffragists –
Herbert Asquith. Evans argues that the strident militancy of the

suffragettes in Britain was an outcome of the lack of support from liberal politicians which was unusual given support from liberals elsewhere in Europe. The Labour Party was engaged in building a united and effective presence in the House of Commons and was challenging the Liberal Party as the party of reform or the representative of working-class interests. At the turn of the twentieth century there was much debate within all sections of the suffrage movements on the question of relating the demand for votes for women to calls for a fully independent Labour Party in the House of Commons and the demand for adult suffrage. The term 'democratic suffragist' was coined by Margaret Llewelyn Davies, leader of the working-class organisation, the Women's Cooperative Guild, to identify and energise those working for unity of the two demands. They covered a broad spectrum from 'progressive' liberalism to revolutionary 'rebel' socialism in complex and constantly shifting patterns of different currents of thought.

Most suffragists brought to their campaigning pre-existing class and party loyalties, and, in the party–political context of the day, the progressives amongst them found these frequently cutting across their loyalty to the cause of their sex. This aspect of British suffrage politics contrasts with the experience in Germany (Evans 1980) and the USA (Tax 1980). Women were active in suffrage movements to enhance both social and political aspects of women's lives and voting was one way for women to directly influence and improve their social and legal situation. By gaining fair representation in government, unfair legal systems could be challenged. Elspeth King notes an illustration of the unjust legal system in Scotland, when in Dundee, Sheriff Gray sentenced a man to 40 days' imprisonment for stealing two pounds of sugar and another 14 days for sexually assaulting a little girl (King 1992: 31). In cases of property versus women's bodily integrity many feminists today would argue that the former is still privileged and the latter devalued.

The vote was not simply an end in itself, and various social advances were expected from extending the franchise to women – liberation from low pay, poor working conditions, domestic violence and prostitution. Needless to say, the liberal hopes in the power of reason were (rather too) high and today many women still suffer under these injustices. Yet, Levine notes Snowden's comment on British feminism in the second half of the nineteenth century:

One after another the citadels of education, science, art, social
services, politics were all attacked and one after the other – with
the exception of the last – the portals of these jealously guarded
male monopolies were grudgingly opened.

(Levine 1987: 156)

In the nineteenth century, arguments regarding women's rights
were often posed in moral and sexual terms and women suffered in
their every-day lives enormously, not least if they were poor or from
'the colonies', and thereby judged impure (Mohanty *et al.* 1991;
Stoler 1997; Walkowitz 1980). A radical aspect of Wollstonecraft's
analysis was her use of colonial slavery as a reference point for
female subjection which added a new element to the discourse of
women's liberation. Ferguson argues that: 'By theorising about
women's rights using old attributes of harem-based slavery in con-
junction with denotations of colonial slavery, Wollstonecraft was a
political pioneer, fundamentally altering the definition of rights
and paving the way for much wider cultural dialogue (1992: 98–99).
This work enabled criticisms of colonial slavery in discussions of
women's rights which attempted to extend analysis to women of
Colour, beyond White norms.

paved the way + black feminism

Women's in/equality: sexuality and morality

Over many centuries women were viewed as the property of men
– as men's daughters, sisters and wives but not considered as individuals. For African people during times of slavery and beyond,
laws and customs subjugated them as property. As will be seen in
the case study for this chapter, ideas concerning hierarchies of
women emerged with the later suffrage feminists in the context
of Imperial feminist attitudes. By the mid-nineteenth century in
Britain, Christian values and virtues and female values and virtues
were seen as identical, and this morality was exported in distorted
forms to those colonies under British rule. Yet also in the Victorian
era in Britain alongside this popular Puritanism, moral hypocrisy
and pornography flourished.

Female chastity assumed importance and was defined within
restricted social and economic boundaries. Nancy Cott (1987)
explains that 'passionlessness' was essential for women's admission
to moral equality, enabling women to develop their moral and
human capacities only by denying their sexuality. From the 1860s

a series of Acts called the Contagious Diseases Acts, were passed, the first in 1864. These Acts can be viewed as a supreme example of the double standard and its embeddedness in political thought and action. The Acts were ostensibly needed to reduce the high rate of sexually transmitted diseases in the armed forces. Police in certain designated garrison and naval towns in southern England were given powers to stop any women they suspected of being prostitutes and compel them to have medical examinations. Bryson notes that such examinations were described as 'medical rapes' involving often brutal and semi-public internal examinations. In 1869, when calls were made to extend the system to the whole of Britain, a major nationwide campaign began under the leadership of Josephine Butler. Many attempts were made in Parliament to repeal these controversial Acts – between 1880 and 1885 more than 17,000 petitions against the Acts were made with over two million signatures and 900 public meetings (Weeks 1989: 20). The Acts were suspended in 1883 and repealed in 1886.

Campaigners such as Josephine Butler spoke out against the double standard which implied that 'fallen women' had no rights and 'male vice' had no responsibilities. The repeal campaign under Butler's charismatic leadership drew thousands of women into the political arena, often for the first time, encouraging them to challenge key forms of male power and control such as that of the police. Walkowitz argues that in denouncing regulation as a bodily invasion and a violation of the constitutional rights of working-class women, these feminists argued that it was the regulation system, not prostitution: 'that doomed inscribed women to a life of sin by stigmatizing them and preventing them from finding altern-ative and respectable employment' (1993: 378). In advocating self-restraint and rescue work, Butler argued against state regulation or repression, and her example inspired women in most European countries to take up the issue of prostitution (and later trafficking in women). The far-reaching implications of these campaigns are summed up by Bryson in terms of: commonality between women, prostitutes and infected wives as victims of male lust; hostility to male sexuality; relating women's sexual exploitation to issues of employment and education; and suggestions that a woman's con-trol of her body/person could not be guaranteed without legal and political rights (1992: 62).

Female sexuality was viewed through ideologies of male sexual 'needs'. Weeks argues that middle-class men had problems fulfill-ing the 'standard of manhood' when sex with one's own class was filled with respect and propriety. This often resulted in middle-class male sexual power being experienced fully in acts with (or against) working class women (Weeks 1989: 39). It could be argued that some men constructed the belief in female passionlessness to service their own ends – 'to help gentlemen cope with their own sexuality' (Cott 1987: 235). Whereas middle-class men wanted to desexualise relations to maintain their own domination over wives and prostitutes, middle-class women wanted this to limit male domination. It is unlikely that prostitutes at this time believed that payment was a means of limiting male domination.

Medical constructions of women as dominated by their repro-ductive systems was apparent in the essentialism of linking women's biology to their destiny, viewing women as inherently weak and unable to achieve their true destiny as mothers if they dissipated their strength by having a career. Nancy Tuana argues that med-ical views of women's illnesses, mental and physical, were influ-enced by accepted theories concerning women's nature: 'Woman's nervous instability was an unquestioned axiom, stemming from the belief that woman's reproductive role placed a strain on her entire system . . . Both philosophers and scientists seem obsessed by this image of woman as mother' (Tuana 1993: 106–107). Such assump-tions were partial and class-based, with the latter argument often deployed to exclude middle-class women from university educa-tion rather than working women from physical work. The *British Medical Journal* in the 1870s notes an American doctor's belief regarding the dangers of education for women: 'It is not merely her mind that is unsexed, but her body loses much of its special charm that attracts men. In America the college woman when she does marry is often barren' (Weeks 1989: 43). In Britain in the 1860s clitoridectomy was attempted as a cure for epilepsy, hysteria, sterility and insanity. Whilst clitoridectomy caused fierce criticism in some circles, the practice of ovariotomy (removal of ovaries) was carried out on thousands of women in the USA from the 1850s. Such medical decisions were clearly racialised as well as class-based and Black and poor women suffered disproportionately.

Women's activism and 'the Cause'

In Britain, little improvement was apparent in women's moves towards their emancipation from Wollstonecraft's time to the mid nineteenth century when women were pressuring for change. Bryson notes that: 'although overshadowed by Mill and the later activities of the suffragettes, women themselves were, by the 1860s, far from silent or inactive' (1992: 52). Such activism involving those women working against the Contagious Diseases Acts is a clear example of this. Many politics books discuss the Parliamentary debates yet little of the political science literature gives any sense of the scale of women's activities and the privations many women suffered for their right to vote – 'The Cause' as Ramelson (1967) calls it. From 1866 onward, a permanent organisation to campaign for women's enfranchisement was established and it took 50 years to win the first victory (1918) and another decade before women and men were equal as voting citizens. Concentration in politics literature has been on 'achieving the vote' so that the longer-term building of women's movements is undervalued. Levine argues that:

> The few years of political clamour surrounding the militant suffragettes from around 1908 until the cessation of their activities on the outbreak of war in 1914 has served to mask effectively not only the alternative feminist tactics of that same period but also the vast range of activity preceding it in the later nineteenth century . . . Even within the period in which the franchise issue climaxed into physical struggle, other feminist issues remained important within the movement. Their eclipse has both narrowed and starved our understanding.
>
> (Levine 1987: 156)

Even after the vote was won it was clear that major issues remained on the feminist agenda: equal rights in marriage and divorce, equal pay, fighting male abuse and prostitution were still being struggled for, at least in part. In publicly campaigning for changes in laws – marriage and divorce laws, child custody, education and employment, and the vote – women were actively attempting to improve their situations. Of course, women's interests and needs differed greatly, with some middle-class campaigns imposing ideas of virtue or morality. As will be seen in Chapter 3 there was an increasing politicisation of working-class women in the late nineteenth and early twentieth century which highlighted problematic images of womanhood (Scott 1993) and a clash of loyalties between class and gender. Important though the suffragettes' public displays of resistance to political domination were, in showing that women were prepared to act and put their lives at risk for their beliefs, this aspect of struggle was just one of those emerging amongst women.

Campaigning for women's enfranchisement involved suffragists in an active attempt to redefine not only female 'roles' but political life. These campaigns took place within liberal politics with the consequent shifts in ideas across national contexts (Evans 1977). In Britain the lack of liberal support for feminism necessitated the extreme suffragette tactics. Within the feminist movements it was clear that clashes of loyalty between gender and class were becoming more apparent into the early twentieth century and were to arise equally strongly within socialist politics (Chapter 3). Just as divergent loyalties of class and gender emerged in the suffrage movements in Britain in the nineteenth century so issues of race, class and gender affected the movements in the USA. In the USA the dual involvement of women in **abolition** and suffrage highlighted the two major sources of participation – the experience shared with European women of severe restrictions in their public lives and a second derived from the so-called 'ante-bellum reform politics', particularly the anti-slavery movement (Dubois 1978: 22). Like their European counterparts involved in food rioting, US women who engaged in the abolitionist movements stepped out of the limited domestic sphere into the public arena. Some active women had to resist their communities to work against slavery. Spender notes Angelina and Sarah Grimke having to stand against their Southern Quaker community in order to publish works such as Angelina's 1836 *Appeal to the Christian Women of the South* (Spender 1983: 217). Women attending the 1840 Anti-Slavery Convention in London soon realised the full impact of the male double standard when they were refused participation, being curtained off and barred from the debates. The anti-slavery activism in association with suffrage campaigns, was to raise the spectre of racism in women's politics and more broadly across many political tendencies.

Yet the anti-slavery movements in Britain and the USA were in large measure quite conservative groupings of liberals who had specific and limited aims in terms of ending what they viewed as the barbaric practices of slavery. The activists did not envisage emancipation in terms of Black people's citizenship or specific rights for women. Activists within the suffrage movement in the USA had used arguments equating (white) women's situation with that of Black men – as if Black women did not exist. It is clear that the potential of the history of women's activity is immense for revising existing understandings of particular periods or issues and feminist historians are engaged in projects which interrogate both the histories of feminism and imperialism (Burton 1994; Haggis

1990; Hall 1992; Jayawardena 1995; Midgley 1998; Mohanty *et al.* 1991). The Case Study for this chapter focuses on the changing emphasis from abolition feminism to suffrage feminism in Britain in the context of later debates in feminisms in Britain.

Case study: British imperial feminism — roots and legacies

This brief study examines some changes in feminist perspectives of abolitionist feminists and those of suffrage feminists towards slavery, imperialism and anti-colonialism to assess their significance in considering later feminist developments. The racialised and gendered developments in British feminism at the stage of 'high imperialism' (1880–1914) impacted on ideas of 'sisterhood', racial superiority and gender hierarchies among women. Given that much feminist thinking about politics from the 1960s considered liberal, socialist and radical legacies from the nineteenth century, it is particularly significant to look at the imperialist roots of some feminist thinking with respect to the cross-cutting impact of gender and race/class divisions in tracing current developments.

Clare Midgley notes that key themes in recent feminst work recognise the importance of:

- studying both colonisers and colonised;
- recognising female agency – White women's active role in promoting colonialism, contributing to colonial discourse and using empire as a sphere of opportunity; colonised women's active negotiations with and resistances to imperialism and colonialism, and their oppositions to the patriarchal domination by both colonisers and men in their own communities;
- understanding the ways in which the varied forms of feminism in Britain and its Empire were heavily influenced by shifting and differential relations to imperialism and anti-colonial nationalisms (Midgley 1998: 14).

In this context Hurtado (1989) has argued that women's relation to White men affects their focus – the different relationships experienced by white middle- and upper-class women, working-class women and women of Colour, to White men helps in understanding some White feminists' concentration on gender as the key focus. For women of Colour their relations with White men have been generally mediated by state institutions and their political activity reflects this. In particular, political struggles such as reproductive rights, race and class played historical parts in population controls and sterilisation abuse, so that

for women of Colour 'abortion rights' have a different significance than
for many White women. Chandra Mohanty argues that ideologies of
womanhood are informed by class and race as well as sex:

> Thus, during the period of American slavery, construction of
> white womanhood as chaste, domesticated, and morally pure had
> everything to do with corresponding constructions of black slave
> women as promiscuous, available plantation workers. It is the
> intersections of the various systematic networks of class, race,
> (hetero)sexuality, and nation, then, that position us as 'women'.
> (Mohanty 1991: 13)

This is another exmaple of the ways in which dualism and binary
oppositions, identified by Coole (see p. 21 above) can be seen to
be put to work against women's interests and in the creation of
'women's positions'. In the context of the histories of feminism, for
White and Black women, both arise in relation to other struggles.
Often White feminist arguments rest on gender as the sole (or main)
axis of struggle rather than analysing the racial (White) consolidation
of struggles, such as those of colonialism. In arguing that White
women need to analyse 'our relationship to race, ethnicity, class and
sexuality' Ann Russo (1991: 299) suggests that racism is as much an
issue for White people as for people of Colour because White
people are implicated in racial formations.

In her work on liberal middle-class British feminists, Indian women
and imperial culture, Antoinette Burton (1994) identifies 'imperial
feminism' as emerging with the organised women's movement in
Britain in the period 1860–1914. Midgley outlines the proto-feminist
roots of this in the female anti-slavery activities. Attempts to place
female anti-slavery in relation to work on imperialism and feminism:
'entails the adoption of a critical perspective on existing historiography
in both fields'. Understanding British women's anti-slavery activities
needs to be within the imperial framework as: 'the eradication of
slavery became a major justification of Britain's continuing imperial
expansion in the Victorian era'. In turn, British women's anti-slavery
politics needs to be placed within the history of feminist development
as: 'it is not generally viewed by historians as a feminist campaign . . .
[due to] the tendency among contemporary white Western scholars
to identify as feminist only those movements which have an exclusive
focus on gender-based oppression' (Midgley 1998: 163). In viewing
female anti-slavery as a form of Western proto-feminism, various
aspects of their roots out of which 'imperial feminism' emerged can
be seen: leading anti-slavery activists moved into leadership roles in
women's movements in the 1860s and 1870s; feminist organisations

drew on abolitionist networks; and women made specific links between the two campaigns. Josephine Butler labelled the feminist campaign against the Contagious Diseases Acts the 'new abolitionism' and shifted from campaigning in Britain to fighting their implementation in India (Midgley 1998: 164).

In tracing the similarities and differences between the ideological perspectives of the female anti-slavery campaigners and the liberal feminists of imperial feminism Midgley (1998: 165) shows that anti-slavery campaigns noted the common humanity of African and European peoples and common degradation under slave systems whereas later feminists tended to show White Anglo-Saxon women as superior as much by virtue of their race as nationality. This can be related to wider shifts in Britain after the 1850s towards accepting biologically based racial hierarchies. The complexities of cultural constructions of White women's sexuality associated with that of Black men is highlighted by Ann Laura Stoler in tracing colonial discourses on the impact of White women's presence within European colonial communities: 'Allusions to political and sexual subversion of the colonial system went hand in hand. The term "Black Peril" referred to sexual threats, but it also connotated the fear of insurgence, of some perceived nonacquiescence to colonial control more generally' (1997: 21). In these contexts concern over protection of White women was often provoked by threats to the cohesion of European communities so that: 'colonial accounts of the Mutiny in India in 1857 are full of descriptions of the sexual mutilation of British women by Indian men despite the fact that no rapes were recorded' (ibid). Images can become realities in terms of dominance and perceived power.

This Case Study shows the complexities involved in thinking through feminisms in terms of political and cultural constructions of 'others'. The ways in which the projects of Western feminism and imperialism were intertwined have relevance for our later considerations of anti-racist international visions of political change. The imperial Western feminist movements were clearly situated within the context of Britain's imperial expansion and conceptions of 'others' arose within this. Western women thought of their mission as leading 'their victimised non-European sisters out of patriarchal oppression under the mantle of empire' (Midgley 1998: 176). Yet the validity of this 'imperial feminism' was challenged from an early date by the activism (rather than the assumed passivity) of Black women developing their own movements for emancipation.

Summary

Western philosophy has generally viewed women as less than men through a series of variations on the Aristotelian theme that to be female is 'a kind of deformity, albeit one that occurs in the ordinary course of nature. It has pictured the female identity in the same way that biological science has pictured female embodiment – that is, as an imperfect or incompletely achieved version of the real (male) thing' (Frazer *et al.* 1992). By contrast, feminism rejects at the outset the premise of male superiority, and argues that if women view the normative structures of ethical theory (of what should be), as inadequately grounded in their own experience, then the fault lies with the theory.

- Women were viewed as being weak and dependent and were unable to own property or to gain economic independence.

- When women did as was required of them and aimed to 'please' men, these characteristics were then viewed as 'natural'. As a result ideas about women were constructed so that women's 'role' was seen to be concerned with 'private' domestic issues. Politics was regarded as a public activity and thus considered not a suitable realm for women.

- Wollstonecraft and other thinkers pointed out that 'morality' for women, within conditions of subordination, becomes concerned with respectability and modesty – women's sexual reputations are important. A woman's virtue was made contingent on her *sexual reputation* whereas men had a civic role in which public virtues were extolled.

- Feminist thinking recognises the 'social construction' of women as arising out of the *social power of men* to develop notions of femininity and in turn, to judge and subjugate women accordingly. Police powers under the Contagious Diseases Acts were a powerful example of this and the double standard such powers upheld.

- In challenging the male arena of public political participation the demands by women for the vote and for married women to own property were *radical* demands. As such men were threatened by them, some believing that giving any autonomy to women would see the collapse of society.

- Clashes of loyalty were apparent for many suffragists between class and gender. Decisions had to be taken about working for full adult suffrage, including working men, or concentrating on gaining middle-class women's rights.

- Eventually women gained the vote after working hard for the 'war effort'. After the war many working women were returned to their domestic duties.

- British imperialism had an impact upon feminist thinking as British feminists drew on ideas of Empire and contributed to debates about the nature of colonised societies. 'Imperial feminism' still has relevance within feminisms today.

Further reading

Coole, Diana (1994 [1988]) *Women in Political Theory: From Ancient Misogyny to Contemporary Feminism* Hemel Hempstead: Harvester Wheatsheaf, 2nd edn 1994

Evans, Richard J. (1977) *The Feminists: Women's Emancipation Movements in Europe, America and Australasia 1840–1920* London: Croom Helm

Rossi, Alice S. (ed.) (1974) *The Feminist Papers: From Adams to de Beauvoir* New York and London: Columbia University Press

Wollstonecraft, Mary (1992 [1792]) *A Vindication of the Rights of Woman* (edited with an introduction by Miriam Brody) London: Penguin Books

Chapter 3

Socialist thinking and women's liberation

Individuals in large numbers, male and female, forming volunt-
ary associations, shall become a mutual guarantee *to each other*
for the supply of all useful wants, and form an unsalaried and
uninsolvent insurance company against all insurable casu-
alties; *where perfect freedom of of opinion and perfect equality*
will reign . . . where children of all will be equally educated and
provided for by the whole.

Thomson and Wheeler 'Appeal' 1825
(Coole 1994 [1988]: 163)

True emancipation begins neither at the polls nor in courts. It begins
in a woman's soul. History tells us that every oppressed class gained
true liberation from its masters through its own efforts. It is neces-
sary that woman learn from that lesson, that she realise that her
freedom will reach as far as her power to achieve her freedom reaches.

Emma Goldman 'The Tragedy of Woman's
Emancipation' 1910 (Shulman 1996: 167)

Chapter outline

As the title suggests, this chapter is concerned with aspects of socialist thinking, including Utopian **Socialism**, **Marxism**, **anarchism**
and **Bolshevism**. The writings on the oppression of women and
women's liberation are considered within various socialist visions
and projects. Key ideas regarding women's domestic ties and the
'socialisation' of such labour are considered. Links between economic exploitation and sexual oppression are more clearly apparent within Utopian and anarchist thinking than within Marxist and
Bolshevik theories.

- Of the many forms of socialism which developed during
  the nineteenth century, the focus is on Utopian Socialism

and Marxism, which in early forms *explicitly* addressed questions of women's oppression and liberation;
* The writings of Emma Goldman and Alexandra Kollantai are considered as examples of anarchist and Bolshevik thinking on the woman question, against the background of the Russian Revolution in 1917.

Introduction

As discussed in Chapter 2, the feminist creed formulated by liberal thinkers such as Wollstonecraft and Mill was effectively concerned only with middle-class women. The ideology of 'married family life' espoused was not a reality in most women's lives. Considering this dominant ideology of male breadwinners and female domestics Levine observes that:

> As an ideology, however, it was highly effective in ordering people's values according to its precepts. . . . If it was effective in dismissing unmarried and working women alike as society's failures, if it was effective in polarizing the traits of masculinity and femininity in the popular imagination, then surely its effects were palpable.
>
> (Levine 1987: 12)

With the spread of industrialisation across Europe and North America during the nineteenth century, women workers were becoming more visible. Women had been working long before this time yet it was during the nineteenth century that the woman worker became a troubling figure – her existence was viewed as a 'problem'. In assessing this 'problem', Scott argues that it involved: 'the very meaning of womanhood itself and the compatibility between womanhood and wage-earning; it was posed and debated in moral and categorical terms' (1993: 399). Much has been made of the transfer of work from home to factory and women's problematic relation to combining productive activity with childcare. Interpretations of women's work within industrialisation which focus on industries such as textiles, obscure other areas of employment such as domestic service, in which far greater numbers of women were employed and which showed greater continuity with women's previous occupational histories. The interpretation of separation of home and work institutionalises functional and biological differences between men and women as a basis for social organisation.

Scott examines: 'how the dilemma of home versus work emerged as the predominant analysis for working women; how this related to the creation of a female workforce defined as a source of cheap labor and fitted only for certain kinds of work'. In so doing, Scott attributes change to the discourse of gender: 'which elaborated, systematized and institutionalized a sexual division of labor' (1993: 402).

It is apparent that distinctions according to sex were not unique to nineteenth-century debates, but the discourses on such distinctions were articulated in fresh ways with new economic, social and political effects. Certainly questions regarding gender as a sexual division of labour and women's work outside and within the home, in production and reproduction, featured in the socialist theorising. As we see in Chapter 4 such debates were to flower in feminist thinking of the 1960s and 1970s in terms of the oppositional aspects of women's work inside and outside the home, their involvement in reproduction and production and their varying relation to capitalist and socialist modes of production.

It was in the nineteenth century that we see women of the new urban working classes starting to raise their voices in calling for their rights, primarily as workers. Vogel comments that: 'In the quarter-century that preceded the First World War, a powerful working-class movement, represented by trade unions and socialist parties, arose in virtually every European country. The new working-class parties shared a commitment, however abstract, to the eventual transformation of capitalist society into classless **communism**' (Vogel 1983: 95). The movements for women's rights in Europe and North America were mainly a middle-class phenomenon. Working-class women tended to operate within the labour movement (political and industrial) and not necessarily to struggle for women's rights. There were a few areas on which women's movements focused across a broad range. Evans notes that many middle-class women were aware of social problems associated with industrialisation such as poverty, disease, slum dwellings, appalling working conditions and poor wages in factories: 'Indeed, a major impulse behind the emergence of feminism and the mobilisation of middle-class women for the feminist cause lay in the growth of social welfare organisations designed precisely to deal with problems such as these (Evans 1977: 144).

Many histories of socialism begin with the aftermath of the French Revolution, viewing France as the cradle of Utopian Socialism and Utopian Communism. Of the varying strands of socialism, which used ideas from many areas of Enlightenment rationalism, romanticism, materialism, natural rights theory and utilitarianism, I concentrate principally on Utopian and Marxist, and to some extent anarchist, as these theories had great influence during the nineteenth century and beyond, on ideas concerned with overcoming the oppression of women and creating more egalitarian societies. With the growth of industrial **capitalism** and with the Bolshevik Revolution in 1917, many of these ideas were given specific focus. From this time onwards another type of system – socialist democracy – could be looked to as challenging that of liberal capitalist democracy. This was to have political repercussions well into the twentieth century and the 'collapse of Communism' in Central and Eastern Europe in 1989. For later feminist thinking, although Marx and Engels did not elaborate on considerations of women's liberation by earlier socialist thinkers, the impact of their work was felt in their method of analysing human social organisation and reproduction as well as in their vision of the establishment of socialist society in progression towards communism. While Evans (1977) notes that for Marx and Engels the emancipation of women was a marginal question barely alluded to, it could be argued that Engels produced the first **materialist** analysis of women's oppression.

Background

It is clear from the history of women's suffrage struggles that concern with aspects of political participation such as voting rights shows only one part of the vision for women's liberation and benefited mainly one stratum of women. Involvement in class politics of workplace democracy affected many more women across a broader range of issues. The replacement of feudal states with democratic class societies and principles of popular sovereignty highlighted the oppression of working people apparent under capitalist industrialisation. Some working women were so poor that their wages were insufficient for them to survive on and there were fears that these women would turn to prostitution and crime. The biggest area of employment for women in Britain in the nineteenth century was domestic service. Often the attitudes of middle-class women were condescending, viewing working women as in need of moral guidance. As has been noted, racism was also emerging within women's politics. Rossi notes divisions in the aims and tactics of suffragists in the USA, who used the anti-immigrant ethos to further their cause – votes for middle class, educated, moral Protestant women – who could be counted on to use their votes 'wisely'. Yet radical and reform feminists had a larger perspective:

> they were intensely urban and cosmopolitan and saw the future within the framework of an urban, industrial society. Secondly, they were critical and questioning about the impact of social institutions upon human freedoms. They were also intensely secular, no longer involved in theology and the church. The passions that had been expended on religious issues by the moral-crusader feminists were expended on political issues and economic analysis and reform . . . Lastly – and this element was shared by radicals and reformers – their concern was as much for working-class women as for middle-class, educated women.
>
> (Rossi 1974: 473–474)

It is clear that struggles of a qualitatively different type were developing from the many strands of socialist analyses of working people's oppression under capitalism. These various strands encompassed differences in terms of their social democratic politics and the beliefs of ethical socialism which predominated in Britain. Some radical feminists noted by Rossi were not wary of examining such institutions as the church or the family – seeing religion as dead and the family on the wane or in need of restructuring. However, there was no wholesale rejection of the church and religion. As outlined in Chapter 2 movements for the liberation of workers were developing alongside the burgeoning struggles for women's rights. Most of the branches of socialism of the later nineteenth and early twentieth century did little to embrace women workers in the struggle. Some loyalties could be seen to be divided across race and gender and class, with nationalism and patriotism creating clashes in time of war. As socialism was about eliminating oppression for all working people so, as with liberal struggles for the vote, feminist input in socialist circles had first to ensure the inclusion of women workers. This inclusion expressed itself in the struggles for trade union representation for women before proceeding to articulate women's specific needs within a socialist framework. In this context work – domestic and public, productive and reproductive, paid and unpaid, valued and undervalued – was to become, for feminists, a key issue in both theoretical terms and in practice.

Utopian ideas

Explicitly socialist ideas were known from the 1820s in Europe with Utopian Socialist figures such as Henri Saint-Simon (1760–1825), Robert Owen (1771–1858) and Francois-Marie-Charles Fourier (1772–1837) yet they did not form a coherent grouping and renounced any references to their ideas as 'utopian'. Marx and Engels used the term Utopian Socialist for those who wished to replace capitalism with a co-operative and rational society by means of reform rather than class conflict and **revolution**. The Utopian Socialists attempted to outline, often in great detail, a way of social life which would be in harmony with the true nature of humanity. Their societies were to be creative and dynamic and Fourier, particularly, looked forward to the 'full flowering' of humans. These early socialist thinkers explicitly included women's needs and a feminine perspective within their theories. Saint-Simon wrote of women's emancipation as an integral part of the emancipation of the 'useful class'. It was Fourier, a Saint-Simonian, whose eccentric writings were to influence most subsequent theories of socialism, who focused consistently on overcoming women's oppression. He argued that social progress could be measured with regard to the progress of women: 'the extension of privileges to women is the general principle of all social groups' (Evans 1977: 154).

Diana Coole argues that Marx and Engels were impressed by Fourier's critique of marriage and symbolic equation between women's liberation and social principles:

> For a century, virtually all socialists would accept the need for collectivized housework and child-care – advocated by the Utopians but described most fully by Fourier – as an essential component of female emancipation, . . . not until Alexandra Kollontai wrote in the twentieth century, would the tradition retrieve Fourier's crucial association between women's equality and sexual freedom, such that society might be founded on libidinal relations.
>
> (Coole 1994 [1988]: 173)

Yet, as will be seen, when Kollantai wrote about sexuality, Lenin and other Bolsheviks regarded this as distasteful. In his work, Fourier envisaged the possibility of communities based on principles that were identified with the feminine, so that rather than expecting women to conform within a male-defined world, women would be able to make their communities in their own images. It is clear in such theories that women's concerns *are* central to a new morality. Unlike some later Marxist arguments, economic change was not viewed as sufficient to *change* the existing order. The key differences between the Utopians and Marxist socialists was their belief in reform and persuasion, rather than force and conflict, and their creation of communities based on their principles. In both Britain and the USA the work of Anne Wheeler and William Thomson, *Appeal on Behalf of Women* (Thompson 1983 [1825]) was widely discussed and formed a solid basis in feminist thinking. In France, Utopian Socialist women included Claire Demar, Flora Tristan and Suzanne Voilquin. Perhaps the best known, Tristan (1803–1844) wrote the influential *The Workers' Union* (1843) with its links to the ideas of workers' model communities put forward by Owen and Fourier. Tristan's ideas were taken up by a group of socialist feminists in Paris during the 1848 revolution (Watkins *et al.* 1992: 81). In noting the commonalities and differences between British and French Utopian Socialists Coole notes that Owen's *The New Moral World* sought to replace marriage with naturally chosen monogamy, while Fourier's *The New Amorous World* valued unrestrained sexuality expressed in polygamous, bisexual encounters. The value accorded to the feminine in French writing is: 'in many ways a more interesting and enduring contribution to socialist feminism than the sometimes prosaic and ambivalent statements concerning sexual equality' (Coole 1994 [1988]: 171).

These thinkers did not advocate violent revolution yet they wished to see the existing order replaced and to create radically different societies in which: 'women would gain equal rights with economic and legal independence; private property relations would be dramatically altered (less so in French models) and the division of labour, prevailing family forms and sexuality will be challenged' (Bryson 1992: 28). The work of many of the Utopian Socialists, especially the Owenites, overlapped with that of other working-class movements such as the Chartists. Whilst Chartism was a much bigger movement involving tens of thousands of women campaigners and activists, Barbara Taylor argues that: 'throughout the 1830s and 1840s concern with the question of women's own status was much more closely identified with [Owenite] Socialism than with Chartism' (1983: 266). However, support for feminism was still limited as ideas of male breadwinners and domestic wives were increasingly popular images among working people. The failure of Utopian Socialist aims lent a lack of historical 'weight' to their work, yet, as Bryson notes, the Utopian Socialist ideas represented an important if brief alliance of liberal, socialist and feminist ideals, which challenged distinctions between private/public and made interconnections between legal, political, economic and personal subordination. This alliance formed an important bridge in that: 'For the next 150 years, liberal campaigns for political and legal rights were largely separate from socialist preoccupations with the class struggle, while the idea of personal oppression frequently disappeared from the agenda' (Bryson 1992: 34). It is important to recognise that Utopian Socialism was much more than a 'primitive phase' leading to Marxism, and certainly it provided key aspects of future socialist thought concerning ways of overcoming the oppression of women and achieving women's liberation. Some of the ways in which the key divisions between liberal and varying socialist analyses impacted upon feminist thinking and, in turn, how feminist writing about personal oppression found expression, are explored in Chapter 4.

Marxism and women's liberation

The essence of socialist theory is that of *equality*, an egalitarianism premised on the eradication of oppression based on class, race, gender or any other social inequity. The Marxist materialist conception of history explains the ways in which humans can act upon their environment, in a politically conscious movement, to create more equal situations in which human potential can be developed. Both Karl Marx (1818–1883) and Frederich Engels (1820–1895) stated that liberal ideas of justice and individual rights and on human nature were by no means universal or immutable but the product of a particular historical period and as such they could be changed. In Marxism the belief in human consciousness as all-important was challenged in favour of concentration on the organisation of society – man's mastery of nature was a motor of history. Marx and Engels viewed nineteenth-century capitalism as an important form of human society for accelerating this mastery while at the same time its economic system contained the seeds of its destruction in favour of the creation of a classless communist society. Basically Marx viewed the economic system as determining (in the final analysis) the limits of change, and socialism required a particular stage of development of capitalism for its realisation.

Class conflict – the economic exploitation of workers by bourgeoisie – was the dynamic for change. Crudely reduced – the coming to consciousness of the mass of workers, of the injustice of their exploitation and their realisation of their power to effect change – could lead to the development of a revolutionary situation in which the capitalist order would be overturned and a socialist society organised. A classless communist society would be developed from the stage of socialist organisation. Their ideas were popularised in key works, such as *The Communist Manifesto* 1848 (in Tucker (1978)). They were not available in English until later in the century.

Socialist political movements explicitly stated that women's liberation was an *integral* part of the *communal* revolutionary project. Marx and Engels did not place women in the centre of their analyses, and indeed had little to say about women, yet key aspects such as the socialisation of domestic work, envisaged by Engels in *The Origin of the Family, Private Property and the State* (1884) as another stage towards equalising relations between men and women in society, had profound impact on later debates. While the ideas of thinkers such as Marx and Engels had far-reaching implications within societies at the time of their distribution, the overwhelming influence of their works came to fullness with the Russian Revolution of 1917. Engels outlines both the appalling conditions under which women had to labour and the changed nature of public/private aspects of familial oppression: 'With the development of the modern individual family, the administration of the household lost its public character. It became a private service and the wife became the first domestic servant, pushed out of participation in social production . . . The modern individual family is founded on the open or concealed domestic slavery of the wife, and modern society is a mass composed of these individual families as its molecules' (*Origin* in Rossi 1974: 486). This formulation of women's participation in social production and the question of individual–society relations became a central theme in much socialist–feminist analysis (Chapter 4). Engels' concentration though, was more on prehistory than the family in capitalist society, and on the family generally, rather than on women's oppression in particular. His critique of household work becoming privatised under capitalism, and of women's position as 'slaves of the workers', each alienated from the other, is powerful, but he viewed the family solely in the context of the social division of labour, assessing women's oppression mainly with reference to different forms of ownership. Ideas of women's personal oppression are absent. It is clear that neither

Marx nor Engels attempted a systematic study of the specific oppression of women nor of the gendered nature of power relations. In terms of sexual relations, Engels does not attempt to explore implications of how things will be different under socialism other than to expect that in the new order:

> That will be answered when a new generation has grown up: a generation of men who never in their lives have known what it is to buy a woman's surrender with money or any other social instrument of power; a generation of women who have never known what it is to give themselves to a man from any other considerations than real love, or to refuse to give themselves to their lover from fear of the economic consequences'.
>
> (*Origin* 1884 in Rossi 1974)

This powerful critique of existing sexual relations was based on dominance of economic power rather than that of male power and is more cautious than the writing on free love by the Utopian Socialists. It is more damning of current marital practice than some liberal critiques – although there are echoes of Wollstonecraft's words. Engels fails to recognise male and female sexuality equally: assuming men's greater needs and women's wish to submit; heterosexuality as 'natural'; and that economic factors would outweigh other motivations such as preventing conception. In the classless society Engels foresees male domination over women would cease, yet as the bases of this domination are inadequately theorised then the assumed 'inevitable' harmony between men and women was at best naive, and at worst misogynist, in ignoring the benefits men gain from their dominance.

It was in the area of women and work that Marxism had its most powerful impact on later generations of socialists and feminists. The two essential preconditions for women's emancipation – women's participation in the workforce and the socialisation of domestic work – could not happen under capitalism. They would have to take place in a system in which industry was socialised or communally owned, and within a society in which the nuclear family model was not underpinning private property and profits. Put crudely, liberation was to be gained by workers' efforts to control the external world of work. With this control and the achievement of a socialist revolution it was assumed that the contradictions of women's oppression would be overcome, and the expression of fully human development would be gained, in the socialist revolution. Evans points out that the immediate political impact of this work on women was negligible: 'The influence of Marx and Engels operated rather at a more general and indirect level, for in shaping socialists' perception of society, it also incidentally helped form their perception of women's place in it' (1977: 156).

Socialist critiques and organisation in Germany

At the turn of the century, various socialist voices were raised to warn the suffragists that their goal was limited and doomed to disappointment. August Bebel (1840–1913), a self-educated worker and leader of the Social Democratic Party (SPD) in Germany, published the first edition of *Women under Socialism* in 1879 and it was made widely available in 1883. This precedes Engels' work and in its time was equally influential, yet later neglected. In arguing against liberal aims, Rossi notes Bebel predicted that: 'even with vote in hand, countless women would still experience marriage as a form of sex slavery; that the vote would do nothing to abolish prostitution and nothing to abolish the economic dependence of wives' (Rossi 1974: 496). Bebel argues that women must organise and struggle for their own liberation and later women's organisers in the SPD women's movement, Clara Zetkin (1857–1933) and Lily Braun (1865–1916), aimed to do so. Both women wrote for the SPD's women's magazine *Die Gleichheit* (Equality) yet were divided over the feminist content of their politics. Zetkin proved an excellent organiser in establishing separate local structures for women with national 'agitators' under the communication umbrella of the women's magazine. However, the chief means of gaining Party acceptance of this scheme was her focus on the irreconcilable divide between bourgeois feminism and proletarian women. Declaring that the SPD would not countenance bourgeois feminism brought Zetkin into direct conflict with ideas such as Braun's on women's rights to abortion and contraception. Zetkin's strategy of separation of feminists from socialists did mean the rapid establishment of a large and fairly autonomous women's movement yet it also meant that feminists such as Lily Braun were pushed out of the socialist women's movement. As feminism was viewed very much in terms of reformism Zetkin was able to defeat supporters who wished for co-operation with bourgeois feminists. Yet the split between the feminist and socialist women activists clearly highlighted wider debates over the role of the party and on the nature of socialism. These were to be even more clearly reflected in debates on the 'woman question' after the Russian revolution of 1917–1918 (Buckley 1989) and arose again for feminists in varied form after 1989, with the collapse of 'state socialism' in Central and Eastern Europe and the former Soviet Union (Corrin 1992; Funk and Muella 1993; Einhorn 1993; Posadskaya 1994; Renne 1997). Under the organisation of Luise Zeitz (1865–1922) the SPD women's movement membership reached 175,000 by 1914 with 216,000 women trade unionists. At the outbreak of war the SPD women's movement was clearly the most effective and significant socialist women's organisation in the world and the first women's emancipation movement organised by the working classes (Evans 1977: 162). It is for these reasons that concentration here is on Germany rather than other European polities. Yet the electoral success of the SPD called into question whether it was not becoming part of the system it aimed to overthrow and was becoming less revolutionary. Moves towards reformist pragmatism were symbolised when only one of the SPD MPs voted against support for Germany's war effort. Nationalism and patriotism split many women's movements. Zetkin shared her vigorous opposition to the war with many other women socialists and feminists throughout the world.

Socialism, anarchism and women's liberation

The ideas of some anarchist thinkers deserve mention within the context of socialism and women's liberation; particularly those of Emma Goldman (1869–1940), not least because her distrust of state intervention echoes that of many socialist thinkers, including Marx, when considering aspects of popular sovereignty and face-to-face democracy. In 'Socialism: Caught in the Political Trap' (in Shulman 1996) Goldman notes the dangers of 'scientific' socialism in terms of not recognising the power of the middle classes:

> But I deny that so-called scientific socialism has proven its superiority to Utopian Socialism. Certainly, if we examine the failure of some of the predictions the great prophets have made, we will see how arrogant and over-bearing the scientific contentions are. Marx was determined that the middle class would get off the

scene of action, leaving but two fighting forces, the capitalistic and the proletarian classes. But the middle class has had the impudence not to oblige comrade Marx'.

(in Shulman 1996: 105–6)

She goes on to point out that while Marx was right in that the majority of workers had become poorer, the rise of an 'aristocracy' among the working class who have higher wages and savings or property, meant that they had lost sympathy with revolutionary aims.

Her work combined amazing activism and courageous honesty. Having escaped Czarist repression in Russia Emma Goldman became a revolutionary agitator and key anarchist thinker in the USA. By 1919 she was deported with 248 other 'undesirables' to Russia in the Red Scare of 1919. This enabled her to experience the Russian developments first hand and to write about her disillusionment. Although for Goldman, anarchism was the primary focus, rather than feminism – as socialism was for Zetkin, and as we see, Bolshevism for Kollantai – she shared with these thinkers a recognition of the particularly gendered political requirements for changing social relations in a revolutionary way. Goldman warned, before the state had moved towards rights and welfare for women, that the state could not be a trustworthy vehicle for feminists (Coole 1994 [1988]: 231). In her fiery speeches against capitalism, the state and the family 'Red Emma' spoke, among other things, of free love, prostitution, contraception, war resistance and workers' rights. All of these things mattered to women and to feminist thinkers, yet in her day by her own admission, she was denounced by other feminists as 'an enemy of women's freedom' and 'a man's woman' (Shulman 1996: 4). The doctrines of anarchism, much like the works of Marx and Engels, paid no special attention to women's liberation yet Goldman's writings recognise a radical feminist stance on many issues of sexuality and the family as fundamental to women's oppression.

In 'Victims of Morality' Goldman writes that 'It is Morality which condemns woman to the position of a celibate, a prostitute, or a reckless, incessant breeder of hapless children . . . Religion and morality are a much better whip to keep people in submission than even the club and the gun' (in Shulman 1996). She acknowledged Mary Wollstonecraft as a 'pioneer of womanhood', a true rebel, like herself (Brody 1992) and there are echoes of Wollstonecraft's recognition of women's sexual subordination in marriage in Goldman's *Marriage and Love*: 'The institution of marriage makes a parasite of woman, an absolute dependent. It incapacitates her for life's struggle, annihilates her social consciousness, paralyses her imagination, and then imposes its gracious protection, which is in reality a snare, a travesty on human character' (in Shulman 1996: 7). But unlike Wollstonecraft she was well aware that: 'victories at court or at the polls would be useless with a woman's claiming unrestricted freedom over her body' (Wollstonecraft 1992: 64). In this context, Shulman points to Goldman's recognition in 'The Traffic in Women' that all women are treated as sex objects: 'Nowhere is woman treated according to the merit of her work, but rather as a sex. It is therefore almost inevitable that she should pay for her right to exist, to keep a position in whatever line with favors. Thus it is merely a question of degree whether she sells herself to one man, in or out of marriage, or to many men' (Shulman 1996: 7). It is clear that Goldman's analyses highlight various aspects of women's oppression *as women* – distinct from general economic oppression; they were oppressed by institutions such as marriage, family, puritan morality *in addition* to their problems as citizens and workers.

In her critiques of Russian socialist development in 1921, two years after she had been deported, Goldman denounces the suppression of free speech and the dominance of the party. Rossi notes: 'Ever the anarchist libertarian, she believed that the "triumph of the state meant the defeat of the Revolution"' (Rossi 1974: 508). Yet it was her opposition to the focus on women gaining the vote (within an oppressive state structure) that earned Goldman feminist disapproval in her time. Her writings on this are uncompromising:

> The right to vote, or equal civil rights, may be good demands,
> but true emancipation begins neither at the polls nor in courts.
> It begins in a woman's soul. History tells us that every oppressed
> class gained true liberation from its masters through its own efforts.
> It is necessary that women learn that lesson . . . A true conception
> of the relation of the sexes will not admit of conqueror and
> conquered; it knows of but one great thing: to give one's self
> boundlessly, in order to find one's self richer, deeper, better. That
> alone can fill the emptiness, and transform the tragedy of woman's
> emancipation into joy, limitless joy'.
> ('The Tragedy of Woman's Emancipation' in Shulman 1996: 167)

Goldman's work has become more popular in the last 25 years than it was in her lifetime with the rise of feminist interest and renewed anarchist interest in the problems with which she engaged. Writing in 1974 Rossi views Goldman as: 'a feminist visionary who speaks to the mood of the 1970s far better than she did to the women of her own day' (1974: 508). Equally compelling for twentieth-century feminists were the issues raised in the establishment of 'socialism' in Russia.

Bolshevik revolution and women's liberation

Russian feminism was very conservative until the Revolution of 1905 due largely to the repressive outlook of the authoritarian Czarist regime. Yet women were active in terrorist activities against the regime from the 1860s. Twenty-one out of forty-three people sentenced to hard labour for life between 1850 and 1890 were women and their involvement continued in the Socialist Revolutionaries (Evans 1977: 181). The Socialist Revolutionaries, the first wing of revolutionaries, aimed for the reconstruction of society on the basis of the peasant commune. Maria Spiridonova became their leader in 1917 and led them to their disastrous insurrection against the Bolsheviks in the summer of 1918. The second wing of the revolutionary movement, the Social Democrats, were inspired by Marxism yet their views on women's equality reflected those of the German SPD, principally Bebel and Zetkin. Their most prominent woman leader Alexandra Kollontai (1872–1952) wrote *The Social Bases of the Woman Question* (Kollontai 1977 [1908]) repeating much of Zetkin's belief in separating feminists from socialists. Her later work was concerned more directly with women's situation and considered issues of subordination between the sexes and a new proletarian morality (Coole 1994 [1988]: 225). Lenin brought Kollontai into his government after the October Revolution as Commissar for Social Welfare.

Aristocratic women in Russia won the vote from the Provisional Government in July 1917 yet it was working women in Petrograd who had initiated the Revolution of February 1917. While women are largely absent from political accounts of the revolutionary processes between February and October, Jane McDermid notes: 'women of all social classes participated in the intervening period of turmoil, even if rarely in a leadership role' (McDermid 1997: 17). With the success of the Bolshevik Revolution women such as Kollontai, Krupskaya, Inessa Armand, Zinaida Lilina, Ludmilla Stael and others worked to implement socialist policies for women against a background of famine and civil war in Russia. Lenin believed the politicisation of women would lead to both women's liberation and successful revolution. The duality of women's oppression and the double-edged nature of women's revolutionary participation were apparent. The Bolsheviks needed women's support and participation to overthrow the old order, and the primary concern was to reduce working women's oppression so that they may realise their interests. The old bourgeois laws on divorce and illegitimacy would be replaced by new legislation guaranteeing women's rights to property; abortion and contraception with the abolition of religious marriage and illegitimacy; and marriage and divorce codes based on equal rights of men and women. Of course, the fact that women give birth to children was something that could not be changed and in the survival climate of dire poverty in Russia in the 1920s easier divorces often meant that women were left to care for children alone (Buckley 1989). Similarly, women's oppression by 'household bondage' in the 'petty domestic economy' was also to prove hard to abolish.

Writing by Inessa Armand and Alexandra Kollontai, the first two directors of the *Zhenotdel* (Revolutionary Women's Committee) shared with Bebel, Engels and Marx the belief that women's liberation was only possible under socialism. Like Lenin they realised there would be nothing 'automatic' in this. Change could not come merely from new economic structures or legislation, but changes had to take place within the family, in domestic labour, maternity, childrearing and sexual relations. Both Armand and Kollantai viewed reorganisation of domestic labour and childrearing as fundamental to the transformation of the family. When these thinkers broadened their analyses to the dynamics of sexual relations, Lenin and other revolutionaries disapproved of this as 'bourgeois self-indulgence'. While the 'communist sexual puritan' element of Bolshevik thinking echoes some of that by the Owenites in Britain, it is wholly contradictory to the French Utopian Socialist thinking about the need for sexual revolution. Certain strands of twentieth-century feminist thinking were also divided, in various respects, in their analyses of sexual divisions of labour, between materialist/idealist and structural/cultural frameworks (see Chapter 4).

In the Bolshevik analyses of the socialisation of housework and childcare tasks, the economic benefits of women's participation in the public sphere were overestimated and the high costs (economic and psychological) of making available public utilities for meals, laundry and childcare, were radically underestimated. Kollontai stated that: 'Instead of working woman cleaning her flat, the communist society can arrange for men and women whose job it is to go round in the morning cleaning rooms' (Buckley 1989: 45). Heitlinger (1979) points out that Lenin thought only of the savings in labour time when housework would be socialised, not acknowledging that previously unpaid domestic work becomes waged work requiring equivalent payment. As the gendered nature of domestic work was not analysed, the psychological costs for women were not considered, and this gendered dichotomy in work was to prove a heavy burden for women in the Soviet Union and later 'state socialist' societies. The term 'state socialist' is used descriptively for those countries which came under the Soviet sphere of influence after 1948 (see Corrin 1992).

Impact of socialist theories for feminist debates

From Utopian Socialist writings and experiments in the 1830s and 1840s we see the critique of capitalism from the perspective of a new conception of the individual and the possibilities of social life. The outlook focused on the conflict between the individual and society with a commitment to communities that would unify the personal and social needs of people – some views regarded the bourgeois family as naturally 'good' whilst others advocated free love as a way of undermining the patriarchal bourgeois ideal family. While Marxist political writings provided limited theoretical guidance on the problems of women's oppression and women's liberation, the work of Marx and Engels and their 'scientific' brand of socialism had a significant impact on nineteenth- and twentieth-century feminism in at least five major ways:

- Marx is the philosopher of the oppressed and women are oppressed.
- Marx is also the pre-eminent theorist of revolution and liberal and socialist thinkers recognised the liberation of women as a revolutionary proposition – centring on challenging the 'sacred' social institution of the family.
- Placing family and sexual relationships in an historical context, as other forms of social organisation, meant that they could be challenged and changed.
- The impact of economic factors on the condition of women, as the result of a particular historical stage of

development, made Marx's political economy critique
particularly appropriate to women.

- That Marxism is about *praxis* was important for later
  feminists in outlining the importance of 'changing the
  world' on the basis of practical experience – the impact of
  theory, practice, reflection. New methods of analysis were
  offered for feminist thinking.

Yet the basic Marxist categories such as value of labour, industrial
reserve army, remain ungendered and do not explain why women
are oppressed differently from men. As Marx and Engels believed
all divisions would be overcome in socialist revolution scant regard
was paid to women's greater exploitation. As the proletarian struggle
would allow *all* automatic emancipation, little attention was paid to
sexual relations as these were deemed to be determined largely
by economic relations. It is on these and other crucial issues of
organisation that anarchist thinkers such as Goldman broke with
Marxists. Goldman critically analysed the bourgeois feminists of her
time yet allowed that the exploitation of women took on an extra
dimension in terms of men–women relations and was passionate
in her defence of women's rights to 'be women' whatever that
entailed. Equally passionate about her beliefs in face-to-face democracy she warned of the dangers of state intervention long before
her disillusionment with the situation after the Russian Revolution.
Most notable are the resurrection of her arguments long after
her death in terms of later twentieth-century feminist debates
regarding the state as a vehicle for women's liberation. It was in
part the disputes on these and other issues between the Marxists
and anarchists that dissolved the *First International* (Evans 1977).
As is considered in the Case Study, the impact of the thought of
Marx and Engels on the Russian revolutionaries was also to have
consequences for 'women's liberation under socialism' and to
generate debates regarding socialist feminism internationally.

In their time, for Zetkin, Kollantai and other revolutionaries, the
aims of the so-called 'bourgeois feminists' were insufficient because
they left capitalism intact. It was around this time that the value of
separate women's organizations was questioned, and found to be
counterproductive. This question, of separate women's organisation, has remained a central point of contention in socialist politics
and feminist politics throughout the world. Yet the British situation
was one in which the agitation of middle-class women for higher
education, legal changes, radical movements against the Contagious

Diseases Acts and for birth control, raised women's rights as a very live issue which socialists could not ignore (Rowbotham 1972).

That gender roles and socialisation were not tackled in the revolutionary writings allowed the ill-founded belief that women would be released from their domestic burden without men assuming any new domestic roles. The implications of male–female relations and the means by which women were subordinated to men were nowhere thoroughly analysed. Notions of sisterhood were viewed as out of step with the class-based analysis of Marxists. Such notions of sisterhood in the twentieth century have had to grapple with many questions not least those arising from racism. In questioning bias, prejudice and oppression, analyses of diversity and domination have enriched international feminist debates. In terms of socialist–feminist thinking, questions concerning conceptions of 'socialism' arose after 1989 when many elements of the practical politics of the systems in Central and Eastern Europe became discredited. In the wake of changes in Central and Eastern European politics in 1989 the names of various parties and groups were changed from 'Communist' to 'Socialist' or 'Social Democrat' or 'Left' and so on.

It is well to reiterate the deep reluctance of many socialists to countenance autonomous women's movements or indeed to see that women's oppression raises particular questions for women as social beings. In her conclusion regarding Marx and Engels on 'The Woman Question' Elizabeth Waters notes that they recommended public housekeeping – the socialisation of domestic work: 'In this prescription, there is no recognition of the need for women and men to wage a conscious struggle to transform interpersonal relations, nor of the political requirements of such a task' (Waters 1989: 26). This problem is something to which later Marxist and socialist feminists returned in the later twentieth century (Chapter 4). The old class dualisms as well as the divisions between socialism and bourgeois feminism remain, often implicit, within the arguments around political change to end women's inequality. It is also significant that the socialist developments in the 'Third World' had different antecedents and contended with different forces, not least colonialism (Jayawardena 1986). Sometimes there are new twists in such discussions – certainly 'socialist feminist' activists internationally are now assimilating discussions and decisions which Central and Eastern European women have undertaken in the rejection of so-called 'socialist' values. In turn, women from the so-called 'socialist' countries in Europe are questioning what both the legacies of their old regimes and the market-oriented democracies offer for various women's situations (Posadskaya 1994; Renne 1997). Debates concerning feminist thinking in the liberalising atmosphere of Central and Eastern European countries have gained an urgency as have notions of the 'dictatorship of the market'. It is to the renewal of debates around feminism, liberal, radical and socialist from the 1960s that we turn in Chapter 4 to assess debates on politics from varying feminist perspectives.

Case study: Feminist and socialist internationalism

In nineteenth-century Europe, working-class parties, particularly those influenced by Marxism, strongly supported co-operation between workers of different countries – unity is strength. The Communist Manifesto ends with the slogan: 'Working men of all countries, unite!' (Tucker 1978: 500). Theoretically socialism had to be an international phenomenon, particularly the more capitalism developed into a full imperialist system. In response to this, in the 1860s, there was an attempt, in which Marx himself played a leading part, to form an international socialist movement. This is known as the *First International*, followed in 1889 by a second attempt, the *Second International*. It is in the latter that socialist women in large numbers participated, and in which leaders like Clara Zetkin discussed the establishment of a Socialist Women's International.

International contacts and meetings had also played an important part in stimulating the growth of feminist politics in the late nineteenth century. Women's international organisation, like other international gatherings, was quietened by threats of police repression following the Paris Commune of 1871, which made associations with the word 'International' dangerous. Its revival after the 1880s was largely dominated by American women, who took the lead in founding the *International Council of Women* in 1888 (40 years after the Seneca Falls Declaration). Radicals within the feminist movement were not satisfied with the moderate feminism of the Council and began forming alternative groups. The establishment of the *International Woman Suffrage Alliance* in 1904 formalised this split. The Alliance however remained a minority movement with only seven member countries with suffrage movements over 2,500 strong (Evans 1977: 252).

At an International Socialist Women's Conference, organised by Zetkin in 1907 at the time of the Congress of the Second International, the *Socialist Women's International* came into being. Among the delegates sent were: 19 from England; Germany 16;

Austria 7; Hungary 3; France 3; Bohemia 2; and Norway, Belgium, the USA, The Netherlands, Finland, Switzerland, Italy, Sweden and Russia each sent one delegate. It is perhaps surprising that 19 were sent from England, yet this was not an accurate reflection of the support from socialist women. The three French delegates represented only themselves whilst the single Finnish participant could speak for several thousand Finnish socialist women (Evans 1977: 166).

German dominance was apparent at this 1907 conference. This was in part because of the large number of women within the SPD and partly due to their administrative and political arrangement of the conference. As such, the resolutions passed reflected Zetkin's aims to distance socialist women's politics from those of bourgeois women, particularly in opting for votes for men *and* women (not just manhood suffrage) and in non-cooperation with bourgeois feminists. Such strategic interventions had profound repercussions on the breadth of the internationalism of the *Women's International* and was to cause splits in women's politics for many generations. In the *International* generally countries were responding to their particular political situations and at the outbreak of war in 1914 they took different decisions. This effectively meant the *International* split along the sides of opposing nations as most parties supported their own national war efforts. Yet as often happens in war, as the deprivation and deaths continued people sought an end to war and the anti-war elements were strengthened. When the Bolshevik Revolution succeeded in Russia the anti-war sections seemed vindicated as the revolution not only transformed Russia but the international socialist movement. As Vogel argues: 'For the first time, revolutionaries had fought for and won the opportunity to begin the transition to a communist society, and the effort commanded the attention of socialists everywhere' (1983: 115). Its influence in Asian countries is acknowledged by Jayawardena (1986: 8): 'Influenced by events in Russia, communist parties which had arisen in Asia by the early 1920s – in China, India, Japan, Iran, Egypt and Turkey among others – launched revolutionary movements for social and political change'. In all of these countries the 'woman question' was raised in the early twentieth century with women's emancipation viewed as an essential and integral part of the national resistance movements. As we see in Chapter 8 the growth of feminist politics at the same time as national liberation movements were complex processes (Mama 1997). Key demands grew for democratic rights in the context of resistance to foreign domination and local and religious exploitation.

The forces of capital were ranged against the new revolutionary Russian state and the urgent task of socialists became providing concrete answers to the specific questions of the revolutionary society, not least the 'woman question'. In March 1919 the *Communist International* (Comintern) was established in Moscow to support the Russian government endangered by civil war and foreign intervention. Lenin viewed this as the first step of the International Republic of Soviets towards the world-wide victory of communism. It was at the 2nd Comintern in August 1920 that Lenin's in/famous 21 points were accepted in which all communist parties were to model themselves on the Russian Communist Party with strict discipline in defence of Russia and obedience to central demands and continued vigilance against social democracy. This was the case until 1921 when 'unity from above' meant co-operation with social democrats and later in 1923 with 'united from below' signalling co-operation with socialist workers and trade unions. The consequent history of Stalinist control over much of the decision-making in international communist politics, reversing the belief in world revolution for 'socialism in one country', had a dramatic impact not only on socialist political interventions in many countries, but on ideas regarding women's liberation within socialism.

Summary

- With the spread of industrialisation across Europe and North America women of the new urban working classes began to organise for their rights as workers.

- Socialist theories, particularly Utopian and Marxist, became influential in the nineteenth century and were given a focus with the 1917 Bolshevik Revolution.

- Utopian Socialist writings and experimental communities in the 1820s and 1830s critiqued capitalism from the perspective of new conceptions of the individual and new possibilities of social life, assuming women's concerns as integral, with some theories adopting the 'feminine principle' recognising the need to overcome sexual oppression.

- The anarchism of Emma Goldman shared a recognition, with later socialist thinkers, of the gendered political requirements for changing social relations in a revolutionary way. Goldman believed that the state could not be a vehicle for feminist change.

- There was a deep reluctance on the part of socialists and anarchists to countenance autonomous women's movements or to view women's oppression as raising particular questions for women as social beings. Socialist women activists believed that 'bourgeois feminism' was a divisive distraction from the goal of proletarian revolution. Goldman and several Bolshevik women did write about the specific nature of women's oppression.

- The roots of socialist developments in 'Third World' countries had different antecedents and contended with different forces, not least colonialism.

- Developments within the Communist International (Comintern) and susbsequent political change with Stalinism in the Soviet Union were to have profound impacts upon world politics in the twentieth century and on feminist thinking concerning women's liberation within socialism.

Further reading

Bryson, Valerie (1992) *Feminist Political Theory: An Introduction* Basingstoke: Macmillan Press

Shulman, Alix Kates (1996) *Red Emma Speaks: An Emma Goldman Reader* 3rd edn New Jersey: Humanities Press

Tucker, R.C. (ed.) (1978) *The Marx–Engels Reader* 2nd edn New York: W.W. Norton

Vogel, Lise (1983) *Marxism and the Oppression of Women: Toward a Unitary Theory* London: Pluto Press

Chapter 4

Feminist liberation politics

I myself have never been able to find out precisely what feminism is, I only know that people call me a feminist whenever I express sentiments that differentiate me from a doormat or a prostitute.

Rebecca West 1913 (Rowbotham 1992: 8)

The words 'feminism' and 'feminist' have become emotive words that often provoke hostile reactions. . . . In this study the word 'feminism' is used in its larger sense, embracing movements for equality within the current system and significant struggles that have attempted to change the system.

(Jayawardena 1986: 2)

Chapter outline

Considerations of the 'new' politics of women's **liberation** are assessed in this chapter against the backdrop of dramatic political shifts following the Second World War. Key aspects of these analyses include:

- the spread of communist ideas and societies in Eastern Europe, China, some African countries and India, with consequent reflection on theories and practices of women's liberation through socialism;
- women's liberationists' creation of new analyses of women's lives based on concepts such as **patriarchy** and new styles of politics based on their experiences;
- issues of 'difference' and exclusion in women's politics which generate much debate and re-visioning within feminist thinking.

Introduction

It is now fruitful to turn towards the debates that were engendered in feminist politics in the second half of the twentieth century. In a short overview such as this only the tip of the proverbial iceberg can be touched in outlining the massive growth of activism and analyses of women's politics in the era from the 1960s, some of which is considered in later chapters. Much of this material is considered in Women's Studies readings, which are noted in the text.

The location of a politics of liberation growing out of radical developments is one key to later twentieth-century feminisms, with the term 'women's liberation' taken to place women's struggles with those of other oppressed groups, as something worthy of political activism and analysis. Women certainly learnt from other liberation struggles yet the challenges posed by women's liberation were to differ in form and content from previous movements. The development of Black Power groups, particularly the Black Panther Party, from the Black **Civil Rights** movements in the USA showed how a politics of liberation could challenge an existing order and also how threatening such developments were to those in political structures of power (see Wahad *et al.* 1993). Periods of radical struggle are often followed by periods of repression and backlash. The umbrella term 'backlash' is used to denote attempts at resisting and undermining liberation struggles by the use of force, legal and otherwise. In women's struggles strategies utilised the ridiculing of these politics through the power of revision in the media, particularly press and television. How a struggle is portrayed can radically affect people's perceptions of its aims and their identification with it.

Background

In the three decades after 1914 the experiences of fascism, two world wars, the use of nuclear weapons, economic depression and liberation struggles contributed tremendous human upheaval. In periods of war all human relations are strained, with traumatic consequences of violence, fear, loss, migration and complex settlements.

In recent years the conflict which broke out in the Former Yugo-slavia reiterated for many younger people the ways in which women were bearing enormous burdens in many different ways, yet work-ing to resist the totalising atmosphere of martial mayhem. The use of women's bodies as battlegrounds is a constant feature of war with inhuman tolls being taken on many women across the centuries (Enloe 1993; Corrin 1996; Anthias and Yuval-Davis 1992). The period from 1948, 30 years after the Bolshevik Revolution, saw particular political formations and aspirations taking shape. With Soviet influence in many of the Central and Eastern European countries a breach was made on the continent of Europe – the heart of colonial 'motherlands'. This separation was highlighted with the division of Germany into the German Democratic Republic in the East and the Federal Republic of Germany in the West. Establishing 'state socialism' in Central and Eastern Europe en-tailed the creation of 'Soviet-type' societies working towards very different goals than the liberal capitalist regimes. The development of two German states and societies was like a microcosm of the divided Europe. 'Socialist' (Soviet-type) social policy and women's emancipation have been assessed and debated within Western feminisms and in comparative frames (Bridger *et al.* 1996; Buckley 1989; Corrin 1992, 1994a; Einhorn 1993; Funk and Muella 1993; Heitlinger 1979; Posadskaya 1994; Pilkington 1996; Renne 1997; Scott 1974). Soviet-type regimes in Europe, the success of Maoist communism in China in 1949 and independence in India in 1947, changed the balance of powers in the world. The rhetoric and reality of Cold War politics had a deep impact in the 1960s and beyond.

From 1945 independence was gained in Indonesia, The Philip-pines, briefly in Burma, and later in Malaysia (1957). The State of Israel was established in 1948 and the Korean war (1950–1953) was followed by the Hungarian Revolution at the same time as the Suez Crisis in 1956 and independence in Morocco and Tunisia. The success of the Cuban nationalist and socialist revolution of 1959 under Castro led to the US–USSR confrontation in the Cuban Missile Crisis of 1962. In Algeria the liberation struggle culminated in an independence in 1962 and in Africa national liberation movements were developing in various countries. Ghana was the first independent African state in 1957, Malawi and Zambia left the Central African Federation in 1964 and Unilateral Declara-tion of Independence (UDI) was declared in Rhodesia in 1965 (at the time of UDI political control was assured for the Whites which was condemned by the UN). Rhodesia later became known as Zimbabwe.

The ongoing movement for African Liberation spread to the then Belgian Congo 1960–1965 and against this background continued strengthening of **Apartheid** politics took place in South Africa with the introduction of identity cards for Blacks and suspension of their parliamentary representation followed by bloody suppression (Sharpeville). Over 20,000 women marched to government buildings in Pretoria to protest against the bans in August 1956. The women were all walking in groups of not more than three in order to avoid the ban on processions that day; 9 August is now South African Women's Day. Their rallying call was heard throughout the world: 'Now that you have touched the women you have struck a rock, you have dislodged a boulder, you will be crushed' (for the graphic images developed by South African women see McQuiston 1997). Despite worldwide condemnation South Africa left the Commonwealth and in 1963 established the Bantu state of Transkei. From 1964 the USA was at war with Vietnam until a 'phased withdrawal' was agreed in 1969. The year 1968 became a pivotal year in North American and European 'youth politics' with anti-war demonstrations and protests against state policies from Paris to Prague.

The 'fall-out' from these momentous and literally earth-shattering developments was to be felt for decades, not least in the ideas and politics of some of the feminist movements arising from the ferment of liberation political actions and debates. While feminists in Western Europe and North America were able to concentrate energy on women's liberation struggles many women in other countries were struggling with issues of survival in newly independent states or under authoritarian regimes. For women in Spain under the Franco regime there were few opportunities for political liberation. The situation across Western European countries varied tremendously in terms of the openness for women's liberation politics (see Kaplan 1992). The terms of independence, with legacies of colonialism, left much political work to be done and conflicts such as that between India and Pakistan had immense repercussions (Davies 1993; Haniff 1988; Sharp 1993). Analysing the politics of the Western feminist ideas and movements from the 1960s highlights specific feminist perspectives on politics which are further considered in later chapters.

Feminisms before the 1960s

The period from the end of the First World War to the 1960s was one in which little explicitly feminist activism was visible and few feminist works were published. Yet at this time many women were actively involved in political campaigns. Certainly women in many 'Third World' countries were active in liberation movements; from 1912 in South Africa following the founding of the **ANC**, women took an active role in the struggles against Apartheid. Since gaining the vote in the 1920s, many Western women's activities were taken up with immediate welfare concerns. In the UK for example, workplace struggles for maternity benefits, securing decent health care and family endowments were pursued in the 1930s. These benefits were eventually incorporated into the welfare state proposals after the Second World War. Much has been written about the forcible return of women to 'the home' after major wars in which their skills in factory work and agricultural realms were vital and well utilised. The enforcement of 'domestic ideologies' tend to come to the fore during such times and women in many walks of life are constrained by this. In assessing British women's situations between the two World Wars Deirdre Beddoe notes that: 'Official state policy coerced women back into the home – their own or somebody else's' (1989: 50). Domestic labour remained the major sector of women's employment until 1939. The media were used to attack women who wished to retain 'men's' jobs in factories and even those women claiming their unemployment benefits when employment was unavailable. The power of the press in purporting to represent 'public opinion' against feminist politics has been an ever-present aspect of anti-feminism in the twentieth century. The steady increase in numbers of women entering higher education in many Western countries in the 1940s, and women's entry into previously male-dominated professions, coupled with the economic affluence of the 1950s, enabled some women to gain much more economic and social independence to pursue their own interests. With legislation such as that on equal pay, abortion and the development of the contraceptive pill in the 1960s, the scene was being set for the development of women's liberation politics.

In not finding a great deal of feminist material of the 1950s Spender proposes that this suggests: 'the taboos against any expression of these ideas on the part of women or men may have been greater then than in other recent decades' (1983: 720). In this context, the publication of Simone de Beauvoir's *The Second Sex* in France in 1949 was a tremendous impetus for later feminist thinking. It was popularised in a paperback edition in English in 1953. The 50th anniversary of its publication was celebrated and debated at a large feminist gathering in Paris in January 1999. Rowbotham describes the importance of this 'extraordinary achievement' which first attempted a total synthesis of biological, cultural, historical and psychological destiny of the concept and situation of women: 'By starting the task of disentangling femaleness from femininity Simone de Beauvoir indicated a new and transformed possibility – the movement from passivity into freedom' (1973: 10–11). It is to attempts at developing such movements towards freedom that we now turn in assessing women's liberation politics.

Early politics of women's liberation in the USA and UK

From the 1950s post-war consumerism with its projection of 'happy housewives' in the USA came critiques from feminists, and the 1960s saw rapid developments in self-organisation. Liberal feminism has been a significant strand in the USA with a focus on institutionalised education and legal reform for equal rights. Ideas from *The Feminine Mystique* (Frieden 1963) were widely taken up by middle-class White women across the USA. By 1966 Betty Friedan had founded the National Organisation of Women (NOW) serving as its first President. She was replaced in 1970 by a Black woman, union organiser and civil rights activist Aileen Hernandez (Guy-Sheftall 1995: 163). Very early issues were raised about the partiality of the vision in published works and campaigns, in neglecting the experience of Black women, and on the visibility of lesbian activists (White and Black). Allegedly Friedan had referred to lesbians as the 'lavender herring' and thereby not a focal consideration for women's liberation. Shortly afterwards around 20 lesbians formed a group known as Lavender Menace to highlight lesbian issues for discussion (see Chapter 6). There were many political differences in discussions and campaigning between the liberals and radicals in the USA with racism and sexuality becoming key aspects for consideration. By 1970 'women's liberation' was viewed as an umbrella term with thousands of small groups and collectives. **Collective** working was something developed within feminist political groups so that responsibility was shared and each woman had an equal voice. This was in part to rotate tasks and in part to give women political experience and confidence to contribute, as in mixed gender gatherings men tended to dominate. Some viewed these ways of working as similar to the face-to-face democracy discussed by Marx and Goldman while others likened them to chaos (see *The Tyranny of Structurelessness*, Freeman 1992).

Many women active in the early 1970s women's liberation movements in the UK and USA were involved in the New Left politics but this 'cultural revolution' was still based on sexist values, devaluing women's politics and not heeding their voices. At the 1967 National Conference on New Politics in Chicago issues of women's liberation were viewed as unimportant. The following year the first nationally recognised feminist protest was held at the Miss America Contest in Atlantic City. When some clothing was symbolically 'trashed' (girdles, corsets, bras) the media constructed the myth of 'bra-burning women's libbers', although nothing was in fact burned. The role of the media played a large part in feminist politics from the 1960s with few struggles being deemed 'media sexy' but a novelty value remained in reporting women's marches with banners and singing. Political developments such as international campaigns against multinational exploitation of women or anti-nuclear campaigning were avoided or marginalised in press reporting. Having no 'leaders' also confounded journalists who preferred to speak with 'the leader'.

In the UK much early feminist writing and activism emerged from women who were closely allied with the political Left. The labour movement, concerned primarily with issues of White, working men, was resistant to considering feminist issues. Questions of **family** work and a family wage were challenged with work by Mitchell (1966), Barrett and McIntosh (1982) and Delphy (1984). Liberal feminism was not such a significant strand in the UK but radical feminism was to prove a revolutionary force within UK politics. In 1970 the first Women's Liberation Conference was held in Oxford with four key demands: equal pay, 24-hour nurseries, free contraception and abortion on demand (Rowbotham 1972). In 1972 an alternative women's magazine *Spare Rib* (biblical creation of Eve) was established as was *Ms.* magazine (neither Miss nor Mrs) in the USA. New ideas on sexuality and the social control of women were spread with feminist publications such as Millett's *Sexual Politics*, and Greer's *The Female Eunoch*, both in 1970, and Koedt's article 'The Myth of the Vaginal Orgasm' (written for the

first national Women's Liberation Conference in the USA in 1968).
Simone de Beauvoir's *The Second Sex* was reprinted (generally only
the second part) in paperback. Although there was no overall
co-ordination in UK feminist politics, two of the most successful
campaigning networks focused their co-ordination in 1975. The
National Women's Aid Federations linked groups and campaigns
challenging male violence and supporting abused women, and the
National Abortion Campaign established ongoing co-ordination of
activities.

Early terms of debate

In highlighting the significance of new aspects of feminist debate
it is important to give due recognition to works such as that of de
Beauvoir, as many 'new' feminist ideas were in fact reconsiderations
on key themes in *The Second Sex*. Some feminist writers view de
Beauvoir's work as a bridge between 'old' feminisms and new
women's liberation politics as the ideas it considers span across
each, particularly in terms of women's identities and how these
can be constructed and 'chosen' (Humm 1992). The ways in which
debates were framed and the focus on patriarchal relations were,
of course, original in the context of women's lives from the 1960s.
Reducing complex volumes and discussions to their basics, I highlight some ideas developed in the 1970s which underpinned much
'movement activity' of the time, before considering their development in practice.

As noted Friedan's writing advised women to go out to work to
find financial independence, even if they had to spend much of
their income on domestic work and childcare. Clearly, this was
not an appeal to *all* women, as presumably some women would
have to do the domestic work and childcare. It did not analyse
class, racial and other barriers. Its appeal to White middle-class
American women was in its assertion that women had rights to
financial independence and in questioning men's apparent rights
to block that. Differences between Friedan and radical critiques
are that Friedan wants some women to share male power, whereas
radical critics want to enable most women to challenge it.

A much more radical approach is taken by Kate Millett (1970)
in showing the sexual nature of politics. The partiality and prejudice in previous scholarship serves men's self-interest. Millett sees

men and women as inhabiting differing cultures, the rulers and the ruled, with patriarchy as the basic means of rule. In whatever its form, sexual domination is 'perhaps the most pervasive ideology of our culture and provides its most fundamental concept of power' (1970: 25). A key aspect of interlocking parts of patriarchal systems is socialisation, with men socialised to assume power and women not to, so our thinking must change. Unlike individual solutions, Millett considers the collective lives of women under patriarchal value systems: 'Male supremacy, like other political creeds, does not reside in physical strength but in the acceptance of a *value system* [my italics] which is not biological' (1970: 27).

A similar belief in changing values is noted in Germaine Greer's work: 'If it is obvious that religion declines once people cease to believe in God, it follows that male dominance will decline when people cease to believe in male supremacy and authority' (1970: 15). Millett's focus on the political and collective aspects of women's oppression is counterposed in Greer's emphasis on the personal and individual dimensions, viewing marriage and romance as primary means by which women are subordinated. Both Millett and Greer consider the familial aspects of women's oppression arguing against the objectification of women as sexual objects for men. Greer sees rape as an act of: 'murderous aggression, spawned in self-loathing upon the hated other. Men do not know themselves the depth of their hatred' (1970: 251). In outlining the many, varied male terms of abuse for women, Greer argues against heterosexual relations which involve active (male) feats being imposed upon passive (female) recipients.

Francis Beale's (1970) essay 'Double Jeapardy' in Robin Morgan's *Sisterhood Is Powerful* became the most 'anthologized essay' in the early years of women's liberation publications (Guy-Sheftall 1995: 145). In it Beale analyses issues of reproductive freedom for Black women, recognising the need for White women's liberation movements to be anti-imperialist and anti-racist: 'the system of capitalism (and its afterbirth – racism) under which we all live has attempted by many devious ways and means to destroy the humanity of all people, and particularly the humanity of black people. This has meant an outrageous assault on every black man, woman, and child who resides in the United States' (Guy-Sheftall 1995: 146). Beale outlines how enforcement of the US myth of 'manhood', with men earning good money and driving Cadillacs, and of 'woman' as estranged from all real work, spending hours primping and preening, limited to a sex role, negatively affected the realities of, and the relations between, Black men and women. Recognising that the 'exploitation of Black people and women works to everyone's disadvantage and that the liberation of these two groups is a stepping-stone to the liberation of all oppressed people in this country and around the world', Beale set a radical agenda for feminist politics. This agenda recognises shared oppressions between women but clearly states that: 'Any White group that does not have an anti-imperialist and anti-racist ideology has absolutely nothing in common with the Black women's struggle . . . If white groups do not realise that they are in fact fighting capitalism and racism, we do not have common bonds' (Guy-Sheftall 1995: 153).

Linda La Rue's article 'The Black Movement' (*Black Scholar*, May 1970) objects to the analogy then being drawn in feminist literature between the oppression of women and the oppression of Black people and points to the incompatibility of White role models for Black women: 'If anything is to be learned from the current women's lib agitation, it is that roles are not ascribed and inherent, but adopted and interchangeable in every respect except pregnancy, breast feeding, and the system generally employed to bring the two former into existence' (Guy-Sheftall 1995: 167). In challenging internalised myths about Black womanhood, La Rue concludes that: 'I maintain that the true liberation of black people depends on their rejection of the inferiority of women, the rejection of competition as the only viable relationship between men, and their reaffirmation of respect for general human potential in whatever form – man, child, woman – it is conceived' (ibid: 173). It is clear then, that Black women's critical voices were raised as 'White women's liberation' was proceeding in the USA and elsewhere. That it took a long time for these voices to be heard and understood by wider feminist audiences is explored in depth in Chapter 5.

The term 'sex class' was coined in Shulamith Firestone's *The Dialectic of Sex* (1972) as springing from a 'biological reality', that men and women were created different and not equal. She extends de Beauvoir's analysis in arguing that although this difference did not necessitate the development of one class dominating the other, the reproductive *functions* of these differences do. Firestone points out that removing the biological basis of women's oppression would not guarantee freedom for women and children, on the contrary new technologies, particularly fertility control, could be used against them to reinforce the system of exploitation. Marxian theory is critiqued for not analysing the psychosexual roots of class deeply enough to recognise the need for revolutionary uprooting of the basic social organisation, the biological family.

Recognition of the dangers of theories of women's liberation becoming isolated from understanding other forms of oppression in the 'racist class structure of Amerika' is apparent in Andrea Dworkin's *Woman Hating* (1974). Dworkin acknowledges shared oppression in women's lives while recognising that not all women are in a state of 'primary emergency' as women:

> As a Jew in Nazi Germany, I would be oppressed as a woman, but hunted, slaughtered as a Jew. As a native American, I would be oppressed as a squaw, but hunted, slaughtered as a native American. The first identity, the one that brings with it as part of its definition death, is the identity of primary emergency. This is an important recognition because it relieves us of a serious confusion'.
>
> (Dworkin 1974: 23–4)

Highlighting the different ways in which women are oppressed as women and within marginalised, targetted groups shows that privileging one aspect of women's lives can be exclusionary.

Abbott and Love's book *Sappho was a Right-On Woman* (1972) was the first book to trace the relationship of lesbianism to feminism and it included a breadth of material on lesbian experience as described by lesbians. On its publication Millett commented on the cover of the book that: 'this book begins to fill the terrible need of an entire population of women, until now not only persecuted and ignored, but deprived of any reasonable account of themselves and the sufferings imposed on them by a hostile society'. In her work *Lesbian Nation: The Feminist Solution* (1974) Jill Johnston argued that the word lesbian was no longer about women in sexual relation to one another but signifies activism and resistance towards a woman-committed state.

One book published in the mid-1980s slightly later than these early liberation texts, is of interest for what it represents. It is the *Women: A World Report* published at the end of the UN Decade for Women in 1985 (New Internationalist 1987). This work combines factual analysis with a series of essays by 'some of the world's most contemporary women writers' (book jacket). It is a fascinating read for the politics of the time, particularly the reception that faced Angela Davis on her trip to Egypt to write about the topic given to her for the book which was 'sex'. At the time feminists in Egypt were outraged that rather than considering multiple forms

Figure 4.1 Paid and unpaid work of husbands and wives

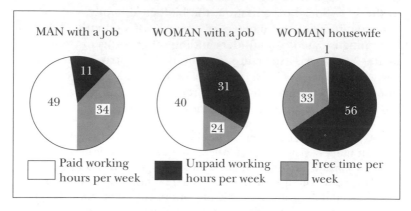

Data from 12 countries in 1975: Belgium, Bulgaria, Czechoslovakia, France, Federal Republic of Germany, German Democratic Republic, Hungary, Peru, Poland, USA, Soviet Union, Yugoslavia.
Source: New Internationalist (1987) © New Internationalist

of oppression which they were facing the UN organisers had chosen 'sex' for Egypt when debates over female genital mutilation were capturing headlines rather than being seriously addressed without fear, shame and guilt overwhelming the debates on strategies for resistance.

The five central topics of this book – work, family, education, politics and sex – are tackled by five writers from rich countries and five from poor countries making different visits to compile their reports. The opening paragraph sets the tone:

> Discrimination against women is a profound and subtle sickness that has lodged itself deep in the subconscious of both men and women as well as in the structure of our societies. This makes it one of the hardest sources of inequality to fight – because it grips women from within and without.
>
> (New Internationalist 1985: Preface)

Some of the evidence uncovered is remarkable and obviously was useful in arguing women's case at various levels in national and international bodies.

As Figure 4.1 shows, women can be seen to work twice as hard as men and housework is invisible work with long hours, which goes unvalued, unrecognised and unpaid. The combination of statistical evidence and personal/political essays made this work a useful anthology for feminists to draw from. Some of the materials produced during this time by the UN were to become useful campaigning tools, particularly the postcard which read:

'Women constitute *half* the world's population, perform nearly *two-thirds* of its work hours, receive *one-tenth* of the world's income and own less than *one-hundredth* of the world's property'.

(UN Report 1980)

The Decade for Women (1975–1985) proved helpful for many women's groups in initiating more international networking, sometimes with interventions at high levels of government and bureaucracy. The tensions between international governmental decision-making and grassroots campaigns remains an area of feminist political work which occupies many women and women's groups today. The Beijing Conference on Women in 1995 highlighted the complexities of 'mainstreaming' feminist political initiatives at the international governmental level.

Issues and alliances

Slogans such as 'the personal is political' created a focus among many different groups of women through community education and **consciousness-raising** groups. Consciousness-raising enabled women to come together in a safe, non-competitive environment to discuss things of importance to them, personally and politically. In this way women could recognise their shared oppressions and differences, and work towards creating positive changes. It was apparent that while 'common' experiences could be celebrated in certain ways, the discussions of oppression in terms of 'race', class, ethnicity, disability were much more difficult issues to assess without fear, shame, guilt overwhelming debates on strategies for resistance. The importance of consciousness, women-only space and of being inclusive arises again in considering coalition politics (Reagon 1983). The political impact of the assertion that 'the personal is political' meant a re-evaluation of 'the political' so that all aspects of our lives are considered as being influenced by wider political, cultural and economic contexts. Issues that were formerly deemed 'personal' or 'women's questions' were now brought into the public arena for debate. In this way, women who knew themselves to be unhappily married could actually question the institution of marriage rather than perhaps blaming themselves or thinking they had been unlucky in their choice of partner.

This generation of more public debate, and small-group 'consciousness-raising' had enormous political influence on campaigns across a range of feminist debates on reproductive health, violence against women, sexuality and how women's bodies were viewed, redefining 'beauty' and images of women. Feminists were able to show that idealised portrayals of marriage and 'the family' were false and racially constructed, so that policy and politics based on them were damaging for women and children. The media popularising of 'happy families' at the wedding of Charles and Diana in the UK in 1981 was one backdrop for feminist analyses on the destructiveness and manipulation of false ideals of 'husbands' and 'wives' and their allotted roles.

Feminist connections and alliances were being formed throughout North America and Northern Europe during the 1970s. Women in West Germany organised simultaneous evening demonstrations in various towns to protest against all forms of violence against women in 1977 and later that year similar UK demonstrations were held. These marches were organised to highlight the realities and the threat of men's violence against women which were constraining women's freedom, and they symbolised aspects of women's campaigning on their own behalf. These events were often lively and loud with torches, banners, percussion and singing, highlighting women's rights to be out after dark without fear. Calls on such marches for 'more policing' are critiqued by Black feminists as Black communities are differently policed and often targetted in 'raids' in which many women and men have lost their lives.

The virtual explosion of women's magazines and journals during the 1970s and 1980s shows the vast creative energies that were unleashed within women's politics during this time. Liz McQuiston's (1997) impressive work on these imaginative outpourings illustrates examples of many feminist magazines – *Women Speak!* Barbados; *Shrew, Red Rag, Spare Rib,* Britain; *Rites, Kinesis,* Canada; *Mujer, Fempress,* Chile; *Courage, Emma,* Federal Republic of Germany; *Manushi,* India; *Banshee,* Ireland; *Emma, Isis,* Italy; *Labrys,* Greece; *Broadsheet,* New Zealand; *Echo,* Senegal; *Speak, Sash,* South Africa; *Manuela,* Brena; *Sauti Ya Situ,* Tanzania; *Big Mama Rag, Off Our Backs, Ms., On the Issues,* USA. Feminist publishing houses were later established in several countries with Onlywomen, Sheba, Virago and The Women's Press in the UK, and Kitchen Table and Women of Color in the USA.

Reversals and 'backlashes'

With the election of conservative governments in many European countries, including Margaret Thatcher in the UK in 1979, and the election of Republican President Reagan in the USA in 1980, the decade of the 1980s was to witness a radical conservatism in much Western politics with nuclear ceilings being raised in the Cold War and considerable social redefinition and change. The agenda was a radical one in that both Thatcherite and Reaganite policies were designed for change and intervention in the social fabric. 'Rolling back the state' was to institute some very radical redefinitions across all layers of society with notions of an 'under-class' being portrayed alongside re-visions of 'classless' societies. Drastic reductions in welfare programmes (both contributory and non-contributory) and changes in employment patterns increased tensions between rich and poor. These political changes affected the advances and defeats in much feminist politics with issues of 'backlash' (Faludi 1992) apparent. Reversals of hard-fought feminist gains were being enforced unevenly, in areas such as equal conditions of work and reproductive health. To some extent it seemed that in Scandinavian countries, Australia and Canada the movement of feminists into government institutions and administration in the 1970s meant more headway in 'mainstreaming' women's issues and thereby avoiding some of the direct consequences of radical conservatism when the economic and political constraints arose later in these countries.

Strands of feminist thinking emerging from the 1960s located debates in shifting political climates across many, varied issues and strategies for change. Much of these political debates can be understood from reflections in numerous feminist anthologies (Hoagland and Penelope 1988; Humm 1992; Jackson 1993; Kemp and Squires 1997; Mirza 1997; Morris 1996; Mohanty *et al.* 1991; Moraga and Anzaldua 1983; Richardson and Robinson 1993; Smith 1983; Spender 1985). There is no satisfactory 'ordering' of strands of feminist politics. I focus on some continuities and breaks with earlier thinking, attitudes towards the state and key theoretical issues which are later expanded upon and critiqued.

Continuities and breaks

Liberal analysis largely presented the roots of women's subordination as legacies of custom and prejudice that could be rectified by legislative change in moves towards equal opportunities and legal and educational reforms. In extending earlier Marxist discussions, Marxist, materialist and socialist feminisms engendered vigorous debates about the roots of women's oppression under capitalism and showed that women's oppression had material foundation. Within the materialist strand a division is generally made between economic materialists such as Delphy and those who viewed sexuality as the prime basis of oppression, as did Rich. While Marxist methods proved useful for feminists in analysing the ongoing causes of women's oppression, the break with orthodox Marxism soon became clear in debates concerning the role of patriarchy.

The key break with past thinking was in the area of radical feminist debates about patriarchy and women's oppression, arguing that at some level all previous theorising was 'patriarchal'. In these analyses of men's control, through men's use and abuse of power, feminist thinkers made incisive investigations into social and political theory and the roots of women's oppression. Analyses of power in its coercive, protective and capacity modes showed a focus primarily on *coercion* for radical feminists, *protection* for liberals and on women's *capacity* to enact change in all strands of feminism. With the use of conceptions of patriarchy and patriarchal relations in feminist critiques, radical feminists were able to make distinctive breaks with much previous thinking on politics and with their views of how change can be achieved.

In recognising that patriarchal systems of control are not inevitable and can be changed, Rich notes that in acknowledging this:

> we tear open the relationship at the core of all power-relations,
> a tangle of lust, violence, possession, fear, conscious longing,
> unconscious hostility, sentiment, rationalization: the sexual
> understructure of social and political forms.

(Rich 1981: 56)

This radical critique shows the powerful impact of theorising the personal as political and the revolutionary ways in which views on human relations and women's oppression could be considered. Recognising how patriarchal relations engage with other forms of social relation, holistic analyses of race, class and gender as interlocking systems of power can be fruitfully accomplished. Avtar Brah points out the usefulness of the term 'patriarchal relations':

> I prefer retaining the concept of 'patriarchal' without necessarily subscribing to the concept of 'patriarchy' – whether historicised or not. Patriarchal relations are a specific form of gender relation in which women inhabit a subordinated position. In theory, at least, it should be possible to envisage a social context in which gender relations are not associated with inequality.
>
> (Brah 1996: 109)

Patriarchal relations can then be assessed in terms of how they combine with other forms of social relation in certain contexts. Some poststructuralist and postmodern critiques consider that fragmentation in our lives makes such political analysis unrealistic as they are reject 'metanarratives' which attempt explanatory theories of interlocking systems of power. Such critiques do not consider it worthwhile to construct general theories of women's oppression and patriarchal theories have been labelled 'essentialist' in this regard (see Barrett and Phillips 1992; Coole 1994 [1988]; Fuss 1990).

I have concentrated debates in subsequent chapters on Black feminist thinking, lesbian politics and feminist disability perspectives partly for ease of analysis but also because key feminist debates grew *out of* aspects of exclusions in feminist politics. Coalitions among feminists in practice continued in various ways with much overlap between individuals and groups. Black feminisms centred the realities of Black women's lives historically in analysing interlocking axes of oppression, showing that issues of race, class and gender are interwoven in our lives. Considerations of what Black 'families' under slavery experienced highlight radically different familial forms (Davis 1982). Shared conceptions of women's situations were important for feminist debates and bell hooks stresses Delphy's focus on the term 'oppression' as important in placing feminist struggle in a radical political framework (hooks 1984; Delphy 1984). That hooks wrote in the same book about 'white supremacy as a racial politic' was not taken up generally across feminist thinking of the time. A fascinating insight into how socialist feminists in the UK were thinking through issues of racism and current political priorities is given in the Special Issue of *Feminist Review* no. 23 1986.

Recognition of the ways in which women are oppressed differently and strategies for overcoming varying levels of oppression are still widely debated. All forms of feminist analysis generally looked towards the belief that being active politically was part of what being feminist was about. Just how to be active and within which contexts again was hotly debated. Different thinking about women's oppression led to radically different ideas on how to focus and generate change. As noted in the introduction, feminisms are not monolithic ideologies but bodies of ideas and campaigns of action which view politics from broad perspectives of 'women', challenging male power and privilege. Attitudes towards the use of the state as a vehicle for women's liberation highlight this.

How to effect change?

The different philosophical traditions from which feminist critiques arise affect their views on effecting change, particularly with regard to conceptions of the role of the state as a potential mechanism for change. Definitions of 'the state' focus on the set of structures which mediate power relations in society, while representing a higher consensus, as shown in its authoritative provision of law and monopoly of coercive power. Liberal feminists have continued to view the state as the main motor for change since this is the arena in which rights can become laws. Marxist, socialist and radical feminists explicitly reject liberal conceptions of politics and view the state as representing the economic forces of capitalism. Marxist and socialist feminists have argued that the state and 'the family' operate in tandem to support capitalism (McIntosh 1978). The state promotes women's oppression variously through regulation of education, representation of sexuality, the underlying gender assumptions of legal, judicial and penal systems (Barrett 1980).

Those radical feminists who reject the state outright as a patriarchal institution share shades of anarchist thinking of the nineteenth century. Radical feminists' belief in working collectively within communities to regenerate or revolutionise society from within, share something of the Utopian Socialist thinking. For radicals, state power is male power and feminism is the 'final critique' of Marxism (MacKinnon 1982). Critics of both Marxist and radical views see the class-based analyses to be as reductionist as gender-based analyses. Yet Bryson notes the radical critique of liberal ideas of state 'neutrality' views state intervention in formal equality as potentially increasing male power: 'for example, state provision of welfare services may involve new forms of subordination rather than independence for women, while legislation to outlaw pornography may be used to censor lesbian literature or to outlaw sex education' (1992: 195). The more nuanced approach from radicals recognises an interconnectedness of patriarchal structures so that the significance and limitations of orthodox politics can be assessed. Laws concerning male violence were assessed by radical feminists in terms of their intersection with enforcement by patriarchal police forces and judiciary. While some liberal and socialist feminists still participated in party politics at various levels, from local government to interventions in policy-making, radical feminists were suspicious of such political participation and viewed it as unproductive.

In recognising that the state deals with different women differently, Bhavnani and Coulson (1986: 84) argue that racism 'places different women in different relationships to structures of authority'. The issues affected range from immigration legislation to health, education and welfare services. Marshall (1994: 127–128) reasons that: 'state subjects are constituted and regulated in both gender- and race-specific ways. In most cases, however, this regulation is not explicit, but implicit, disguised by supposedly neutral categories such as tax-payer, worker, dependant, client, recipient, citizen, consumer and the ubiquitous "family".' In anti-feminist theories 'the family' is viewed as the basic 'natural' unit of society before the state, and viewed in need of protection from state intervention. In reality such arguments support a conservative *ideology* of a particular form of 'family'.

In practice, there has been no single way feminist politics has been considered, organised and acted upon. Feminists have worked both in autonomous groups, establishing services women need (Rape Crisis, Women's Aid, Lesbian Lines) and within existing organisations and structures to reform them. Sometimes one strategy has been more effective at a certain time, but each is made more effective by the existence of the other.

Feminist ideas on liberation

Marxist methods of analysing women's struggles through *praxis* (uniting theory and practice in action) in a dialectical frame of historical materialism are highlighted by feminist thinking. Within this, issues of public/private, paid/unpaid work are important. That humans make our own history (but not as we choose) is a basic tenet of historical materialism and with societies in Europe, China, some African countries and political parties in India developing towards communist organisation, work in all its contested forms became a major focus in feminist debates. The divide between radical politics and liberal feminist campaigns has echoes of nineteenth-century debates between bourgeois liberal views of women's participation in male power being opposed to women's autonomous organisation challenging the state forces. Overlapping loyalties of gender and class again came to the fore for some feminists, although the 'femocrat' discussions in Australia and various European countries in the 1990s brought these strands into connection (Dahlerup 1986). In considering debates on family, motherhood and reproductive health as key aspects (amongst others) of feminist discussions, the varied uses of grassroots campaigns, legislation and/or state forces as instruments for feminist change are a major focus. These debates and political actions and choices engage with the contradictory and changing situations of many women's realities, so there cannot be neat clarification on these complex issues.

Equality and difference – liberal perspectives

The liberal feminist perspectives had a powerful impact in the USA and to a lesser extent in Western Europe, Australia and Canada. Friedan's (1963) work on the 'problem with no name' stirred debates among White middle-class women in the USA with thoughts about work outside the home. With labour market expansion in many Western countries in the 1960s women were entering the workforce in larger numbers and some assumptions were being made on models of full employment which were to be dashed in the 1970s and 1980s. As noted in Chapters 2 and 3 arguments have been utilised by feminist thinkers regarding women's need for equality with men and recognition of their difference from men – often whichever appeared more useful. For most liberal feminists the expectation that women will compete in the labour market with men brings forward ideas on how household work and childcare can best be undertaken to give women equality of opportunity.

Given the different areas in which women need particular consideration if they are to compete with men under conditions other than of discrimination, liberal feminists have argued for many legislative and educational changes in national laws, trade union regulations and gender-awareness programmes. Phillips argues in this context that:

> the tension between calling for equal treatment or insisting on women's special needs is one that remains at the heart of feminist dilemmas. For women to have an 'equal right' to work, for example, they may actually need *more* than men. They need maternity leave; they need workplace nurseries; they need extra safety conditions when pregnant; they may need time off for menstruation.
>
> (Phillips 1987: 8)

Some of the liberal campaigns have been very influential, for example those for equal opportunity policies in schools. Liberal feminists have also been successful in making alliances within the professions such as teaching, journalism, law and medicine, to lobby effectively for changes.

The importance of official networks is signified by Kaplan as legitimating women's issues as issues: 'not just of, by and for women but as *general societal, economic and political* questions' (1992: 28). In the European Union, five directives between 1957 and 1987 identified areas in which women are discriminated against (Hoskyns 1985; Lovenduski 1986). Kaplan argues that in this political activity: 'although the grassroots movements did not at first take much notice of this European framework (nor did offialdom take note of grassroots movements), both levels of activity moved in the same direction of change' (1992: 29). It can be seen that over time the 'mainstreaming' of many feminist issues has brought about a closer identification across feminisms of the usefulness of varying strategic alliances.

Family work – Marxist and materialist perspectives

One of the major feminist contributions to debate has been to widen conceptions of 'work' to include domestic labour and to point out ways in which its invisibility underpins the capitalist division of labour. In the 1970s Marxist feminists found themselves confronting two major problems. They recognised that women's subordination predated capitalism and Marxist theory had no developed means for exploring gender divisions. While Marxism had an analysis of 'the woman question' in relation to the economy, it had no analysis of 'the feminist question' which centred on women's relation to men.

Women's oppression is functional for capitalism – women provide a cheap and flexible source of labour power and their domestic labour services reproduce and sustain more workers. Marxist considerations of 'the family' as subject to changing status in historical development meant that the form of family could be questioned and opened up possibilities for radical changes in viewing sexual relations. What was new about the Marxist feminist analysis was the linking of capitalist and patriarchal systems of oppression. It was apparent that the particular form of family actively promoted within capitalist societies (men as fathers, heads of household and breadwinners and women as mothers, childcarers and subordinate to men) was most suited to supporting both capitalism and patriarchy. While this actual family arrangement accounted for approximately one third of family structures in Britain (Barrett and McIntosh 1992) the *ideology* of this family form as normal and desirable, and ideas about the 'family wage' were powerful in reinforcing women's oppression. This ideology continues to have repercussions for women's lives across many countries today (see Chapter 9).

Mitchell (1974) extends de Beauvoir's analysis of women's oppression from family ideology (of themselves as wives and mothers) in separating the *economic* mode of capitalism from the *ideological* mode of patriarchy. The latter functions through the unconscious. Mitchell's use of psychoanalysis here is important for later feminist debates, especially regarding women's agency, consciousness and cultural politics. Each of the four structures identified by Mitchell – production, reproduction, sexuality and the socialisation of children – needs examination to understand how they maintain women's oppression and to identify potential areas of change. Rather than women entering the workforce in poorly paid jobs, Mitchell argues that women have to enter on the same terms as men, which means putting in order the other structures of oppression, so changes in the 'public' and in 'privatised' arenas are required. Her arguments that a cultural and ideological revolution was required were taken up by radical feminists in various contexts. So, Marxist methods and concepts provided a starting point for many radical theories of patriarchal oppression.

Radical views on family and sexuality

Analysing the 'patriarchal institutions' of family and heterosexuality, radical theories strike at the core of our lives. For Adrienne Rich, failure to examine heterosexuality is 'like failing to admit that the economic system called capitalism or the caste system of racism is maintained by a variety of forces, including both physical violence and false consciousness' (1981: 20). It is not heterosexuality itself that is inherently damaging to women but the *compulsory* nature of it in our societies. In her analysis of motherhood as experience and institution (1986 [1977]) Rich stresses the importance of patriarchal oppression:

> The institution of motherhood is not identical with bearing
> and caring for children, any more than the institution of
> heterosexuality is identical with intimacy and sexual love. Both
> create the prescriptions and the conditions in which choices are
> made or blocked; they are not 'reality' but they have shaped the
> circumstances of our lives.
>
> (Rich 1986 [1977]: 42)

Theories of freeing women from domestic work and childcare and substituting alternative family forms have been considered by political theorists from Plato to Goldman with suggestions for anonymous parenting, female collectives and socialised childcare (Coole 1994 [1988]: 181). These models deny the *experience* of motherhood outlined by Rich. In viewing power here, Rich is centring on the *capacity* element of women's power in seeing motherhood as a potent source of power and energy for women. In much of her work, as in that on motherhood and heterosexuality, Rich's work created space for opposing feminist views to connect. Her ideas on a 'lesbian continuum' include a range of woman-identified experience outside the patriarchal mind-set of 'sex'. As the case study on feminist resistance to male violence against women shows, the ways in which 'malestream' theorising is deconstructed and proved wanting, highlight the powerful capacity of feminist theorising to develop alternative conceptions of how to effect change in our societies.

Family work in international perspectives

Women's labour in families has different aspects depending upon which women are being considered. That Black women in the USA historically worked as carers in White homes is well documented (Davis 1982). As a group: 'women of Color are the lowest paid wage-earners in America. We are the primary targets of abortion and sterilization abuse, here and abroad'(Lorde 1996 [1984]: 20). For radical Black thinkers, the international dimension is integral to Black politics. I consider the international context of women working and the impact of global shifts in capital on women's lives.

In centring the question of the relationship between capitalist patriarchy and the exploitation and subordination of colonies, Maria Mies argues that these questions: 'concern every woman in her everyday life, and the feminist movement in its political goals and existence' (1986: 2). Reducing the incentives for multinational companies (MNCs) to further colonise countries in Asia, Africa and Latin America through the unjust international division of labour Mies argues, could become a focus for feminist-led consumer liberation movements in overdeveloped countries linking with women's production liberation movements in underdeveloped countries. In tandem such movements could enable the 'bourgeois model of the housewife' to lose its attraction as a symbol of progress.

In outlining how the global division of labour operates, Swasti Mitter (1986) explains that the older division of labour, the product of colonialism, was one in which European 'mother' countries provided manufactured goods whilst the 'children' of the empires provided raw materials. The emerging order was legitimised as one of reciprocal benefit in classical economic literature such as Ricardo (1817). The scope of this division of labour declined with the independence of former colonial territories from 1947 with many countries developing their own industrial bases with production policies of import-substitution (IS). When IS policies failed for various reasons, models of export-oriented industrialisation (EOI) were supported by richer 'First World' countries providing capital, whilst the undifferentiated category 'Third World' would provide cheap labour. The developments of computer and satellite technology enabled supervision and separation of production globally: 'The centralization of market and technology, together with the decentralization of production, have turned out to be the major features of the new international division of labour' (Mitter 1986: 8).

Women's marginal role in the mainstream labour movement makes them particularly attractive employees in these 'flexible' arrangements as the key desire is to be able to hire and fire workers at will. A polarised labour market emerged in which women constitute the majority of the 'casual' workers with little job security or benefits, and a small core elite of multi-skilled male workers whose benefits are still supported by trade unions. The key issues for feminists are: 'the extent to which poor women are able to gain greater control over their working conditions and more democratic power over state policies. It has always been difficult for underprivileged groups to define the terms of economic regulation through the state. The aim of alliances should be to facilitate the process.' (Rowbotham and Mitter 1994: 220). The ways in which 'Third World' women have been resisting these conditions are returned to in Chapter 8 in considerations of international and transnational feminist politics.

Our Bodies, Our Selves

Women's health and well-being has been a concern for feminists across the centuries with campaigns to ease poverty, prevent prostitution and male violence against women. Publications such as the Boston Women's Health Collective *Our Bodies, Ourselves* (1973) encouraged women to learn about their bodies and not be dependent on or manipulated by (generally male) doctors and health professionals. Gains made by feminist campaigns remained fragile in hostile climates. That the US Supreme Court ruled abortion legal in 1973 (*Roe* v. *Wade*) must be set alongside the bombing of the first abortion clinic in 1978 and the 'Take Back the Night' march in San Francisco. The marches became symbolic of the injustices caused to women by the threat and reality of male violence, such that they cannot go out safely at night. The National Black Women's Health Project was founded in 1981. Reproductive health gains, such as that of abortion rights under the UK Act of 1967 were challenged in Parliament, and in the USA Black feminists were protesting the ongoing use of long-term contraceptives such as Depo Provera against Black and working-class women. Depo Provera is an injectible long-lasting contraceptive, the use of which was discontinued due to bad side-effects. It is against this background that feminists working against male violence against women, developed new insights into this reality and new ways of theorising which challenged 'malestream' views.

Case study: Feminist analysis of male violence against women

As we have seen, one of the key gains of women's liberation politics was the conscious move to make formerly 'private' issues part of the public agenda for change. Feminist analyses of male violence against women can be seen as a 'successful' area of political work in that at the end of this century this issue is highlighted on most national and international agendas as noted in the UN *Progress of Nations Report* (1997). This does not mean that male violence against women has been considerably reduced, it does mean that this is now recognised as a crime and that women's rights to resist such violence, and to be given support and services, are endorsed.

Developments in feminist analyses of male violence are embedded in feminist practice. Similar ways of working (listening to women's experience, reflecting on how this is constructed, collectively working to change oppressive relations and reflecting on changes) are apparent across the range of feminist resistance. Feminist resistance has long been apparent in specific instances of resistance by women to male violence in order to survive and/or to escape situations of violence. The term feminist resistance is used here to refer to feminist research, support services, theorising and activism to resist male violence. The international nature of feminist resistance to male violence inevitably raises questions regarding the 'global' nature of feminist analysis and resistance (Bunch and Carillo 1992; Corrin 1996; Davies 1994; Peters and Wolper 1995; Radford and Russell 1992). Key issues have been raised regarding accepted myths of 'family', men's rights and suitable behaviour for women. In addition the requisite responses from police, judicial bodies and other state authorities have been examined and found wanting. Feminist resistance has highlighted the differential response by state forces to different groups of women, such as those of Southall Black Sisters as women from minority communities (See Chapter 5). Reflection on the construction of White femininity and 'whiteness' have been linked with knowledge gained on racism in consideration of the operation of judicial systems and enforcement of apparently 'neutral' legislation (hooks 1984; Mama 1989; Smith 1983).

Violence, or the threat of it, is something that women live with every day of their lives all over the world. Male violence against women is the most forceful evidence of the oppression of women.

The central argument in feminist explanations of male violence against women is that all such violence is a product of unequal power relations in society. The term 'male violence' includes a range of violent harm deliberately inflicted upon women – physical, psychological and sexual – concerned with the exercise of power leading to social control by men over women: 'Women are socialised to associate their self worth with the satisfaction of the needs and desires of others and thus are encouraged to blame themselves as inadequate or bad if men beat them' (Bunch and Carillo 1992: 18–19). Despite widespread evidence of much male violence, the extent of this violence has remained hidden for a long time. One major use of power is apparent in the normalising or legitimising of men's violence against women through academic writing, policy making, legislation and enforcement. In turn, feminist resistance has succeeded in challenging such 'normalisation' or 'legitimation'.

In theorising ways in which to consider male violence certain terms have become important. One such is that of 'continuum' which, Liz Kelly argues: 'enables us to document and name the range of abuse, intimidation, coercion, intrusion, threat and force whilst acknowledging that there are no clearly defined and discrete analytic categories into which men's behaviour can be placed' (Kelly 1988: 75–76). This is significant, in connecting women's different experiences of male violence, such that the expressions of: 'men's gender power through the routine use of aggression against women is connected to 'non-routine' assaults, such as rape, which are extensions of more commonplace intrusions' (Kelly 1988: 27). It does not imply any 'weight' as to the situation in which the violence occurs or the 'seriousness' of such violence, but more sensitively reflects the experiences of male violence as named and defined by women and children.

Feminist analysis highlighted the contradictions in much of the non-feminist literature which do not make connections with wider issues of male violence against women. Most of the non-feminist theories are viewed as serving to disguise or deny men's positions of dominance within patriarchal systems. From non-feminist perspectives everyday assumptions arise including aspects of 'rights' within families (men's 'rights' over women and children), understanding of violent behaviour in men as something 'abnormal' (rather than common) and suppositions about how to 'deal with' violence and what are 'appropriate' responses (within 'private' families).

'Domestic' violence or violence in intimate relationships
'Domestic' violence became an overall term used in English to define violence which takes place in or around the home. Kathy Sillard has

pointed out that the term 'domestic' can be used to trivialise such violence (1995: 241). Given that the term does not translate easily into other languages, for example, in Iceland the term translates as the house being violent towards its inhabitants and in the Netherlands as 'cosy violence', various groups now use the term violence in intimate relationships. Violence in intimate relationships includes current or former intimates, violence in the household perpetrated by a woman's partner, parent, child or other relative. The term can also be useful for describing violence suffered by disabled women from carers. Some uses of the term include forms of child abuse and elder abuse. Racism within police forces, social services, the judiciary and other authorities, seriously affects the outcomes of intervention within people's homes (Kilcooley 1997; Mama 1989, 1995; Patel 1990; Siddiqui 1996).

Assumptions from limited, non-feminist perspectives still often shape men's and women's thoughts on how to assess and deal with violent situations. Mary Maynard outlines three significant kinds of definition – legal, professional/expert and those of women themselves. As with all attempts at definition the political nature of male violence means that the narrower, non-feminist proposals in legal or expert areas can and are being challenged by feminist perspectives which have very much built upon the experiences and definitions of women experiencing violence.

Construction of debate
Many of the myths surrounding male violence in cases of violence in intimate relationships, rape and femicide have been powerfully challenged by feminist writers. (Brownmiller 1976; Saadawi 1980; hooks 1984; Kishwar and Vanita 1984; Hall 1985; Kelly 1988; Mama 1989; Patel 1990; Bunch and Carillo 1992; Radford and Russell 1992; Maynard 1993; Corrin 1996). Discussion of such myths is linked with ideologies such as 'woman blaming', men's 'uncontrollable' sexual drives, and considerations of 'privacy' in terms of social control within households. These are often used as 'excuses/ explanations' of male violence. Feminist research formulates questions that are relevant to political work deconstructing such myths and considering the connections and linkages across the range of such violence – in the home, workplace, street corner, violence involving racism, homophobia, xenophobia and other prejudices as well as violence on international and global levels including trafficking in women and in war violence (Davies 1994; Enloe 1993; Corrin 1996).

Women's bodies (and minds) become used as battlegrounds in struggles for control and domination. This is particularly apparent in struggles over laws and social changes that give women some measures of control over their own bodies – be this in terms of abortion, or resisting enforced sterilisation, enjoyment of sexuality (heterosexual and lesbian) and laws that criminalise rape in marriage. The varying responses at **community** and societal levels, and within the international arena, are shaped by specific contexts and women's locations within them.

Education for change
The possibilities of *education* in its broadest sense have been utilised by feminist campaigners in terms of 'changing people's minds' away from myths about male violence and towards better possibilities for women and children. Campaigns were developed to raise awareness within societies and state structures for the need for changes in both attitudes and legislation/policy. Projects such as the feminist-led Zero Tolerance Campaigns in Scotland were designed with clear goals – making *male power* in violence in personal relations, rape and sexual abuse *publicly visible*, and thereby less acceptable and giving politicians a more sensitised awareness of how policy can be effected and implemented to reduce male violence against women.

The Zero Tolerance campaigns have probably been one of the most successful local authority campaigns in the UK. They were feminist initiated and took radical and pioneering approaches, framing issues of male violence in terms of looking at men's behaviour, not women's. The basic insistence was that men take responsibility for their violence whilst showing the political, social and cultural contexts in which violence occurs, which *can be changed.*

The campaign developed a three-pronged approach:

- PREVENTION – active prevention of crimes of violence against women and children
- PROVISION – adequate provision of support services for abused women and children
- PROTECTION – appropriate legal protection for women and children suffering abuse

The primary objectives of the first stage of the campaign were:

1 informing people of the scale of the problem
2 dispelling many of the myths surrounding this issue
3 emphasising the criminality and unacceptability of this violence

The importance of women's movement activists in creating the conditions in which the campaign was able to develop must be acknowledged. Feminists provided the intellectual and political framework for the development of such initiatives. The fact that these feminist principles, values and beliefs are incorporated into a campaign endorsed by local authorities, health boards, trade unions and educational institutions is a definite and tangible 'success' story which is part of a process of challenging the legitimacy of women's oppression (Cosgrove 1996; Hart 1997; Kitzinger and Hunt 1993).

Passionate politics

It is difficult at the turn of this century to convey why the differences between feminist theories and groups took on such oppositional stances in the 1970s and 1980s, certainly given feminist considerations of overcoming binary divisions such as theory/ practice and even right/wrong! Suffice it to say that passionate politics were involved in terms of fervent beliefs and the very broadness of the appeal of 'feminisms' to women meant that sophisticated debates about the nature of women's oppression and creation of change would ensue. As will be seen the 'positions' sketched here are not mutually exclusive and some feminist groups campaign across several levels of struggle, simultaneously, for freedom for all. I have separated discussion on Black, lesbian and disability politics for ease of analysis but Black, lesbian and disabled women and their ideas and ideals have formed part of all feminist strands. Some women, of course, are involved in various coalitions as elements of our identities cannot be separated. Partial feminist discourses, not acknowledging the privileges and power inherent in constructs such as 'whiteness', meant that many women have been viewed as 'different' from a norm which was not articulated.

Networking from the 1970s led to ideas about sisterhood and connectivity with women's consciousness-raising through education and self-discovery. New methods of street politics were developed with direct actions forcing 'personal politics' into the public arenas of debate. Reflection on historical continuities included new visions of culture in women's writings, art and creativity highlighting the subversive power of women's art. Critiques of power revealed the extent to which prejudice and sexism were rooted in language and representations of women, in 'malestream' advertising and art not just in pornography through multinationals. Things were being redefined and re-evaluated (Spender 1985; McQuiston 1997) and these trends have continued until today.

The movement to integrate feminist viewpoints was apparent in the USA with the development of Women's Studies courses in formalised education growing rapidly during the 1970s. In the 1990s the impact of the growth of Women's Studies courses internationally forms an increasing aspect of debates on feminist activism and political incorporation (Stacey 1993; Curthoys 1997). In the first half of this century many women in the UK and USA had less opportunities to study in higher education and certainly to make their voices heard or have their words published. Today barriers remain in various forms. For many women specific forces are ranged against their voices being heard in society and in feminist movements. Later chapters explore the conditions in which despite their involvement in many levels of feminist struggles some women's ideas and politics are not recognised as central to feminist debates. This is not unique to feminist movements as the marginalisation of groups for varying reasons echoes wider social and political oppressions and prejudices.

Summary

- What differentiated the politics of various feminist groupings in the 1970s and beyond was the emphasis that they gave to aspects of explanation of the specific oppression of women and how concepts such as patriarchal relations could help to elaborate this.

- Views differed: liberal demands were for women's equal rights and opportunities and a belief in education; socialist and Black feminists emphasised class relations within an international perspective; radical feminists argued that all previous theorising was patriarchal, their aim was to revolutionise society from within.

- For Black and socialist feminists economic and cultural revolutions are still required to overcome liberal capitalism and challenge international divisions of labour.

- While analyses of difference and diversity have been characterised as a central focus in gender analysis, some thinking about 'difference' crucially neglects issues of power and domination.

Further reading

de Beauvoir, Simone (1988) *The Second Sex* Harmondsworth: Penguin

Corrin, Chris (ed.) (1996) *Women in a Violent World: Feminist Analyses and Resistance across 'Europe'* Edinburgh: Edinburgh University Press

Evans, Mary (ed.) (1994) *The Woman Question* 2nd edn London: Sage

McQuiston, Liz (1997) *Suffragettes to She-Devils: Women's Liberation and Beyond* London: Phaidon

Chapter 5

Black feminist thought

I urge each one of us here to reach down into that deep place of knowledge inside herself and to touch that terror and loathing of any difference that lives there. See whose face it wears. Then the personal as the political can begin to illuminate all our choices.

(Lorde 1996 [1984]: 161)

I grew up in the vast encircling presumption of whiteness – that primary quality of being which knows itself, its passions, only against an otherness that has to be dehumanized. I grew up in white silence that was utterly obsessional. Race was the theme whatever the topic.

(Rich 1993: 181)

Chapter outline

In this chapter the politics of Black feminisms is considered within discourses on **race** and histories of imperialism and colonisation. The political uses of terms such as **Black, White** and **women of Colour** and '**Third World**' are explained within the contexts in which they are used. Issues of institutionalised **racism** are discussed and the ways in which Black feminist theories have moved forward thinking about dominance and resistance. Key points include:

- black feminist discussions exploring how both Black and White women's gender is constructed in various ways, with a focus on issues of class and racism;
- the power and privileges of **whiteness** considered in the context of the denial of White as a racialised category;
- identity/difference issues assessed in terms of: difference as experience, difference as social relations; difference as **subjectivity** and difference as identity (Brah 1996);
- the politics of coalition viewed in the context of international solidarity.

Introduction

This chapter considers the analyses of Black women, women of Colour and 'Third World' women, on politics and feminisms. The terms Black and White and women of Colour are capitalised to note their politicised content – of political and pride terms for Black people and people of Colour and to show the generally non-problematised nature of White power and privilege. We need to differentiate between Black and White as analytical categories and Black and White women as individuals. I use quotation marks around 'Third World' as it is a particularly poor term given its ranking connotations, yet such phrases are hard to dislodge from our literature. The term Black, as used in the USA and internationally, considers African–American experience and politics. When analysing the experience of Asian, Chicana, Latina, Native American (i.e. not White) women, the term women of Colour is used. In the UK, as we see, the term Black was taken as a cover-all political term and is still used broadly in British literature. None of these terms are definitive and for some women terms such as women of Colour are reminiscent of 'Coloured' and not helpful. As 'women of Colour' reflects more the intellectual and political coalitions that joins groups of women it: 'aims to foster unity and unwillingly flattens diversity' (Hill Collins in Zinn and Dill 1994: xv). I use the term Black to consider both the realities of African–American people and politics, and to consider the theories generated by Black women and women of Colour, as in 'Black feminist thought'. Neither 'Black feminist' nor 'White feminist' are clearly defined ways of thinking but are used descriptively and I try to put them into context.

As the work by Guy-Sheftall on African–American women shows, Black women have been present in many struggles over the centuries and the interconnections of racism, class and gender oppression cannot be separated. I do not use quote marks around the word race as some authors do to show that it is a social construction, because this can mean that the lived reality of racism is not recognised in the term. Women of Colour and Black feminists have been involved in theorising ideas about reproductive rights, employment issues, motherhood, lesbianism, disability in the multitude of feminist debates touched upon in this book. Until the 1970s, the resonance of these theories arising from lived experiences were in many ways viewed as 'add on' politics. By 'add on' I mean that it was considered acceptable in feminist and some other progressive politics to add issues of racism or aspects of Black women's experience on to the core of White ideas. Rather than a politics emerging from the recognition of multiple oppression and the ways in which our lives are structured through the prism of race, class, gender, sexuality and disability, much White feminist politics centred upon White experience, which was of necessity privileged. The privilege of whiteness did not mean that many White women were not oppressed as women, as lesbians, as disabled women but their lives were structured differently than those of Black women and women of Colour who experienced racism in their everyday lives. In part, Black feminist movements grew in particular ways through the experience of this marginalisation from White women's liberation movements, as well as the desire for centring the international dimension of feminist struggles. There are many reasons why groups choose to work separately and in coalition. For Black women in Western countries it was a necessity to work together separately from White women who had not challenged their own racism. In working with other Black women, Black feminists were able to work together recognising a centrality of Black experience internationally and to develop inclusive politics of liberation.

In writing of experience, the historical and individual experiences of women are considered to understand how certain images/subjects were constructed as well as to understand what women's lives were like. Experience is important for feminist thinking not only in terms of recognising the realities of women's lives but in developing an understanding between experience, social power and politics. The notion of identity politics grew out of considerations of experience. Whilst identity politics remain important in feminist thinking, it is identification with working toward change in political struggle that is central to much feminist activism. Mohanty points out that certain 'Third World' critiques challenge liberal humanist ideas about subjectivity and agency. In particular Alarcon, Ford-Smith, Anzaldua and Sommer suggest: 'a notion of agency which worked not through the logic of identification but through the logic of opposition' (Mohanty 1991: 8). Chris Weedon argues that: 'Theory must be able to address women's experience by showing where it comes from and how it relates to material social practices and the power relations which structure them' (1987: 8). Black feminists theorise about how Black women's lives have been structured through racialised discourse and racist social practices and power relations within various societies over time so that much biased and prejudiced thinking needs to be de-constructed.

Obviously Black women's experiences are vastly diverse but certain aspects of how their lives have been structured by race and racism hold similarities and enable collective engagement. These issues are highlighted in my later discussion of the impact of post-modern thinking on feminisms.

There was 'tokenism' in the early days of women's liberation politics when Black women and women of Colour invited to feminist events were expected to 'speak for' Black women. Such tokenism often did not allow a Black woman to speak on issues of motherhood or disability as she was considered an 'expert on race' and only, or primarily, interested in race issues. It is still the case in some UK universities that many women of Colour are expected to teach on race issues whatever their knowledge, preference or job specification. In similar ways disabled women were invited to speak on disability issues and 'for' disabled women. As we see in Chapter 7 disabled women's lives are affected by intersections of race, class, sexuality in varying aspects, and differences in their impairments need recognition in this context. Out of Black feminist thinking has come the recognition of the need to consider whiteness, the privilege afforded to White women, that has much of its roots in the historical realities of **colonialism** and immigration. The term 'White' needs to be regarded as a racialised category in order for us to understand some of the realities of people's lives and work towards overcoming racism.

Critiques by Black feminists of political thought in terms of **ethno-centrism**, racism and partiality had impact within feminist thinking, generating many creative and challenging analyses of political thinking. Ethnocentrism makes White ethnic realities the centre of thinking so that all experience is universalised from this position with models developed that characterise, and thereby deny the specificity of, Black women's experiences. For many Black feminists the realities of resisting racism and sexism or being expected to place priority on one, has to be considered. In the study of the work of Southall Black Sisters (SBS) the unity of theory and practice are apparent in their relationships and their work against oppression at all levels. Their work brings together Black feminist theories regarding women's oppression and the practices of supporting women and resisting racism.

In examining the starting points and consequences of women's liberation politics key questions are posed. Why was 'difference' important in feminist critiques? Here considerations are raised about why White feminists viewed 'others' as different, with whiteness viewed as the norm. How have Black feminist analyses moved forward thinking about oppression, racism and resistance? Has this made conceptual shifts in political thought possible? What is the 'politics of experience' and how does power operate in building gendered and racialised subjects. How does feminist thinking relate to anti-racist, 'Third World' and post-colonial studies? I will attempt to situate some of these arguments but lack of space prevents a full analysis.

Race and racism

From a biological perspective there is only one race – homo sapiens, the human race. In writing about 'races' people generally mean groups marked as different from other groups on the basis of various traits (skin colour, physique) the choice of which have developed historically and arbitrarily. The concept of race is therefore a social construction so that Black and White people were invented over time. Racial prejudice is sometimes wrongly described as being based on irrationality. Often political prejudices are founded on rational (not 'correct') arguments and have profound consequences. Philomena Essed points out that: 'This semblance of common sense and so-called logical thinking, in turn, makes specific prejudices seem acceptable' (Essed 1990: 10). Racism, the complex mix of prejudice and discrimination based on an ideology of racial domination and oppression, functions to justify the oppression of specific racial/ethnic groups and perpetuates differences in power (Essed 1990; Miles and Phizacklea 1979; Sivanandan 1982). Stuart Hall explains how certain ideologies become 'naturalised' in the world of common sense: 'Since (like gender) race appears to be "given" by Nature, racism is one of the most profoundly "naturalised" of existing ideologies' (Hall 1995: 19). As such, ideologies of racism become taken for granted and people tend to become unaware of the historical and cultural constructions in society. It can be argued that generations of school pupils in Britain learnt their racism at school from the histories of imperialism with the 'good' British adventurers going out to 'civilise the natives' – of India, African countries, Latin America or elsewhere.

The term 'Black people' was created during the trans-Atlantic slave trade. Before this time people from specific ethnic and linguistic groups, villages, towns, regions, religious communities were called Ashanti, Bantu, Ibo, Yoruba and so on. When slave ships transported people from the African continent they were: 'deliberately mixed up on New World plantations, especially in North America, and collectively called "African", "negroes", "blacks", "niggers", "Sambo" and so on, by their masters' (Jordan and Weedon 1995: 308). This collective name-calling lumped them together as if they were one people rather than peoples of many identities. The arbitrary nature of this construction of race has had inhuman consequences. From the hundreds of thousands of bodies thrown off slave ships to waiting sharks, Australian Aboriginal children having their heads kicked off, deaths in Hitler's gas chambers, to the lynchings, racist murders and incarceration of Black people today, the reality of race and racism is an inescapable fact that every person of Colour lives with (Baldwin 1964; Davis 1982; Gilbert 1978; hooks 1992a; Jordan and Weedon 1995).

Racialised images are representations of a politics of domination which have become so embedded in television, film and popular culture that it can be hard to separate out fiction, fact and fabrication. Ideas about Black men's sexual prowess merge into myths of Black male rapists whilst the sexualised images of voracious Black women slide into myths of castrating matriarchs. The influence of these historical experiences is clearly expressed in the stereotypes of Black women portrayed in the media and elsewhere. Michelle Wallace writes of various stereotypes that have appeared over time of Black women – The Mammy, The Black Matriarch, The Harlot/Sex Goddess; The 'Tragic Mulatto' and more recently, the Welfare Mother (Wallace 1979). In her work Millsom Henry shows that despite their American origins such portraits continue to influence some of the ways in which Black British women are viewed (Henry 1993: 2). Often media constructions show familiar figures such as the devoted 'Mammy' or 'natives' who may appear as noble and simple or cheating and devious. Hall points out that when the particular versions fade, traces are still apparent:

> Today's restless native hordes are still alive and well living, as guerilla armies and freedom fighters in the Angola, Zimbabwe or Namibian 'bush'. Blacks are still the most frightening, cunning and glamorous crooks (and policemen) in New York cop series.
>
> (Hall 1995: 22)

This highlights the pervasiveness of racism structured into racialised discourses and how the racialised images proposed as part of our everyday world, need to be recognised as such in order to understand the frameworks in which they are set up (see also hooks 1992b).

Is gender an important factor in race and racism? Avtar Brah points out that racism constructs the female gender differently from the male gender. For example: 'black women slaves in the Americas were racialised *vis-à-vis* white women by the attribution of "masculine qualities" which were thought to set them apart from "the gentility of white womanhood"' (Brah 1996: 157). As many issues of 'race' and racism are structured into our daily lives, it takes time and energy to work against the ways in which our outlooks and opinions can become prejudiced and partial. One example of this within feminist thinking is in considerations of the term 'difference'.

Difference

In political theory difference and equality are often placed alongside each other. Radical Suffragists and the Utopian Socialists recognised claims that women brought to politics different talents and perspectives than men. In some early feminist thinking difference was often placed in opposition to equality, with men. In this section I am more concerned with difference *from*, than difference *per se*. Black feminist analyses do not address difference in terms of equality but of liberation which is a project about resistance and about freedom for all. Given its pliable nature, Avtar Brah (1992) outlines four ways of thinking about difference in the context of interconnections of race/ethnicity with feminism: difference as experience, difference as social relations, difference as subjectivity and difference as identity. In considering *difference* here, I first assess the partiality of early White feminist analyses and examine what such considerations of difference have meant for feminist political alliances.

Analyses of paid and unpaid work and family lives were key starting points of feminist critiques of patriarchal relations. Questions regarding 'which women?' then became essential. The experiences of Black women are absent from early White feminist analyses. In concentrating on White, often middle-class, heterosexual non-disabled women's lives, and generalising from such experiences, feminist criticism of women's oppression was developing in a particular bubble. It was apparently difficult for White feminists who were coming to consciousness of their own oppression, to recognise that their partial analyses were in fact denying the realities of many women's lives.

In highlighting their own experience as central, White feminists were sidelining or writing out the experience of women of Colour so that everything that was 'not White' became 'different'. Such early feminist critics of male dominance failed to recognise the tendency to universalise their own experiences, with the consequent denial and negation of Black women's histories and everyday realities. There was a loss *for all* in such partial analysis. Any inability or unwillingness to question our own understandings does not fall within a feminist mode of learning: particularly in learning from our own and *other women's experiences*, understanding the *construction* of those experiences and *working collectively* for change. Here the difference can be seen in the political priorities of Black women. Issues about listening to women's experiences and learning from the conditions which constructed those experiences are important here. As we will see, modern Black women's experience recognises how **slavery** and colonial oppression constructed issues regarding family, work and reproductive health *differently* for them than for White women.

When White feminist thinkers did begin to acknowledge their partial analyses, their 'tolerance' was still within the bubble of a central White point from which 'others' differed. As Audre Lorde confirmed in a speech made in 1979: 'Advocating the mere tolerance of difference between women is the grossest reformism . . . Difference must not merely be tolerated, but seen as a fund of necessary polarities between which our creativity can spark like a dialectic' (*Sister Outsider* [1984] in Lorde 1996: 159). Here it is apparent that Lorde is far-thinking in her outlook and her belief in the power of women's and feminist creativity. In speaking at a New York conference in which she is on the only panel with input from Black feminists and lesbians, Lorde raises issues regarding the power relations apparent within institutionalised education. It was mainly White, middle-class feminists who had access to publish their work and to organise academic conferences and gatherings. Given the partial analysis apparent in White feminist thinking of the 1960s and 1970s, it was feeding into the construction of 'othering' women and thereby into racism. Rather than recognising and celebrating diversity, the tendency was to see 'others' as expressing 'difference' *from* White feminist thinking. We see here developments from non-acknowledgement (of domination) to toleration (of difference) leading to the belief in expression, and celebration, of diversity. Such developments have remained at the level of 'theory' in many ways, and anti-racist resistance within feminisms is still often viewed as an 'add-on' aspect of some feminist politics (see Case Study).

Central to Black women's lives are the many-layered aspects of racism, institutional and interpersonal, intentional hurts and unintentional woundings. The need for recognising the weakness induced, for *all* women, by partial analyses is argued again by Audre Lorde:

> In a world of possibility for us all, our personal visions help lay the groundwork for political action. The failure of academic feminists to recognize difference as a crucial strength is a failure to reach beyond the first patriarchal lesson. In our world, divide and conquer must become define and empower.
>
> (*Sister Outsider* [1984] in Lorde 1996: 160)

It is in this feminist dialogue of the late 1970s in the USA that the expression of diversity was becoming recognised as more powerful than that of mere 'difference' thinking. The use of the term 'women of Colour' also enabled differentiation of the experiences of all women deemed to be 'not White'. These debates took various directions over time recognising the African–American historical path from slavery, alongside analyses of colonialism and post-colonialism. The UK usage of the political term Black without a parallel term for women of Colour generates complex analyses within Black British feminist thought (see initially Brah 1996; Mirza 1997).

Whose experience?

Within the partial analyses of White feminists in the 1960s and 1970s it became apparent that issues of public/private experiences of women's work, motherhood and family were revealing key aspects of misunderstanding or misrepresentation. As has been considered in Chapters 1 and 2, 'malestream' theorists often relied on arguments of women's inferiority due to physical weakness to support claims against women's equal rights with men. The social positioning of many White women made it difficult to criticise such beliefs. Sojourner Truth, born Isabella Baumfree as a slave in New York, took the name for her journey and the truth of her telling.

In her amazing and important, though insubstantiated (see Guy-Sheftall 1995: 35) speech delivered in 1851 Truth asks 'Aren't I a Woman?' – an early critique of the social construction of 'women'.

> That man over there say that womin needs to be helped into carriages and lifted over ditches, and to have the best place everywhere. Nobody ever helps me into carriages, or over mud puddles, or gives me any best place! And a'n't I a woman? Look at my arm! I have ploughed and planted, and gathered into barns, and no man could head me! And a'n't I a woman? I could work as much and eat as much as a man – when I could get it – and bear the lash as well! And a'n't I a woman? I have borne thirteen children, and seen 'em mos' all sold off to slavery, and when I cried out with my mother's grief, none but Jesus heard me! And a'n't I a woman?
>
> (Truth 1851 in Guy-Sheftall 1995: 36)

Truth spoke of the majority of Black slave women in the USA forced to work alongside their male counterparts, engaging in very strenuous activity equal to that of men and seeing their children sold into slavery, yet not allowed a mother's tears or indeed to be recognised as mothers, as women. This shows that ideologies of womanhood are as concerned with race and class as they are with sex. Truth's words are still powerful today because she is clearly asking 'which women?'. For the lives of 'free' Black women continued to be structured under racist conditions, so that gender could not be separated as a primary focal point of struggle.

Black women were able to call on first-hand experiences of expectations that they should function as men in public and women in private – often to be sexualised, raped and to bear children for slave owners. Until recent times in both the USA and South Africa sexual intercourse and/or marriage between Black men and White women was a criminal offence, punishable in the case of Black men, by death (Jordan and Weedon 1995: 281). That White men had been raping Black women for centuries without censure speaks volumes on the sexual policing policies and the constructed images of Black men as rapists and Black women as sexually voracious.

As slaves were viewed as chattels, women slaves' ability to bear children became another source of oppression for women. Angela Davis explains that: 'Slaveowners naturally sought to ensure that their "breeders" would bear children as often as biologically possible. But they never went so far as to exempt pregnant women and mothers with infant children from work in the fields' (Davis

1982: 8). Slave women were denied experiences of mothering their children into adulthood (as were slave fathers) because children born to slaves were sold into slavery. Yet even under the inhuman conditions of slavery familial relations were generated in ways which allowed slave women and men to humanise their environments. Davis notes Gutman's demonstration of the development and maintenance of slave family relations. For consideration of the ways in which slaves resisted the construction of the perpetual 'child' or repressed 'savage' and maintained domestic arrangements, kin networks and enlarged communities see Herbert Gutman's (1976) *The Black Family in Slavery and Freedom 1750–1925*. Such different histories of work and family relations have been overlooked or ignored by many political analysts. White feminist ideas about womanhood, family, motherhood, work, community were not engaging with the realities of Black women's lives. The ways in which the lives of Black women and women of Colour had been differently structured by colonialism and imperialism in African countries, Latin America, India and elsewhere were/are not being theorised as a central feature of (White) feminist analyses.

In writing about 'Third World' women Chandra Talpade Mohanty recognises the need to move away from essentialist notions of 'Third World' feminist struggles based on biology and culture, and suggests a focus on the political links chosen between struggles. Women's politics, anti-racist, and national liberation politics cannot be separated. Mohanty states that: 'Third World is defined through geographical locations as well as particular socio-historical conjunctures. It thus incorporates so-called minority peoples or people of color in the USA' (1991: 2). The challenge of 'Third World' feminisms to White, Western feminisms has been the inescapable link: 'between feminist and political liberation movements. In fact, black, white, and other third world women have very different histories with respect to the particular inheritance of post-fifteenth-century Euro–American hegemony' (Mohanty *et al.* 1991: 10).

As we have seen the histories of race and racism have developed in many different and inhumane ways. It is in this context that 'Third World' feminists argue for: 'the rewriting of history based on the *specific* locations and histories of struggle of people of color and postcolonial peoples, and on the day-to-day strategies of survival utilized by such peoples' (ibid: 10). The analyses arising from 'Third World' feminist writings raise fundamental questions in relation to feminist ideas of 'what we know' and how knowledge has been historically constructed. Rethinking ideas of resistance, community and agency in everyday life are also required.

Black British feminism

Political Black women in the UK in the 1970s were involved in Black radical and Black women's politics. The first Black women's group in London was the Brixton Black Women's Group, set up in 1973 by women who had been involved in the Black Power movement organisations. Women angered by the suppression of gender issues in the Black movement held meetings and were joined by women alienated by the reluctance of the women's liberation groups to address the realities of racism. Amina Mama writes:

> At the local level black women organised political campaigns and cultural activities and serviced their communities through the establishment of women's centres, advice lines and refuges for women facing abuse. In the course of these activities, a great many underwent a process of self-discovery and change, developing their identities in various ways.
>
> (Mama 1995: 3)

In their newsletter *Speak Out!* the Brixton Black Women's Group wrote of their Black feminism as being part of many struggles, as Black people and as women: 'It is in the context of an understanding of our oppression based on sex, race and class, and the recognition of our struggle being part and parcel of the greater struggle for the liberation of all our people from all forms of oppression, that black feminism is defined for us' (Mama 1995: 4). The late 1970s and 1980s were times of intense politics around racist policing and immigration harassments. Community groups organised campaigns against racism in education, employment, health, housing and welfare services. Within the development of these campaigns Black British people were redefining what it meant for themselves to be Black in the UK. The consciousness of Black identities was concerned with creating new ways of being and rejecting the centuries of imposed imperialist beliefs.

As we have seen, in the USA the term Black is generally used for people of African descent or heritage. In the UK this term was adopted by coalitions of African, Caribbean and South Asian organisations and activists in the late 1960s and 1970s, as a political term. Avtar Brah explains that in the UK:

They were influenced by the Black Power movement in the USA, which had turned the concept of 'black' on its head, divested it of its perjorative connotations in racialised discourses and tranformed it into a confident expression of an assertive group identity . . . Eschewing 'chromatism' – the basis of differentiation amongst blacks according to lighter or darker tone of skin – 'black' became a political Colour to be claimed with pride against Colour-based racisms'.

(Brah 1996: 97)

Class, especially in the UK, was an important constitutive element in the emergence of the concept of Black as a political Colour and Brah comments that in the UK this politics is best understood as part of the British New Left (Brah 1996: 97). This strategic use of 'black' remains contested in the UK in both personal and community terms as it can deny the cultural specificities of many diverse groups. Distinctions need to be made between the use of the term 'black' by subordinate groups in resistance and its use by governments and local authorities to allocate resources (Cain and Yuval-Davis 1990).

In considering the critiques of certain Black feminists in the USA (hooks 1982; Hull *et al.* 1982; Smith 1983; Moraga and Anzaldua 1983; Lorde 1996 [1984]; among others) it is clear that these thinkers address issues related to inseparable interconnections of say, being female, Black, lesbian, working class, disabled, mothers. In this way, Magdalene Ang-Lygate argues, these North American feminists: 'Speaking from a variety of cultural backgrounds and social positions, insisted for example that the privileging of "race", Colour and descent over and above other social categories, say of nationality, class, sexuality and so on, obscured the experiences of women's complex identities' (Ang-Lygate 1997: 169).

Heidi Mirza shows the construction of a national British identity built upon a 'hegemonic white ethnicity that never speaks its presence'. For the three million 'ethnic minority' people in the UK, as officially named and noted in Census surveys:

What defines us as Pacific, Asian, Eastern, African, Caribbean, Latina, Native, and 'mixed race' 'others' is not our imposed 'minority' status, but our self-defining presence as people of the postcolonial diaspora. At only 5.5 per cent of the population we still stand out, we are visibly different and that is what makes us 'black'.

(Mirza 1997: 3)

In claiming their space and naming themselves within Black British feminism, Black feminists in the UK are acting on their own behalf in challenging those who contrive to deny them speech, identity and their space. Mirza recognises that when considering race the subject is male; gender the subject is white and in class discourse race has no place (Mirza 1997: 4). Given this, Black women occupy a place in which questions can be asked that have not yet been asked or imagined and Black British feminists are engaged in a subtle project:

> a project in which over the last 20 years we have attempted to invoke some measure of critical race/gender reflexivity into mainstream academic thinking. In telling our different story, in exposing our personal pain and pleasures, black British feminists reveal *other ways of knowing* that challenge the normative discourse. In our particular world shaped by processes of migration, nationalism, racism, popular culture and the media, black British women, from multiple positions of difference, reveal the distorted ways in which the dominant groups construct their assumptions. As black women we see from the sidelines, from our space of unlocation, the unfolding project of domination.
>
> (Mirza 1997: 5)

Here we see the direct challenges to the heart of academic thinking about how knowledge is gained, how we come to 'know' things and how such knowledge can be used to create 'other ways of being'.

Challenging what we 'know'

In giving radical challenges to both 'malestream' thinking and to particular partial feminist analyses, Black feminist analyses have shifted the ways in which some of us think. As noted in Chapter 3, blanket notions of 'sisterhood' as universal were challenged early on in socialist and bourgeois women's groups and in early women's liberation groups between heterosexual and lesbian feminists. The ideas of liberation for women arising out of a shared oppression 'as women' with conceptions of 'women as victims' were challenged by bell hooks: 'Bonding as "victims", white women liberationists were not required to assume responsibility for confronting the complexity of their own experience' (1992a: 392). It is on such complexities that Black feminist thinkers focused their attention in formulating 'new' ideas concerning domination and resistance.

Feminist thought can give power to women through knowledge – understandings of how women's experiences are constructed in everyday life and in discourses, with consciousness around how oppression can be structured, mediated and experienced. In turn, this can influence ways of resistance. In her work on Black feminist thought Patricia Hill Collins aims at intellectual rigour, excellent research and accessibility because:

> Theory of all types is often presented as being so abstract that it can be appreciated only by a select few. Though often highly satisfying to academics, this definition excludes those who do not speak the language of elites and thus reinforces social relations of domination.
>
> (Collins 1990: xii)

By placing African–American women at the centre of her analysis Hill Collins aims to show the richness, diversity and power of Black women's ideas as part of a long-standing intellectual community and to counteract the tendency of mainstream scholarship to canonise a few Black women as spokespersons. There are dangers in such projects of appearing to view all Black women's experiences as similar and in claiming 'special knowledge' yet one main aim is to offer some subordinate groups of Black women *new ways of defining their own reality:*

> By embracing a paradigm of race, class and gender as interlocking systems of oppression, Black feminist thought reconceptualises the social relations of dominance and resistance . . . offering subordinate groups new knowledge about their experiences can be empowering. But revealing new ways of knowing that allow subordinate groups to define their own reality, has far greater implications.
>
> (Collins 1990: 222)

This work proposes a way of theorising that is not additive, rooted in 'the either/or dichotomous thinking of Eurocentric, masculinist thought' (Collins 1990), but an approach which considers systems of oppression in an inclusive way. This ties in with core feminist notions of the 'personal as political', listening to women's experiences and learning from the power relations within which they were constructed. In this context the recognition of the construction of whiteness and White femininity in opposition to all 'others' is an important concern.

Whiteness

Many feminists (amongst others) have long recognised that we, humans, are more than our gender and/or ethnicity, we are many-layered and complex beings that can change our minds and actions in the dynamic processes of our lives. Political and economic oppressions are also dynamic realities, but positive changes are slowed by misconceptions and misrepresentation. This can lead to misunderstanding and feed into oppressive situations. Whiteness in politics means much more than ethnicity and within feminist thought this is given recognition. As Avtar Brah explains: 'Discussions about feminism and racism often centre around the oppression of black women rather than exploring how both black and white women's gender is constructed through class and racism' (Brah 1996: 110). In considering the racial erasure and denial of power and privilege which whiteness can provide, Kum-Kum Bhavnani shows the ways in which White women become implicated through the denial of White as a racialised category:

> White skin frequently signifies power and privilege – 'the rightness of whiteness' – and this can be accompanied by a resounding silence emanating from white women about this aspect of political, economic and ideological inequality . . . What such a silence does is to deny that the need for many feminists to view as central to their task the manner in which a person develops into defining themselves as white is as important as focusing on the experience of Black women, and thus that one of the goals of feminism is to work towards the removal of the apparently natural power and privilege often accorded to white women in relation to Black women (and sometimes to Black men). If 'whiteness' is unpacked, it is then possible to see not only how gender relations are expressed in racialised contexts, but also how racialised structuring is informed by gender inequalities.
>
> (Bhavnani 1993: 33)

That women have different and conflicting interests cannot be denied despite some notions of 'sisterhood' which centralise domination by men over women. What Bhavnani is clearly stating is that language, common sense, ways of thinking have been framed within imperialist and patriarchal histories, so that it is necessary to ask *why* Black women's experiences have been erased and denied.

Unwillingness to question *how* issues of power structure our lives can create further misery for people. In her memoir about her adult life, bell hooks writes of the lack of response of her university colleagues in a feminist class to her comments on Black women's experiences: 'They listen to me but they don't hear. They don't have to hear. This is what it means to be among the colonizers, you do not have to listen to what the colonized have to say, especially if their ideas come from experience and not from books' (hooks 1998: 98). This highlights not just a lack of knowledge of how Black women's experiences have been differently structured but the lack of any *need* to know. This is what Helen (charles) highlights in discussing her work on whiteness:

> Shifting the focus of 'race' and Colour into the protected sphere of whiteness enables us to look carefully at how to speak, read, think and write of 'feminist whiteness' as a politic. It is never very clear how the apparent neutrality of (non-) Colour is perceived.
>
> (Helen (charles) 1992: 33)

Helen (charles) writes the shape of her name to show how many 'family' names of Black people come from the conditions of slavery in which names were not freely chosen. By asking White women to consider their racialised positioning, Helen (charles) is analysing the possibilities of increasing understanding and accessibility of how 'race' and 'racism' are changing and how feminists can contribute towards such examination and **deconstruction**.

Postmodern thinking has been important in considering the ways in which identities are constructed and deconstructed. Postmodernists reject any grand theories, such as those regarding the causes of women's subordination or male domination. Such considerations have been influential in analysing the differential impact of post-colonial politics and the repressive policies of New Right politics in people's lives. Recognising a variety of subject positions and the complexities of how we form our identities broadens our range of analyses. In viewing different histories, rather than a History, possibilities are opened for charting the various routes which women and groups negotiate in their lives. In arguing that the category 'woman' is unstable or fluid, some postmodern arguments remove the bases on which women collectively choose to act in resisting oppression and to voice their politics, such as lesbian or disability politics. These are complex debates and have been considered in detail by many feminist thinkers (Brah 1992; Flax 1990; Modleski 1991; Nicholson 1990; Riley 1988; Weedon 1987). The eclectic nature of postmodern thinking has proved useful in deconstructing some of the ways in which questions have been posed about women's agency and diversity among women. A key point is that acknowledging and even celebrating difference has no grounding if it is separated from the structural power relations that produce it. The basic aspect of this debate for Black feminisms has been that of recognising diversity in coalitions for change, in recognising the interconnections as well as the specific nature of each oppression. It is in this context that politics of coalition are important.

Coalition politics

Much has been written within feminisms about the concept of sisterhood. From the 'sisterhood is powerful' of 1970 to 'sisterhood is global' (1984), both anthologies edited by Robin Morgan, it was apparent that within feminisms was a desire for international solidarity. But what was this solidarity to be based upon? Felly Nkweto Simmonds points out that in the early 1980s: 'Sisterhood as a central ideology of feminism was being called into question at personal/political and local/global levels, as a theory and as an experience' (Simmonds 1997: 21). These questions were being posed by Black feminists such as Hazel Carby (1982) who argued for White feminisms to account for the historical and contemporary position of Black women. This would challenge some of the central categories and assumptions of mainstream, White, feminist thought. As noted, bell hooks sums up the rejection of a false sisterhood based on 'bonding as victims' (1992: 392).

In her consideration of political solidarity among women, Bernice Johnson Reagon discusses coalition politics. Reagon is a founder member of the female acapella band *Sweet Honey in the Rock* and her talk on coalition was given at the West Coast Women's Music Festival in California in 1981. Coalitions are not about creating safe spaces where people can hide, no space that is 'yours only' or just for people who are like you. In showing that our differences as women are real and can be a strength only when fully acknowledged, Reagon gives the analogy of a room full of people who are the same, women, yet someone comes in who happens to also be somebody else: 'And then out comes who we really are. And at that point you are not a woman. You are Black, or you are Chicana or you are Disabled or you are Racist or you are White. The fact that you are a woman is not important at all and it is not the governing factor to your existence at that moment' (1983: 361).

Here Reagon is talking about bigotry, which *everyone* learns to have, and that women gathering together is no longer about nurturing but about *coalition building*. This concerns recognising our different prejudices and challenging them in a way that we still work together, making political alliances and forging a principled politics of inclusion.

Given the dangers and difficulties involved in such work, it is important to consider the value of coalitions and alliances between different groups of women. June Jordan recognises that: 'I would say about coalitions what I said about unity, which is what for? This issue should determine the social configuration of politics. . . . It seems to me that an awareness of the necessity for international coalition should not be hard to come by in many spheres of feminist discourse because so many of our problems, apparently have universal currency' (1994: 263). These debates about inclusive, principled, international alliances and viewing problems on a global dimension are returned to in Chapter 9.

It seems that 'unlearning' racism is a slow process and reminders are needed in thinking about which women are speaking and/ or being spoken of, and in engaging with issues of inclusion and exclusion in dominant representations. The need to recognise the complexities of such power relations present in different women's lived realities is essential to any feminist strategies of change. There are many dilemmas and contradictions faced by women in simultaneously taking on a multiplicity of struggles as can be seen from the work of Southall Black Sisters.

Case study: Southall Black Sisters

Black Women's Tradition – Struggle not Submission
Southall Black Sisters was founded in November 1979 when a small group of Asian, African and Caribbean women came together following the Southall uprising against the National Front and the government. Southall is in Middlesex, near London, and is an area divided by politics and class as well as religious differences. Asians who settled there were mainly from the Punjab and Sikhs, Hindus and Muslims are all present in Southall. Hundreds were arrested and injured in the police operation to stop mass protest against the National Front presence in Southall in April 1979. Blair Peach was killed by Special Patrol officers and a defence campaign followed.

Mandana Hendissi recalls that: 'The early organisers felt that yes, they were very angry about what was happening to black people – increasing racial attacks, institutionalised racism and increasing fascist activitiy particularly in Ealing – yet there was no mention of women's oppression' ('In Conversation' *Against the Grain [ATG]* Southall Black Sisters [SBS] 1990: 10). It was apparent from the outset that those involved in Southall Black Sisters wanted to work through various aspects of their experiences to be able to effectively campaign on several levels. In discussing the early days, Avtar Brah explains:

> We made a conscious decision to move beyond sloganism and develop solidarity on the basis of a mutual understanding of both the similarities and differences in our experience as Asian and Afro–Caribbean women and to translate this understanding into practice. . . . Our aim was to devise effective strategies for working within our own communities – for challenging the specific configuration of patriarchal relations of these communities as well as in the society at large – while actively opposing the racism to which all Black people, men and women, are subjected. We had to make connections between our oppression in Britain and that of women in the Third World.
>
> ('The Early Days' *ATG* in SBS 1990: 13)

Clearly these were not straightforward goals – translating experiences into practice by bringing together the aspects of gendered oppression within their communities, and the wider patriarchal and racist oppression within British society. Uniting theory and practice through action was emphasised and self-definition as Black was important: 'As Asians and African–Caribbeans we shared common experiences of colonialism imperialism and contemporary racism in Britain . . . It is a political term that united us' (Siddiqui 1996: 95).

Several aspects came together in the development of Black feminist politics within Southall Black Sisters:

1 activism against racism within British society and attempts to theorise from Britian's colonial history to the institutionalised racism of British state structures;

2 challenging leaders within their communities on issues of women's oppression and thereby challenging notions of unified communities;

3 creating a sense of identity in opposition to the dominant white feminist agendas and generating active political coalitions.

In the space here for consideration of these critiques I take an example of each, yet this touches only the surface of deeper debates and practical examples of the unity of theory and practice apparent from their work over the past 20 years.

1 Action against British racism
In challenging women's oppression within an anti-racist discourse SBS has had to analyse many contradictions. This has involved questioning the uneasy alliance between socialists and community leaders in terms of a 'hands-off' approach to Asian family relations from 'multi-culturalist' perspectives. In this approach notions of 'cultural difference' were used obscurely rather than working to recognise, and develop theories of racism from, Britain's colonial history.

Connections between male abuse of power and anti-racism surfaced in 1992 when SBS was involved in the campaign for the acquittal of David Avondale for wrongful arrest. As one of the men in the campaign had been convicted of rape SBS tried to gain discussion of the issue but the result was that both SBS and some men left that campaign. In analysing the racism apparent in the policing of Black communities, Pragna Patel notes the contradictions of helping women suffering 'gang' violence and assisting mothers of boys in 'gang' trouble with the police. The constructed myths about the youth in Southall, coupled with public relations exercises undertaken by the police (since their failure to apprehend the officer who killed Blair Peach and subsequent racist image) involved trade-offs with community leaders who enjoyed a divide and rule aspect to their liaison. Often self-organisation becomes the only realistic option ('Southall Boys' *ATG* in SBS 1990: 54).

2 Challenging notions of unified communities
In considering progressive political analyses on the Left in Britain and conservative, traditional community thinking, the critiques from Southall Black Sisters strike at the foundations of such ideas. Despite the work of SBS being considered a betrayal in some quarters, Rahila Gupta writes: 'We have not left the anti-racist struggle. We did not undermine it. Instead, we brought an anti-racist perspective to the women's movement and a feminist perspective to the black struggle. We took on the dynamics of the contradictions that our dual focus posed ('Autonomy and Alliances' *ATG* in SBS 1990: 56). Following campaigns such as that to secure the release of Iqbal Begum with Birmingham Black Sisters, members of SBS decided to take part in a film considering violence in Asian communities. Rather than impose constraints upon themselves by avoiding discussion before a racist public, Gita Sahgal notes that:

> we wanted both to discuss domestic violence and expose the way in which the multi-cultural consensus oppressed women. . . . We

were conscious of our heritage and wanted to present ourselves
and the women whom we worked with as strong, militant women
who were fighting back.

('Fundamentalism and the Multi-Cultural Fallacy' ATG
in SBS 1990: 18–9)

The apparent complicity of state authorities with community leaders
in presenting examples of 'community needs' created dangerous
situations. Hannana Siddiqui points out this aspect in the work of SBS
concerning restrictions on Asian girls: 'the overall response of schools
and social services to the problem of arranged marriages and the
restrictions young Asian girls face has been that of non-intervention
or reconciliation in the name of multi-culturalism' ('BMWs and
Samosas at the Seaside' ATG in SBS 1990: 42). The fears of 'White
liberals' in terms of not wishing to know about problems within Black
communities is apparent both from anti-racist men and from White
feminists. There are clearly problems with the way such 'knowledge'
is or can be used, yet this does not negate the need for a full
understanding of the various experiences of women and the conditions
within which such experiences are structured and shaped over time.

3 Developing Black identities and working with White feminists
In her hilarious piece entitled 'N.O.W. or Never', Smita Bhide sums
up some of the contradictions raised when SBS worked with various
women, including those from Women Against Violence Against
Women (WAVAW), as *The Network of Women* to organise a national
demonstration of Women Against Male Violence, in London in 1986.
Contradictions and confusion reigned as lack of time prevented the
working through of differences in analysis. Their analyses differed in
that for SBS: 'Our analysis was based on a socialist perspective of the
economic position of women but combined with an awareness of the
very real power that patriarchal ideologies exert over women's lives,
regardless of class, or economic resources, community, culture or
religion' (*ATG* in SBS 1990: 32). Attempts to raise issues of race and
class in debates with the White feminists in WAVAW were not
successful. In this context, Annette Kilcooley writing in the later
1990s offers an explicit example of the ongoing need for awareness
of, and sensitivity to, a holistic approach:

> Black sisters were outraged when white feminists, campaigning
> around safety for women, marched through areas where Black
> people lived, demanding safer streets for women and better
> policing. For which women, they asked – and for whom were they
> demanding better policing? Certainly not for Cherry Groce who
> was shot by a police inspector in Brixton in 1985, while police

raided her home apparently seeking to arrest her son... Not for
Cynthia Jarret either who died during a police raid of her home in
north London in 1985, while police were seeking to arrest her son
who didn't even live there. Nor for Joy Gardner, whose death in
London in 1993 was precipitated by policing activity at her home.
(Kilcooley 1997: 34)

Here we see the advantages of white skin privilege in terms of how
'the state deals with different women differently *and* has different
policing strategies for Black and white groups' (Kilcooley (1997): 34).
Being conscious of the many-layered complexities of women's
experience and positioning does not mean that collective action
becomes impossible. As this study of Southall Black Sisters shows
undertaking actions within various struggles simultaneously is one way
in which to develop inclusive, principled coalitions to enact change for
the better in people's lives.

Summary

Critiques by Black feminist thinkers of political theory and
feminisms have highlighted the partiality of thinking around the
ways in which women's lives are differently structured by political,
historical, economic and cultural conditions.

- Use of terms are important. Black, White and women of
  Colour are all political terms. The use of 'Black' varies in
  the USA and internationally it signifies African–American
  experience. In the UK it is a political term for people who
  are not White. In the USA the term 'women of Color' is
  used for Chicana, Latina, Asian women and those distinct
  from African–American or White–American.

- Racism is a complex mix of prejudices and discrimination
  based on ideologies of racial domination and oppression.
  It functions to justify the oppression of specific racial/
  ethnic groups and perpetuate differences in power. The
  arbitrary nature of the construction of race has had
  inhuman consequences for millions of people over time
  across the world.

- Issues of difference are important for feminisms. Women's difference *from men* was important to analyse in early difference/equality debates. For Black feminist thinkers questions of difference *from* a White, middle-class norm are important. Avtar Brah (1996) outlines four ways of thinking of difference in connections with race and feminism: difference as experience; difference as social relations; difference as subjectivity; and difference as identity.

- Black feminist analyses have challenged how knowledge has been constructed and offer new ways of defining reality by rethinking social relations of dominance and resistance.

- Whiteness includes power and privilege, recognises how for White women gender is also constructed through class and racism.

- Rather than 'universal sisterhood' some Black feminist thinkers have proposed coalition building on the basis of identification with shared goals. A recognition for international or 'transnational' coalitions recognising specific locations and histories of struggle is required.

Further reading

Collins, Patricia Hill (1990) *Black Feminist Thought: Knowledge, Consciousness and the Politics of Empowerment* London: Harper Collins Academic

hooks, bell (1982) *Ain't I a Woman? Black Women and Feminism* London: Pluto Press

Lorde, Audre (1996) *The Audre Lorde Compendium: Essays, Speeches and Journals – The Cancer Journals 1980, Sister Outsider 1984 and A Burst of Light 1988* introduced by Alice Walker, London: Pandora

Mirza, Heidi (1997) *Black British Feminism: A Reader* London and New York: Routledge

Southall Black Sisters (1990) *Against the Grain: A Celebration of Survival and Struggle, Southall Black Sisters 1979–1989* London: Southall Black Sisters

Chapter 6

Lesbian politics

It is a serious and brave act each time one of us comes out, because for some of us the danger is real. . . . Always, we must be on our guard because violence against us is lurking. We are women, we are lesbians, we have no race privilege.

(Silvera 1991: xv)

The ceremony took place the Saturday before Gay Day 1988 . . . Trin's parents and many of of her twelve siblings and their spouses attended. Trin's parents made the wedding dresses that both brides wore that day.

(Jay 1995: 112)

Chapter outline

This chapter is concerned with debates about **sexuality**, and the politics through which lesbian feminist analyses have challenged dominant discourses on sexuality and women's power.

- The personal realm of sexuality and **sexual** practices was shown to be politically important in changing dominant conceptions of how we 'should' live. Recognising the shifting nature of discourses on sexuality, within political structures that change, is significant.
- The use of morality in discourses concerned with **sex** and sexuality can be seen in ideas concerning what is deemed to be 'natural/unnatural' or 'normal/abnormal'. Intersections of sexuality with gender issues, racism, class prejudice and disability politics can be viewed within these processes of *normalising and othering*.
- We see the ways in which lesbian politics has challenged the nature of dominant discourses on sexuality and has had an impact in transforming political conditions and feminist ideas and practices.

Introduction

I turn now to consider lesbian politics in the light of self-organisation, developing lesbian identities, and the contradictions that lesbian arguments and activisms have posed for orthodox views of sexuality and heterosexual institutions such as marriage and 'the family'. Questions are raised by lesbian critiques for feminist thinking, for **gay** liberation politics and more widely within discussions about human rights. Complex debates have been generated regarding the political nature of lesbian existence, from lesbian **separatism** to queer politics, with campaigns highlighting discrimination and prejudice within institutionalised education, welfare services, social and political policies and the ways in which public intolerance is created and continued. The focus is on shifting theoretical debates arising from political campaigns.

The changes from viewing lesbianism as a perversion which needed policing, to an illness which needed treatment, to an unfortunate condition to be recognised and finally to the recognition that lesbians are women choosing to love other women, have taken centuries to play themselves out. As with issues of class, gender, racism and disability politics it is possible to see the ways in which historically specific definitions and constructions are contested and the roles that feminist theories and social movements have played. In some countries lesbians are still punished by law and in most countries social and political prejudices make the experiences for women of 'coming out' quite traumatic (see Markowe 1996). That lesbian thinking poses difficult questions to non-lesbian feminist principles and practices is apparent not only in the early exclusion of lesbian politics from feminist movements and in the resistance to engage with some of the political debates that lesbian feminist theories have raised. In working through these issues I signpost the major debates highlighted by lesbian activism for 'malestream' thinking and within feminisms and wider political coalitions.

Terms of debate

As we have seen, theories of sexuality from the nineteenth century had profound impacts on women's lives. In the history of thinking on sexuality it is not until the twentieth century that any challenges are made to the dominance of heterosexual paradigms. As noted in the Case Study on male violence against women in Chapter 4, the power of 'normalising' discourses is strong. These may be concerned with ideas of men's rights to violence or with the 'natural' ideas about heterosexuality which construct homosexuals as 'other'. The terms 'natural' and 'normal' are ones which we have seen to need caution, given the 'natural' attributes incorrectly applied to (mostly White) women's lives from at least the eighteenth century regarding their inherent weakness and inability to be 'good' mothers and workers, or to undertake full citizenship. For Black women, during slavery it was assumed that they were 'naturally' inferior to the White people who owned them so could be raped and used as 'breeders'. Nineteenth-century imperial propaganda was also concerned in Britain with the decline in 'national stock' and concerns for the 'imperial race'. There are echoes here for late twentieth century discourses on racism. Generally in the nineteenth century sexuality was seen as something dangerous and morally corrupting, with men's 'natural needs' opposed to (often conflicting) ideas of women's chastity, 'vile appetites' or 'passionlessness'. As we have seen prostitutes were blamed for vice not men demanding sexual services. The important use of morality in debates about gender and sexuality was apparent in attempts to control people regarded as abnormal or deviant. The interaction of sexuality with other aspects of life such as class, gender and race can be seen within these processes of 'othering'.

Just as in the nineteenth century when women working as prostitutes were viewed as moral threats to 'good women' and social order, so were seen to need state regulation, so the view that lesbians and gay men posed similar threats to society led to the denial of their full citizenship based on their sexuality. Official discourse regarding stable families meant that economic and social pressures were towards the 'socialisation of procreation'. Many would argue that this discourse has changed little at the end of the twentieth century.

The construction of lesbian subjects

Discourses on sexuality are important in considering the social construction arguments. The term *discourse* basically means to talk about and discuss something. Foucault suggests that each discourse is structured around core themes and connections which define the terms in which statements can be made (1972; 1976). Discourses can define 'problems' and produce 'norms' against which *abnormality* can be viewed. In the same ways in which prostitutes were viewed as abnormal women so were lesbians. Discourses can become institutionalised in policy decisions and organisations. We can see this not only with regard to sexuality but with regard to prejudices around race and in the medical models of disability. The discourse on lesbian politics generated new possibilities for **subject positions**, group solidarities and social movements. As noted, social construction theories were important in challenging dominant views of homosexuality as abnormal. Feminist theorising on lesbian identities opened up the possibility of developing a different history of lesbianism in which diversity can be acknowledged. The down side of such expression can be seen in the labels that are often applied which imply some groups are 'social problems'. For lesbian mothers this type of labelling occurs as orthodox views see mothers traditionally as 'good' and lesbians as 'bad'. Such institutionalised prejudices can mean that mothers lose custody of their children if courts decide their lesbianism makes them 'unfit mothers'. Legacies of nineteenth-century thought remain with us in many such attitudes. So, while the production of new subject positions allows lesbians to organise to resist dominant discourses, the processes of *othering* can have dramatic consequences for the ways in which we see ourselves and are seen by others, as well as what choices we feel we can make. The material effects on people's lives can be seen in many ways, particularly in the intersection of sexuality with disability and race.

In Chapter 1, basic distinctions between biological facts of 'sex' about females and males, and cultural constructions of gender, being women or men were made. In addition, we have seen that essentialist views emphasise the 'natural basis' of various aspects of life. When considering sexuality, essentialist views assume normal and abnormal aspects which can be found in different societies at various times. For **essentialists**, heterosexuality and homosexuality are viewed as distinct forms of sexuality, with lesbianism and male homosexuality seen as different versions of the same abnormality. Bisexuality is not possible within such constructions. For *social constructionists* there is no 'natural' or pure sexuality because sexuality is *produced* through various processes of regulation and control. Sexuality is developed through human action and history rather than biology or innate sex drives and is a social phenomenon which cannot be taken out of its social context. The confusions and contradictions caused by traditional ideas about sexuality are being challenged by new discourses. In this way changes in attitudes can change policy and can also change the ways in which we think of ourselves and how others view us.

In using the terms 'sex' and 'sexual' Esther Saraga argues that 'sex': 'may involve a range of different behaviours, with or without vaginal penetration, such as masturbation or looking at pornography; it may not involve two people; and the sexual activity may not be heterosexual' (Saraga 1998: 42). In defining the broad term 'sexuality' Saraga explains that: 'What is considered "sexual" is not fixed. There is a huge variation in the social meanings attached to it. Because of these ambiguities and complexities, and the many aspects of human experience that may be seen as "sexual", we have used the broader term "sexuality" in this chapter to encompass sexual practices, desires, identities and gender distinctions' (ibid). In our consideration this broad definition of sexuality is used in charting the politics of lesbian sexuality and we again see issues of *difference* arise and hierarchies of power in terms of who conforms more closely to the supposedly unproblematic heterosexual norm, and who is the most 'other'. These rankings change over time and across various cultures and societies and the ways in which they are challenged by lesbian feminist activism is a key focus.

Developing terms of debate

Lesbians have been around as long as humankind. Recorded instances of lesbian living generally stretch back to the women-loving women associated with the Greek poet Sappho who lived on the island of Lesbos around 600 BC. The term lesbian comes from these women, also called Sapphists. Donoghue writes of the formation of networks: 'For the most part lesbians were thought of as connected not over space, in a social network, but over time, as a secret cultural tradition' (Donoghue 1993: 243). Over the centuries lesbians from all countries and backgrounds have found diverse and often daring ways to express themselves, much of which is only now being discovered.

Since the beginning of the twentieth century sexologists (scientists of sex) and psychoanalysts, such as Ellis and Freud, have argued that sexual satisfaction was important for women as well as men, but this meant heterosexual sex and if women did not enjoy this then they might require treatment and could be labelled 'frigid'. This approach reinforced the idea that heterosexuality was the 'normal' path for women and that sexual relations within 'the family' were 'naturally' rewarding. Women's sexuality must be harnessed to procreation and motherhood. Yet, these 'scientific' views were seen as a step forward in attempting 'value-free' approaches to sexuality rather than those based on religious beliefs about evil and sin. The main approach to theorising sexuality from feminist perspectives since the 1960s has been that of social constructionism, with sexualities being *mediated* by culture and history.

In Britain the word 'homosexual' was used from around 1870 to mean 'same' sex. The term 'homophobia' has since been used to denote an irrational fear of homosexuals. This term has been challenged in its application to lesbians as it is argued that it is rational for men to fear lesbians as lesbianism is a political challenge to the institution of heterosexuality (see Kitzinger and Wilkinson 1993). **Homophobia**, as noted by Lorde, is: 'The fear of feelings of love for members of one's own sex and therefore the hatred of those feelings in others' (1996: 99). This explanation shows how fear can be translated into direct prejudices. In 1972 Abbott and Love described a situation in the USA in which: 'Being gay is *ipso facto* a challenge of sex–control/sex–denial . . . Authorities usually suggest that the only way out of their pathetic state is personal cures' (1972: 186). Rather than acknowledging difference, Abbott and Love argue, society has to create a different truth, and so has built in misery, guilt and neurosis for homosexuals to make the 'victims look guilty' (ibid: 187). Developing positive identities in such conditions was almost impossible.

Homophobia is embedded in our social institutions and the effects of anti-lesbianism are important for all women. Those who feel the direct consequences of hetero/sexism, homophobia, racism and other arenas of oppression suffer their effects and have to deal with the consequences but *all people* suffer under such prejudices. This is in the understanding that those who oppress cannot be 'fully free' if they have need for domination. Challenging heterosexism and homophobia within institutions and ourselves is not easy. As Audre Lorde, with her honesty and openness, has pointed out:

To assess the damage is a dangerous act. I think of how even as a feminist lesbian, I have so wanted to ignore my own homophobia, my own hatred of myself for being queer. I have not wanted to admit that my deepest personal sense of myself has not quite 'caught up' with my 'woman-identified' politics. I have been afraid to criticize lesbian writers who choose to 'skip over' these issues in the name of feminism.

(Moraga and Anzaldua 1983: 33)

The internalisation of oppression through social conditioning and political repression takes courage and determination to overcome. In assessing the effects of homophobia Barbara Smith considers: 'I think that in addition to affecting lesbians' emotional health, homophobia also affects the mental health of heterosexual people. In other words, being homophobic is not a healthy state for people to be in' (Smith and Gomez in Silvera 1991: 40). In continuing this discussion Jewelle Gomez points out the compounding features of such oppression and the dangers of people of Colour embracing homophobia: 'because we're embattled psychologically and economically as an ethnic group. We are ourselves in a very weakened position if we allow the system to pitt us against each other' (ibid). The differential impact of prejudice continues to be challenged in various campaigns.

Developing lesbian identities

Lesbian political activism has included work towards: recognition of lesbian politics within feminism; rights for lesbian mothers; decriminalising homosexuality; **AIDS** awareness in challenging negative governmental responses, racist perceptions and public lack of knowledge; and campaigns aimed at eliminating discrimination against lesbians at all levels of society. Lesbians have been involved in major feminist initiatives and in campaigns with gay men to challenge homophobic legislation and actions. The original resistance from gay men and lesbians to police repression at the Stonewall Inn in New York in 1969 was the spark that ignited the Gay Liberation campaigns. Lesbians involved in both Women's and Gay Liberation had to fight both sexism and heterosexism. As noted in Chapter 4, divisions over the non-recognition of lesbian issues within feminist movements became apparent early in the women's liberation politics of the USA and Europe. These debates emphasise the interrelations between some of the major theoretical controversies and the activism from which they arose.

As women lesbians suffer gendered oppression and in acknowledging their lesbianism, lesbians suffer injustices similar to those experienced by gay men. These include oppression at the level of state legislation and injustice of social prejudices and stigmas associated with ignorance and bigotry. Lesbian identity is not apparent from birth and the need for self-acknowledgement means that lesbians generally have to make difficult choices and often become politicised by so doing. The term **coming out** is generally used to summarise the processes which lesbians go through in their self-acknowledgement. Some Black and disabled women also use this phrase to describe choices being made in terms of fully identifying with aspects of their identities (Campbell and Oliver 1996). The implications of using various strategies to move through conflicting **cultures** and subcultures show that:

> the old reductionist notion of 'coming out' is not an act, but rather a never-ending and labyrinthine process of decion and indecision, of nuanced and calculated presentations as well as impulsive and inadvertent revelations – a process, in short, as shifting as the contexts in which it occurs.
>
> (Hall 1995: 137)

Here it is apparent that *context* is important in considering the shifting nature of what it is to be recognised as lesbian and lack of awareness of the complexities of lesbian existence, certainly in situations outside her ability/possibility to change. The term 'lesbian' describes a range of identities and practices of women within their diverse histories and contexts. The construction of sexuality varies among and within countries and communities. The term 'coming out' is used to summarise the processes which lesbians go through in their self-acknowledgement.

Not all feminist lesbians view lesbian politics as their primary or sole site of struggle. Barbara Smith recognises that 'political lesbians of color' have made connections between oppressions and: 'challenged the "easy way out" of choosing a "primary oppression" and downplaying those messy inconsistencies that occur whenever race, sex, class and sexual identity actually mix' (1993 [1982]: 100). Choosing to identify with an aspect of ourself that is viewed negatively by the wider society is necessarily a difficult experience. In the same way that Black people reclaimed the word 'black' which had been used to devalue their identities, some lesbians positively use the term '**dyke**' which had formerly been used to insult lesbians. In claiming such words for 'our own' the negative connotations are reduced and their power as terms of abuse is lessened.

Legislation and sexual reform

As is the case for other oppressed and marginalised groups, changing legislation can help lesbians to enjoy full civil and human rights, yet unless attitudes change, the effectiveness of such laws is curtailed. Lesbianism has not been legally prohibited in much of Western Europe but almost every country in Europe has, at some point, decreed a ban on male homosexuality. In 1861 the maximum penalty for sodomy in England and Wales was reduced from capital punishment to life imprisonment. The 1885 Criminal Law Amendment extended the scope of law to cover acts of 'gross indecency' between men, making sex between men illegal. In this way the person was becoming criminalised. From 1885 to 1967 in Britain all homosexual acts between men, in public or private, were illegal. As with prostitution, the law was used to regulate who was 'right', with homosexuals clearly being in the wrong. Despite initial provision for the protection of women and girls, it excluded lesbians because, as the story goes, Queen Victoria could not believe that sexual love between women could exist. Weeks (1990) also describes a member of the House of Lords deploring that making public such an offence to women who had not heard of it, nor thought of it, would be a great mischief. Diane Richardson (1992) argues that as dominant views of heterosexual sex focused on male penetration of women, so sex between women was more difficult to categorise and was rendered less visible and in some ways viewed as 'harmless'. It was not until the 1950s that positive changes in public opinion regarding homosexuality in the UK were recognised. The increased policing of offences of 'indecency' in the UK led to more homosexual men committing suicide and public opinion was repelled by police excesses. The belief was growing that, although still not morally acceptable, legal remedies were not adequate. The Wolfendon Committee, established to examine issues of prostitution and homosexuality, published its Report in 1957, recommending decriminalisation of homosexual acts in private for men over 21. Actual law reform was not enacted until 1967 in

England and Wales, 1980 in Scotland, 1982 in Northern Ireland and in the Isle of Man in 1990. In this context it is notable that the UK had the highest age of consent for homosexuals in Europe until 1996 when it was lowered from 21 to 18. This was temporarily brought into line with heterosexual consent at 16 but the House of Lords blocked the Bill and further legislation was required to equalise homosexual and heterosexual sexual regulations before the law.

The background to decriminalisation in the UK was that of a liberalisation of thinking in areas such as those of abolition of capital punishment and decriminalisation of suicide and abortion. Restrictions on the 'promotion of homosexuality' remain in the form of Section 28 of the Local Government Act 1988 which makes it illegal for a local authority to 'intentionally promote homosexuality' or to promote the teaching of 'the acceptability of homosexuality as a pretended family relationship' in schools. The insidious mixture of British legislation which makes invisible lesbian sexuality while proscribing 'positive images of homosexuality', conditions a climate which has led to women and girls believing they are 'the only one' or are ill in some way for being lesbian. A recent study showed the alarming statistic that 14 out of 18 young lesbians had attempted suicide, many more than once (Bridget 1993). Even walking hand in hand can be risky as lesbians can be charged with public order offences such as 'breach of the peace', 'insulting behaviour' or 'indecent behaviour'. At some of the large political rallies in the 1980s, police waited outside the parks until lesbians or gay men left holding hands and they arrested them on public order offences. Anti-discrimination legislation is badly needed to ease this negative situation. In such conditions, lesbians have had to struggle hard for recognition as lesbians and to develop positive images of themselves and their lifestyles. Despite prohibitive legislation and social prejudice in many countries, lesbians are organising and assessing their situations as can be seen in the Case Study and other lesbian writings (Moraga and Anzaldua 1983; Ratti 1993; Reinfelder 1996; Silvera 1991).

Identifying 'the lesbian'

In *The Second Sex* (published in French 1949 and in English 1953) Simone de Beauvoir offers a 20-page chapter on *The Lesbian*. At the outset she recognises the range of lesbian lives:

We commonly think of the lesbian as a woman wearing a plain felt
hat, short hair, and a necktie; her mannish appearance would
seem to indicate some abnormality of the hormones . . . Nothing
could be more erroneous than this confounding of the invert with
the 'viriloid' woman. There are many homosexuals among harem
inmates, prostitutes, among most intentionally 'feminine' women;
and conversely a great many 'masculine' women are heterosexual.
Sexologists and psychiatrists confirm the common observation that
the majority of female 'homos' are in constitution quite like other
women. Their sexuality is in no way determined by any anatomical
'fate'.

(de Beauvoir 1988: 424)

This exposition, using the then common parlance of 'inverts' and
sexology, identifies lesbians as womanly and not within either the
confines of biological determinism or of male-dominated relations
in which women have to be secondary. As such, lesbianism can be
seen to pose a threat to 'malestream' thinking and dominance.
Adrienne Rich points out that: 'Lesbian existence comprises both
the breaking of taboo and the rejection of a compulsory way of
life. It is also a direct or indirect attack on male right of access to
women . . . an act of resistance' (Rich 1981: 652).

In questioning the secondary nature of woman's 'roles' de
Beauvoir writes of the positive choices that some lesbian women
are able to make:

Among women artists and writers there are many lesbians. The
point is not that their sexual peculiarity is the source of the
creative energy or that it indicates the existence of this superior
type of energy; it is rather that, being absorbed in serious work,
they do not propose to waste time in playing a feminine role or in
struggling with men. Not admitting male superiority, they do not
wish to make a pretence of recognizing it or to weary themselves
contesting it.

(de Beauvoir 1988: 431)

This work was important in challenging long-held beliefs about
lesbianism as something abnormal merely because it did not fit
the confines of the dominant ideology of heterosexuality. It is
understandable for women to choose to be free of male domination yet within a male power hierarchy such choices by women
would appear 'masculine'. What is remarkable about de Beauvoir's
analysis is that she views being lesbian as a choice, that is at once
motivating and freely adopted. That lesbians can choose to reject
heterosexuality is something I discuss further in considering lesbian

politics of sexual liberation. That de Beauvoir was writing in this way in the 1940s was something quite revolutionary, even if it was not recognised as such at the time.

Lesbian lives – real and imagined

Until the late 1960s there was little possibility to consider lesbian politics in terms of movement activities supported by political theories, yet writings on lesbian lives are apparent from very early times. In her work on seventeenth- and eighteenth-century Britain, Emma Donoghue shows how aspects of lesbian existence have gone unrecognised, been silenced or written out of historical accounts:

> It is a history which, in its combination of stories of lesbians ignored by society's leaders and lesbians persecuted by them, lesbians celebrated as exceptional women and lesbians silenced as deviants, has much to teach us about survival in our similarly contradictory cultures at the end of the twentieth century.
>
> (Donoghue 1993: 267–68)

The richness of this history is clearly being recovered and should no longer be in doubt. Yet, contradictions in nineteenth- and twentieth-century writings, by sexologists, psychologists and other 'experts', display an unwillingness to recognise lesbianism whilst at the same time emphasising its distasteful 'unwomanliness'. Ideas concerning 'images of women' come to the fore again here. Sojourner Truth recognised that in dominant constructions, 'women' did not have strong arms (or strong characters) and were not Black. In similar ways, the ideas that 'women' could be lesbians or bisexuals were contradictory to prevailing European constructions of passivity and 'women's' need for male protection. Contradictory perceptions were apparent in debates on how women's sexual expression could be considered and controlled (Davis 1982; Donoghue 1993; hooks 1984; Jeffreys 1985; Smith 1983; Weeks 1990).

Some modern Western media images of lesbians tend towards seeking incorporation within heterosexual ideologies of 'femininity'. In many Western countries, the recent surge of media interest in lesbians has centred largely on the 'heterosexual male gaze' in promoting 'non-threatening' images of lesbians which often do not translate into any realities. While President Clinton embraced the television character 'Ellen' (actor Ellen Degeneris) when she came out in her show, her series was discontinued. In the UK, lesbian television characters in 'soaps' appear to be concerned with promoting 'positive' images of lesbians in terms of young, White, traditionally feminine women who are not a threat to heterosexual male images of 'passive' women, and could even be considered quite 'chic'. An antidote to such images is that of *The Lesbian Idol* which contrasts the lived-out lesbian identities of figures such as Martina Navratilova and k d Lang (Allen 1998). The politics of such representation raises issues of integration and 'outsider' politics (Allen 1998; Humm 1997; Kabir 1998). While such developments can be important in changing the nature of some debates, underlying oppressions remain. As Ruth Magnani says:

> I believe that on the surface things have changed, quite a lot.
> There's a lot going on in the media about us, and people discuss
> it more. But it's very different when it's near home. On your
> doorstep! I still think parents are very shattered if they find out
> their children are gay or lesbian.
>
> (Magnani 1992: 89)

Despite the popularity of academic discourse of lesbian identities, the realities for many lesbians across the globe show that much discrimination and prejudice remains based on negative judgements of lesbians as bad and deviant.

Carving out lesbian politics – separatism and feminisms

Divisions between heterosexual and lesbian feminists were emerging very early in the women's liberation campaigns. Abbott and Love set the scene very clearly:

> For the most part activist Lesbians have had to put much of their
> energy into fighting a Gay Liberation battle in Women's Liberation
> and a Women's Liberation battle in Gay Liberation. Lesbians have
> had to struggle to make a place for themselves. . . . The egalitarian
> rhetoric of today's Women's Liberation promised much for
> Lesbians, but in the early days there were few deliveries on the
> promises. . . . Many women will not even say the word Lesbian.
>
> (Abbott and Love 1972: 107)

The label *lesbian* was used perjoratively within the media and wider society, to discredit feminist politics. Rather than resisting these 'patriarchal power plays' many feminists and some lesbian feminists took defensive stances, arguing that there were no lesbians in the feminist movements.

Abbott and Love detail the ways in which the media, particularly newspaper journalists, agitated 'lesbian baiting'. The issues were about partiality in thinking and action. All women could not be free if lesbians were oppressed, yet circular arguments were being posed that unless lesbians kept quiet the women's liberation movements would be discredited. Ti-Grace Atkinson draws an analogy between the purging of lesbians from Women's Liberation movements and that of militants from the American Labour movement in the early twentieth century: 'Communism' was to the labour movement what 'lesbianism' was to the women's movement. The practice of 'lesbian-baiting' was designed to contain the women's movement very much as 'red-baiting' had been designed to tame the labour movement (1974: 133). Lesbians were being excluded and silenced at this time and Black lesbians were being further marginalised within White, heterosexual dominance. Lorraine Bethel, a Black lesbian feminist critic, writing on Zora Neale Hurston, remarked that for a Black woman, already twice an outsider, to choose to assume still another 'hated identity' is indeed problematic (Rich 1981: 657; see also Hull *et al.* 1982).

Given the hostility and lack of support from within women's liberation groups some lesbian activists separated to establish groups which developed devastating critiques of patriarchal sexuality. Small non-hierarchical lesbian groups such as The Furies, Lavender Menace, Radicalesbians, Gutter Dyke Collective, Redstockings, the CLIT Collective and Revolutionary Lesbians were active in debates in the USA. The 1970 Radicalesbians argued for the 'woman identified woman' defining lesbianism widely in political and ideological choices distinguished by desires, self-perceptions and experience, rather than in social categories or sexual practices. For them 'lesbian' became one of the categories by which men divided up humanity (Hoagland and Penelope 1988). In UK feminist politics, discussions arose from the Leeds Revolutionary Feminist Group paper on 'Political Lesbianism: The Case Against Heterosexuality' (1981) regarding whether or not heterosexual feminists were 'collaborating with the enemy' by giving their emotional and sexual energies to men. In April 1981 Onlywomen Press published a collection of letters and papers from lesbians and non-lesbians debating the place of sexuality in feminist theory and practice – *Love Your Enemy? The Debate Between Heterosexual Feminism and Political Lesbianism* (Leeds Revolutionary Feminist Group 1981).

Direct questions were being posed regarding why heterosexual feminists choose to remain sexual partners of men when men remain so powerful within patriarchy and heterosexual living is neither natural nor unchangeable. As heterosexual identity is assumed by default, radical lesbian feminists argue that heterosexual women have not made a commitment to heterosexuality which parallels lesbians' commitment to lesbianism. Such 'default' identities are less well theorised than oppositional or oppressed identities – 'lack of reflectiveness is the privilege of power' (Kitzinger and Wilkinson 1993: 32).

Rather than an either/or approach Rich argues that lesbian feminists can ask *different* questions: 'beyond individual cases or diversified group situations into the complex kind of overview needed to *undo the power men everywhere wield over women, power which has become a model for every other form of exploitation and illegitimate control.*' [my italics] (Rich 1981: 663). Simple examples, like why two women cannot walk along holding hands, can underline Rich's point about asking different questions of what underlies the use of male power over women. It is in avoiding thinking in oppositional binaries that Rich sees lesbian strength as challenging the male ways of thinking about sex as a commodity. Spender argues that: 'It is no mean feat to dissociate intimate relationships from the mind-set of "sex" as a rationale for viewing other human beings as a resource for available use' (1985: 194). Rich is pointing up the lack of *choice* for lesbians within the compulsory heterosexual dominance. Lesbians set about creating their own choices in a variety of ways.

Lesbian communities and cultures

Feminists coined slogans such as 'Our Bodies, Our Selves' as a call for women's autonomy in the integrity of their bodies and in sexual expression. An early article by Koedt on the 'myth of vaginal orgasm' opened up new thinking about women's sexual pleasure, outside the confines of men's sexual power, exercised through actual or threatened physical violence and 'romance'. As women are able to enjoy full sexual pleasure without men this not only meant redefinitions of sexuality, but was another challenge to the orthodoxies of 'hetero-patriarchal' politics. The broader understanding of the term lesbian certainly extended possibilities, as Jill Johnston argued, for a lesbian nation as *the* feminist solution:

> The word lesbian has expanded so much through political
> definition that it should no longer refer exclusively to a woman
> simply in sexual relation to another woman . . . The word is now a
> generic term signifying activism and resistance and the envisioned
> goal of a woman commited state.
>
> (Johnston 1974: 278)

Struggles within feminist and gay politics emerged on issues of
dominance, of male power and of heterosexuality, often arising
from fear and around issues of control and prejudice. Julia
Penelope argues that lesbians withdrew from gay male politics as
an act of survival, and that this separation was important in establishing ideas about *lesbian identity* and *community* (Hoagland and
Penelope 1988: 45).

Lesbians celebrate their development of lesbian cultures because
the non-recognition of lesbians is something that has to be constantly addressed, not least by having to choose to keep *coming out*.
As social inequalities can be legitimated through dominant discourses of heterosexuality, it is vital for lesbians to express, and
continue to create, their cultural expressions *as lesbians* for themselves in pride and in resistance to attempts to dominate and
negate lesbian lives. In not understanding the delight for lesbians
of establishing 'women identified women' communities, it was
difficult for some non-lesbian women to overcome perceptions of
lesbianism as a negative choice rather than a celebration of women:

> it often seems to be difficult for heterosexual women to imagine
> a lesbian culture focused on women rather than, as they see it, a
> culture without men. Even those with a more feminist awareness
> still tell their stories in resistance to men, in distinction from men,
> yet still want the powerful ear of that necessary other.
>
> (Marlatt 1991: 130)

Issues of **identity politics** and *difference* are also significant in considering lesbian cultures because of questions raised regarding
interlocking aspects of oppression. A Black lesbian mother cannot
ignore the fact that her oppressors make the connections in their
treatment of her (see Hull *et al.* 1982). Lesbian mothers are not
considered 'real' mothers, lesbian families of close friends and loves
are not viewed as 'real' families, yet lesbians have to live the un-
reality of imposed heterosexuality, with heterosexual images all
around and heterosexual public displays of affection smiled upon.
For two lesbians to choose to hold hands or sneak a kiss walking

through any town or city can be a daring and risky act. Given the self-identification and acknowledgement involved in *coming out*, to oneself and friends, family, colleagues, the need for lesbians to celebrate their cultural creativity within community settings is strong, as their existence is so often repressed.

Certainly during the 1980s in many Western countries, there were flourishing lesbian community groups, businesses (often wholefood co-ops), and lesbian alternative entertainments with cabarets, music, poetry, singing and dramas. This scene changed into the 1990s, in part because aspects of lesbian cultures became 'mainstreamed' with lesbian styles and phrases being taken up by heterosexuals, and due to the impact of repressive politics of the New Right in many countries. Lesbian unity was also frail, as it often entailed a cost, of negating differences. Michal Brody argues that the strength of early lesbian identities was fragile, with the focus heavily weighted towards unity in lesbianism: 'When the time for conflict arrived, as it inevitably does in any groups . . . we had ignored the major differences for so long that we had no skills or common language to work with' (1993 [1985]: 537). There are still rich cultural gatherings, Lesbian Festivals and international political conferences, at which hundreds, and sometimes thousands, of lesbians gather to discuss the differing contexts of their lives and cultural and political expressions for lesbians in planning future collaboration. One such gathering took place in Bologna in June 1998, '*Differenza oltre I confini*', which loosely translates as 'differences across borders' (see *Diva* July/August 1998). In Rome in 2000 a large festival and conference for lesbians is planned to coincide with World Pride.

Lesbian politics has given rise to debates about culture and ethics of lesbian living. Many anthologies illustrate the strength and diversity of lesbian cultures in many countries (Covina and Galana 1975; Faderman 1981; Grewal *et al.* 1988; Hoagland and Penelope 1988; Hull *et al.* 1982; Jay 1995; Lesbian History Group 1989; Martin and Lyon 1972; Moraga and Anzaldua 1983; Neild and Pearson 1992; Ratti 1993; Reinfelder 1996; Silvera 1991). The varieties of ways in which lesbians choose to live, raise many issues regarding monogamy, coupledom and continuums of friendship/ lovers. Donoghue argues against Faderman's (1985) elevation of lesbian coupledom:

> This reduces the rich variety of lesbian culture to its most privileged
> form, the exclusive pair-bond. So many of us have been left out of

such history: celibate women, lesbian friends, women who have
more than one lover at a time, and all of us who experience
lesbian culture not just as a nation of couples but as many
communities.

(Donoghue 1993: 222)

Discussions regarding different ways of thinking about being
together and how lesbians relate to one another opened possibilities for considerations of lesbian ethics.

Lesbian ethics

Lesbian ethics are about basic concerns of relating to one another
in principled ways. Thinking within traditional ethical boundaries can undermine lesbian communities. Any group establishing
a positive identity, in opposition to prejudice from the wider
community, needs to withdraw from the values and structures of
the dominant society while establishing positive ways of living
and being. Sarah Hoagland argues that lesbian existence creates
conceptual possibilities to effect shifts in thinking and transform
consciousness. Rather than starting from traditional concepts in
Anglo–European ethics, such as duty, she considers what was happening in lesbian communities (1994: 199). Hoagland is pointing
out the importance for lesbians of politics in making life mean-
ingful. The contrast given between a heterosexual feminist giving
up time with her man to attend a 'Reclaim the Night' march and
lesbians creating their reality, which is then brought into homes,
bars, cafes, bookshops is one example. In this way, it is argued,
rather than seeing political participation as some form of sacri-
fice, many lesbians enjoy community activism as a vital part of life.
Focusing on both self and community, and the intermeshing of
these within the lesbian world, does not view lesbians as subsumed
into groups, but recognises that concepts of choice and creation
can be explored differently within a lesbian ethic.

Between femininity and an ethic of dependence, and masculinity
and an ethic of independence, Hoagland argues that from lesbian
lives there is another possibility. Rather than a 'lesbian nation' idea
this type of community is: 'something like a context or a place of
reference . . . how we understand our lives is affected by the context
to which we refer for meaning. This is true of how we understand

even our most inner feelings' (ibid.: 203). A belief in the power of ideas and changes in consciousness that can be achieved through communities goes back to ideas of Utopian Socialists. In modern times, research is continuing into lesbian communities (see Taylor and Whittier 1998).

Critiques by Black and 'Third World' lesbians living in the South and in the North question any 'given' ideas about communities of women and about notions of 'home' and of the privilege in separation rather than needs of association with birth families and mixed (men and women) communities. At the same time the knowledge that lesbian loving does entail a different way of relating across perceived boundaries is apparent as Cheryl Clarke explains:

> when the black and white woman become lovers, we bring that history and all those questions to the relationship as well as other people's problems with the relationships. The taboo against intimacy between white and black people has been internalized by us and simultaneously defied by us. If we, as lesbian–feminists, defy the taboo, then we begin to transform the history of relationships between black women and white women.
>
> (Clarke 1983: 136)

There are many ways in which lesbian living and loving challenge accepted norms and myths about how we can choose to love in ethical, caring, passionate, challenging, joyful and political ways. Yet, as disabled lesbians point out, many orthodox ideas about lesbian living remain locked into ideas of stereotyped images of lean, active non-disabled lesbians 'fitting' certain social norms.

Just as women face difficulties in unlearning patriarchal ethics around duty, care and responsibility so too it is often difficult to recognise remnants of hetero-patriarchal attitudes to sex and sensuality, especially as these are reinforced through education and dominant cultural expressions. Rich emphasises the power of lesbian resistance as 'the erotic sensuality which has been precisely, the most violently erased fact of female experience' (Clarke 1983: 25). In recognising the power of the erotic, Audre Lorde reminds us that 'Eros' involves self trust and is an energising force of power and information within our lives: 'I find more and more women-identified women brave enough to risk sharing the erotic's electrical charge without having to look away, and without distorting the enormously powerful and creative nature of that exchange'. In this way: 'we do that which is female and self-affirming in the face of a racist, patriarchal, and anti-erotic society' (Lorde 1996: 111–112).

A different ethic of loving and sensuous self-expression underlies much of the strength of lesbian resistance. Silence, rather than 'difference' is a force in the oppression of women, and in the powerful coming together of women, lie possibilities for full expression and change.

Overlapping prejudices

Where homophobia coalesces with racism, Black lesbians' lives entail difficult 'choices'. In her writing Akanke speaks of choosing not to 'come out':

> Being 'closeted' is not a choice I wish to make. Nevertheless because of the pervasiveness of racism it is one that I *choose* to make. Being black, however is not a choice. As a black woman my colour is my most obvious feature, not my sexual preferences. Within British society, black people's lives, sexuality and culture are regarded negatively. Our colour often dictates our level of income, housing and educational attainment.
>
> (Akanke 1994: 102)

As Black lesbians raising Black children in a 'white, racist, sexist, homophobic society' Akanke and her partner Terri recognise that they are 'fighting a system that threatens to devour "our" children' (Akanke 1994: 102). For Akanke being 'out' holds no attraction as it is another potential weapon to be used against their children.

In examining the experience of Black lesbians in the UK, Anne Hayfield argues that: 'we must examine the racism that exists against all Black people, the sexism against all women and the homophobia against all lesbians and gay men. These discriminations are inseparable' (Hayfield 1995: 186). In overcoming aspects of multiple prejudice it is possible to 'fit' into one group while being aware of contradictions. In a group discussion Ranee from KOLA, Birmingham Black Lesbian and Gay Group speaks of her experience of going into groups and realising that she did not quite fit:

> Going into the groups, the clubs and the pubs helped me say 'Yes, I'm a lesbian'. But I also became very aware that they were predominantly white, and they didn't take anything into account

about being accessible for black people because they weren't
dealing with racism within the groups. So it was like getting into a
group and having your identity, but also knowing that within that
group they could oppress you.

(KOLA 1994: 59–60)

The intersections of hetero/sexism, racism, class prejudice and
disability oppression with institutionalised homophobia generate
many layers of oppression and reaction. In her anthology on disabled dykes developing new cultural forms, Shelley Tremain (1996)
argues against the prejudicial linguistic practices of dyke cultures,
and progressive movements generally, in privileging terms such as
'seeing', 'hearing' and 'visibility' without considering the implications for disabled people. Tremain asserts that some current notions by which disabled people are regarded as *asexual* beings, and
dyke identities as *sexual* identities, mean that disabled dykes cannot exist: 'I contend that the notion according to which disabled
dykes do not exist currently *conditions* the ways in which dykes are
represented in every sphere of lesbian cultural production, and in
fact circumscribes what constitutes those cultures' (1996: 16). In
this context feminist challenges to compulsory heterosexuality are
questioned by disabled feminists who point out that such notions
do not reflect the realities of many disabled women who are considered asexual. A wider focus, for lesbian and non-lesbian disabled
women, needs to be considered (Hearn 1991; Shakespeare *et al.*
1996; Tremain 1996). Before lesbians can be 'out', in whatever
form, recognition and celebration of *all* lesbians and dykes and
their cultures is crucial or myths are perpetuated and oppression
continued and reconstructed.

Lesbian political struggles

Feminist analyses and activism have changed the context of debates
regarding sexuality. Some feminist lesbians have chosen to work with
men as well as women and for many feminist lesbians the primary
community is with women. Being feminist and lesbian may not be
reason enough to work together in effecting particular political
changes. In working in political coalitions towards liberation for
all, key questions remain concerning the sites of struggle and how
we define the context of our politics. Ideologies of marriage and

'the family' are challenged by lesbian existence, yet state forms and welfare policies are structured within heterosexual frameworks of 'family wages' and dependent 'housewives/mothers'. Many women, lesbian and otherwise, do not 'fit' these incorrect conceptions. For lesbians, basic social policy issues such as housing, pensions and health care do not recognise same-sex partnerships. Income maintenance for women who do not live in 'real' families is inherently problematic within a dominant society prejudiced against lesbianism. Hayfield (1995) analyses discrimination through immigration laws, education and housing which shows how Black lesbians are acutely vulnerable to discrimination. For many reasons, lesbians are active in various areas of political life, and in challenging homophobic legislation it is recognised that unless autonomy for all is achieved lesbian oppression will remain.

In the UK recent activism has included challenging unequal rights for lesbian mothers, lesbian access to fertility treatment, single parents' benefits, unequal ages of consent for heterosexual and homosexual men and the 'Section 28' which has implications for sex education in schools and safe-sex information being freely available to young lesbians and gay men. Thousands of lesbians marched on protests against this legislation and were active in publicly challenging the repressive climate in which it was enacted. Jackie Stacey (1995: 284) argues that Section 28 is another example of patriarchal control of sexuality, reinforcement of compulsory heterosexuality and protection of the 'nuclear family' and it can also illustrate a moral panic: 'through which sexual identities have been regulated and defined. In both contexts, Section 28 demonstrates the importance of the power to define the terms of sexuality for the successful reproduction of the dominant culture'.

The context, of how definitions of sexuality were included and excluded from the public debate, how particular discourses were legitimated and others marginalised, is crucial as there was a reworking of certain feminist discourses on sexuality which had gained public currency and legitimacy in the 1970s and 1980s. There was also the context of health with the background of AIDS awareness being used to create even more hostility and pathologisation of homosexuality: 'prevention of the spread of AIDS was easily associated with the prevention of the spreading of homosexuality itself' (Stacey 1993: 285) Homosexuality thereby became associated with promiscuity, disease and a risk both to public health and morality.

The involvement of lesbians in the AIDS epidemic in the USA charts shifting political engagements. Stoller argues that: 'when the 1970s ended and the AIDS epidemic exploded, most lesbians and gay men were living essentially parallel lives, organized primarily around the separate themes of female values and feminism for the women and masculinity and justice for the men' (1998: 369). As the nature of the epidemic, and the state and local responses, changed so too did the activism and community involvement. Research in the USA on 'hidden', or unrecognised, lesbian activism considers that: 'The increasingly hostile political climate within society toward homosexuals in the 1980s seems to have resulted in greater co-operation and unity within the movement' (Cavin 1990: 330). This alliance appears fragile as it is essentially one-way, in that lesbians feel they support gay men's issues around AIDS while most gay men do not support feminist health issues such as breast cancer and abortion (ibid). Many men and women were, and are still, losing friends with the spread of AIDS reaching appalling proportions throughout the world, especially in Sub-Saharan Africa which has over 80 per cent of known cases (UNDP Report 1998). Some wider collaboration with disability groups, and with African coalitions, on AIDS educational, health and support work continues to provide links in debate and activism. The coalitions that emerged between lesbians and gay men led to some new critiques of sexual identities and practices, with various theories such as those around 'queer' identities generating debates (Evans 1993; Jeffreys 1994; McIntosh 1993; Smyth 1992; Stein 1992).

Many changes introduced in the USA and Western Europe by retrenchment in the 1980s around AIDS politics and controlling the terms of debate cannot be viewed as 'just' a backlash that reintroduced 'Victorian' values. Rather than concern with private sexual acts, the focus became the *social reproduction* of sexual identities and life styles through state institutions. Discussion around the political aspects of discriminatory legislation reinforced feminist arguments regarding the social construction of sexuality by highlighting particular situations such as education, the media, leisure activities which could be instrumental in reproducing sexual identities. As 'education' in its broadest context became viewed as a site of 'promotion' of homosexuality, feminists considered what this meant for lesbians in their everyday lives (Abelove *et al.* 1993; Epstein 1994; Stacey 1993; Wilton 1995).

International perspectives

Any international politics is grounded in historical realities of migrations, slavery, colonial domination, resistance to oppression and the impacts of changing political, economic climates and new mechanisms of global exploitation. Difficulties are faced by lesbians who have migrated and become part of 'minority' cultures and lesbians living in parts of the world where feminist perspectives are not apparent and support for lesbians is negligible. As we have seen, the growth of feminist writings and activism in the 1970s and 1980s generated a strong focus on Western countries in the unfolding story of lesbian politics. Lesbians from all over the world have migrated into these 'over-developed' countries and have told their truths in various ways. In North America, the use of the politics of race to condemn lesbians is not uncommon: 'The rhetoric is lethal and well understood by immigrants and their children, who are unceasingly chastised for shedding their "culture" and acquiring the degenerate and destructive values of white societies' (Shah in Ratti 1993: 113). My focus in the Case Study is on feminist lesbians and the realities of their political experience across different continents and regimes in 'Third World' countries.

Case study: 'Third World' lesbian lives

Lesbian existence is being uncovered in many cultures across the ages. From Sappho's writings, to temples in Khajuraho and Konarek in India, built more than a thousand years ago (Donoghue 1993; Jay 1995; Ratti 1993; Reinfelder 1996; Silvera 1991). In considering lesbians living in Africa, the Caribbean, South and East Asia and Latin America we see a picture of diverse struggles within different contexts yet with some similar aspects of prejudice and oppression.

The strength of the much-repeated old myth that lesbianism is a Western or a White phenomenon is challenged by many lesbian voices: 'one of the most conventional myths in India is that any form of lesbianism is a product of Western decadence' (Thadani 1996: 56). Divisive tactics are still used associating lesbianism as negative. In Indonesia Gayatri shows that: 'Women's groups using feminist ideas are frequently labelled lesbian, with the result that they try and distance themselves from the issues of female homosexuality or related issues of sexuality' (1996: 90–1). The Indonesian government controls sexuality strictly and the only sex recognised outside the institution of marriage is that of men with prostitutes.

The repressive nature of state policies and institutions inhibits lesbians in Malaysia and these policies act as barriers to the growth of a national lesbian movement. The political aspect of lesbianism is often missed by lesbians in Malaysia as: 'the invisibilizing of lesbians in society, the lack of political dimension to lesbianism and of emancipatory movements such as feminism or a gay movement – fits into the large context of the repressive and authoritarian nature of the state' (Nur and A.R. 1996: 77). For Black African women in Namibia resisting the scars left by apartheid means resisting the 'beauty' standards imported from the West, with hair straightening and skin bleaches, and the hatred of black women: 'who were despised by whites both for their blackness and their womanhood. Standing up proudly for one's identity as a black Namibian woman takes courage. How much more courage does it take to break the culture of silence and stand up proudly as a black lesbian!' (Frank and Khaxas 1996: 112). The strength of feeling that lesbianism is 'not African' or part of the Namibian culture is challenged by historical records. Despite the lack of support within the SWAPO government Namibian lesbians are coming out, developing lesbian identities and community organisations.

In the process of discovering 'our own diversity' Rakesh Ratti discusses the issues that gay and lesbian South Asians struggle with:

> sexism and misogyny manifested by gay men; friction between lesbians and gay male communities; racist attitudes that are rooted in both color and caste consciousness; the reality of bisexuality and its stigmatization in both the heterosexual and homosexual worlds; and the tightrope we must walk in learning from, networking with, and teaching our Western sisters and brothers.
>
> (Ratti 1993: 12–13)

Across these many, sometimes conflicting, aspects of diversity, various alliances and coalitions continue to be formed, with newsletters and publications on lesbian lives being produced. Following their input into the founding meetings of the Asian Lesbian Network in Bangkok in 1990, lesbians in 'Anjaree Sarn' began publishing a bi-monthly in Thai in 1993, with stories, news and letters from all over Thailand and abroad. Members of Anjaree participated in the 1995 Fourth World Conference in Beijing.

It was at Beijing that, for the first time, an open lesbian addressed a plenary session of the UN. In her moving testimony, Palesa Beverly Ditsie, 23, pointed out that South Africa's interim constitution is the first constitution in the world that explicitly forbids discrimination on the grounds of sexual orientation: 'I come from a country that has recently had an opportunity to start afresh, an opportunity to strive for a democracy, where people govern and emphasis is placed on human rights'. Ditsie explained that Nelson Mandela was loudly applauded in his opening speech to the South African Parliament when he declared that never again would any South African be discriminated against because of their sexual orientation (Anderson 1995). The success of lesbian intervention within the 1995 UN conference is summed up by Reinfelder who states that more than 40 countries indicated that their interpretation of the *Platform for Action* would include prohibiting discrimination on the basis of sexual orientation under 'other status'. One important clause remains in the text:

> The human rights of women include their right to have control over and decide fully and responsibly on matters relating to their sexuality, including sexual and reproductive health, free of coersion, discrimination and violence.
>
> (Reinfelder 1996: 26)

As we have seen, legislation is an important aspect of being able to claim full citizenship and human rights but can only be effectively implemented if attitudes are changed positively towards lesbians in every aspect of their lives.

Some of the issues raised in this Case Study are returned to in Chapter 7.

Summary

- Despite the existence of lesbians throughout the ages, it was only after the resistance of lesbians and gay men to state repression that the coalescence of feminist politics with gay liberation politics enabled lesbian feminists to claim their identities.

- Lesbians extended the feminist critiques to patriarchy by challenging and deconstructing the institution of heterosexuality as neither natural nor inevitable.

- The use of morality in discourses about sexuality is apparent in attempts to control people regarded as abnormal or deviant. These discourses emphasised *choice* for women and men to be able to define their own sexuality, opening possibilities for new subject positions, so that lesbians and gay men could 'come out'. The interaction of sexuality with other aspects of life such as class, gender and race can be seen within these processes of 'othering'.

- Lesbian activism in feminist politics was used to divide feminisms and the emergence of separatist groups of lesbians led to radical rethinking of sexual politics and questions about women identified women. The separatist challenge was seen as the ultimate expression of the 'personal is political' and led to repercussions throughout feminist politics.

- In the 1970s and early 1980s radical visions of lesbian nations, practical developments establishing lesbian communities and collectives in housing and health and in creating cultural celebrations, emerged in a climate of intense political debate. In developing lesbian cultures and communities lesbians are affirming the positive aspects of their existence which are *still* denied in heterosexual cultures.

- Changing legislation can help lesbians to enjoy full civil and human rights, but *attitudes* must be changed to make legal changes effective.

Further reading

Abbott, Sidney and Love, Barbara (1972) *Sappho was a Right-On Woman: A Liberated View of Lesbianism* New York: Stein and Day

Moraga, Cherrie and Anzaldua, Gloria (eds) (1983) *This Bridge Called my Back: Writings by Radical Women of Color* New York: Kitchen Table Press

Reinfelder, Monika (ed.) (1996) *Amazon to Zami: Towards a Global Lesbian Feminism* London: Cassell

Rich, Adrienne (1981 [1980]) 'Compulsory heterosexuality and lesbian existence' *Signs* 5(4): 631–660

Chapter 7

Disability, feminism and body politics

All forms of prejudice have at their heart a refusal to identify with a person's reality setting them apart from common humanity. This is a very important part of the prejudice experienced by disabled people based as it often is on an assumption that the quality of our lives is so poor that they are not worth living – and therefore an unwillingness to identify with our reality.

(Morris 1996: 6)

I wish to live whatever life I have as fully and as sweetly as possible, rather than refocus that life solely upon extending it for some unspecified time. I consider this a political decision as well as a life-saving one, and it is a decision that I am fortunate to be able to make. If one Black woman I do not know gains hope and strength from my story, then it has been worth the difficulty of telling.

(Lorde 1996 [1980]: 332)

Chapter outline

Disability politics are considered in the light of the self-organisation and social movements of disabled people, civil rights issues and transformations in our understandings of **disability**. Assessment is made of discourses on disability and the construction of images of 'the disabled' and how the perspectives of disabled feminists have challenged, and had impact on, feminist theories and disability politics.

- The significance of medical models of disability are considered and what the recent challenges to such models have meant for disability politics and self-organisation.
- Change in the ways in which disabled people viewed their lives is assessed as a major impetus to self-organisation,

challenging the power of professionals and the medicalisation of disability and generating developments in service provision and community care. Alliances with other groups and organisations, in the UK and internationally, are considered in the moves towards developing suitable anti-discrimination legislation (ADL).

- The terms disability and disabled are used throughout, except for terms in quotations. The British Council of Disabled People, the umbrella organisation in the UK for groups of disabled people, use these as preferred terms to identify with the social oppression faced by impaired people.
- Disabled feminist critiques are analysed on prejudice and oppression of disabled people, malestream disability politics and feminist analyses which exclude the experiences and realities of disabled women's lives in perspectives on 'women'. We have seen that constructions of 'women' are various and complex. This chapter points up the exclusion of disabled women's realities, how their experience of disability intersects with other oppressions.

Introduction

Disability politics highlights the need for change in many arenas of our lives, from attitudes, to legislation and a whole range of ideas about ideal appearances and efficient workers. What is entailed, in recognising others' realities and listening to their experiences within the context of our lives, is the need for *change*. Such changes in attitudes, beliefs, ideas, practices and prejudices are not always easy to accept and 'take on board'. Recognising and acknowledging *prejudice* is vital for engendering change, as the destructive force of this contributes to creating further barriers between disabled and **non-disabled** people. On the problems of negative attitudes and prejudices Lois Keith acknowledges that:

> Disabled people have to work continually against destructive forces which see us as powerless, passive and unattractive. It seems that no matter how cheerfully and positively we attempt to go out into the world, we are bound to be confronted by someone whose response to our lack of ordinariness, our difference from the norm leaves us feeling powerless and angry. Trying to understand the

complicated feelings which arise out of our everyday encounters with the world is central to the lives of all disabled people.

(Keith 1996: 70)

The recent growth of literature and media coverage on the experiences of **disabled** people, through the increased effectiveness and visibility of disability politics within communities and at national levels, gives widening scope for the development of such changes. Disability groups' tactics of challenging prejudicial media misrepresentations of disabled people have been effective in deconstructing them. As had been noted, modifying legislation plays only a minor part in developing change unless attitudes are transformed.

Disability in not a 'new' issue. In the history of humankind some people have lived with **impairments** from birth, through illness, accident and war. In the context of war there are currently over 100 million land mines in six countries and millions are still produced each year with someone injured, impaired or killed every 20 minutes. Disabled people come from many different backgrounds, are women, men, children, Black, White, people of Colour, heterosexual, gay, rich, poor, of all ages and many languages including various sign languages. Indeed language has been a key site of struggle for disabled people in respect of terms used to communicate disabled people's realities and in everyday phrases such as 'stand on your own feet' or 'walk tall' (Lois Keith 1994). The way in which disability has been viewed has changed over time. Medical models apparent throughout history have only been significantly challenged since the 1970s and then sometimes only partially and in certain countries. We have seen that terms such as 'natural' and 'normal' are often used in opposition with aspects of women's lives constructed as 'unnatural' or 'abnormal'. In this chapter the term *disability* is shown to be a contested one, open to varying definitions.

Throughout history and across the many different societies in which disabled people have lived, the realities of much of their lives are only now becoming a focus for study. Much of the history of disability in the UK focused on dominant beliefs in the permanent nature of 'handicaps' and the reliance of voluntary efforts to provide 'relief'. Gordon Hughes argues that: 'Such interventions assumed a state of "natural" dependency. However, as the nineteenth century unfolded, such views and practices were increasingly fused with and "colonised" by medical classifications by means of which mental and physical impairments, "insanity", and unacceptable behaviour such as crime became "one class of entity namely disease"' (Potts 1982: 6 in Hughes 1998: 67). This medical discourse became the dominant 'expert' construction of disability until well into the twentieth century.

Until a range of issues across the diversity of disabled people's lives is analysed with studies of how the experience of impairment and the oppression of disability have become gendered, racialised and segregated in various ways, there are dangers that disabled people's political issues will just be 'added into' other movements and not become a central focus of consideration. By the 1980s a transformation in the ways in which disability is understood was taking place and there was a growth in co-ordinated self-organised groups and coalitions of disabled people challenging prevailing political and social attitudes and policies. The seeds of the modern development of self-organisation by disabled people in Britain can be seen to have grown from the situation following the Second World War. The experiences of disabled people in subsequent generations were shaped by policy decisions and actions arising in the late 1940s onwards. Yet it is argued that disabled people have long been involved in self-organisation whether such collective work was termed a 'movement' or widely recognised in society (Mason in Campbell and Oliver 1996: 18).

Early developments

The focus here is on political and policy developments after the Second World War but it is important to remember that aspects of charitable approaches to welfare present in the nineteenth century remain and still have influence in certain areas. As with other aspects of social policy in the developing welfare state, key pieces of legislation were passed regarding disabled people. The Disabled Persons (Employment) Act of 1944 was enacted to ensure reasonable access to paid employment for disabled people. The Education Act of the same year suggested that educating disabled children in mainstream schools was the most acceptable form of education, and the National Health Services Act of 1948 established a range of acute care hospitals. In the 1948 National Assistance Act provision was made for local authorities to provide community-based or residential services for disabled people.

Campbell and Oliver (1996: 28–29) argue that each of these acts failed disabled people in various ways. The Employment Act failed largely because successive governments refused to enforce it while the Education Act became a means for developing a large range of segregated schools with both power and influence which still remain generally unchallenged today. The Health Services Act mainly confined disabled people to geriatric wards until the 1960s when some young chronic sick units were set up. Finally the National Assistance Act meant that local authorities tended to choose to provide fewer community-based services and often bought residential services from charities.

Social and political movements tend to gather momentum in times of great political upheaval and/or when groups of people are being oppressed and find political structures and policy unresponsive to their needs and demands. As noted in Chapter 3, Marx believed that when working people came to consciousness of the reasons for their oppression and recognition that they could act for change, then political change could develop. One precondition for such development is for people to be able to 'come together' in some way to recognise and debate mutual aspects of their oppression. Such a coming together literally, and in terms of consciousness of shared oppression, was not easy for disabled people in the 1960s in Britain as Judy Hunt suggests:

> What was happening was that there were two parallel groups of disabled people. There were those who lived in the community and nothing really began to happen. They were struggling with one set of issues and they were coping somehow in the community. Then there were those people who were in hospitals in chronic wards, geriatric wards and so on.
>
> (Campbell and Oliver 1996: 29)

This reality shows that despite debates over service provision both community and hospital-based services were failing disabled people and many were living in oppressive situations in which their autonomy, freedom of movement and access to other disabled people were severely circumscribed. Jenny Morris considers disabled people's expectations of Community Care in her book *Independent Lives* (1993a).

Restricted realities

In order to understand the position of disabled people during these decades and something of the wider social and political frameworks which structured much of their opportunities, an example of the ways in which disabled people have analysed their experiences across a range of institutional and community-based settings is useful. Considering the experiences of eight visually impaired women who spent their school years in a residential school for partially sighted girls in the 1950s and 1960s, Sally French (1996) shows how these testimonies give recognition to the various oppressions these girls and women faced. Opened in Brighton in 1893, the institution, the Barclay Home for Blind and Partially Blind Girls (begun with a £500 donation) aimed to teach industrial skills to these girls from workhouses and very poor homes. Davis argues that the National Assistance Act of 1948 fostered the use of segregated services such as these run by charitable voluntary organisations for disabled people which have since become powerful vested interests in disability services (1996: 125–126).

When trained, the girls and women at the Barclay Home worked for several or many years, earning just a living, making crafts for sale. One pupil, Harriet, remembers being grabbed by the hair, thrown across the dormitory and beaten with a wire coat-hanger. She was beaten very early in her life at the school:

> We went to bed at half past five in the evening and we didn't get up until seven o'clock in the morning, *but we weren't allowed to get out of bed to go to the toilet.* I was very unsettled because I'd gone to foster parents at the age of three and then to school at the age of five, and one night I wet the bed. The prefect on duty realised what had happened . . . and put me in the bath, but one of the matrons came along. She picked me up out of the bath, just as I was, soaking wet, and gave me the hiding of my life. It really hurt – you know what it's like when you're wet. I yelled and screamed, it terrified me [my italics].

> (French 1996: 31)

While girls tell similar tales of control and abuse in comparable institutions, in terms of what they had to eat, the work they carried out, the lack of human warmth in staff attitudes to them, what is particular about the situation for disabled girls is the physical and psychological constraints placed upon their actions and also the restrictive or experimental ways in which their impairments were viewed. These ranged from not allowing the girls to read closely as it may further damage their sight ('sight-saving') to later ideas of forcing them to wear uncomfortable contact lenses because such 'scientific advances' would appear prestigious for the school.

Writing of the abuse received at the school in the early 1950s, June Monkhouse remembers being rapped over her knuckles so forcefully that her chilblains bled and she shared with others the experience of being severely reprimanded and made to feel that *her lack of sight was something punishable* [my italics] (Monkhouse 1980). French notes that not only does such abuse continue in institutional care today but that children viewed as 'different' or 'difficult' are more likely to suffer abuse. The long-term effects of such experiences include lack of self-esteem and confidence, considered in the words of Stella:

> I don't think you ever get over something like that 100 per cent. But having said that as long as you can earn your living, have a nice home, and be independent then your life is not a failure, but there's a cloud hanging over you because you can remember a lot of bad things.
>
> (French 1996: 47)

The above-related experiences tell tales of far more than institutional abuse. In training these girls with impaired sight for physical and often menial work, not offering them academic education and controlling their segregated environments, the authorities in charge of this and many other institutions were in fact aiming to make these girls 'fit into' social and political contexts designed for, and to further the interests of, non-disabled people. Disabled people, often described as 'handicapped' or 'invalids', were often made to feel ill and dependent and thereby unable to exercise any autonomy in their lives. It was in the 1970s that this situation began to be effectively challenged by disabled people.

Civil rights movement

Having considered how the various welfare Acts passed in the 1940s failed disabled people in a variety of different ways, it is significant to note that these measures were not requested by disabled people nor were disabled people consulted on their implementation. Such legislation was framed and implemented in paternal modes which not only established dependence but expected gratitude. Criticism of the ways in which welfare policies have been implemented do not undermine the usefulness of certain benefits but serve to ensure a critical appraisal of the ways in which such measures support or act as barriers for disabled people in moves towards independence, full citizenship and integration. Negative attitudes and paternalistic attitudes towards disabled people have been prevalent in British society for a long time. With regard to legal treatment Ken Davis argues that: 'For over four centuries in Britain, where disabled people have been among those singled out for legal treatment, we have been dealt with as problems in need of special treatment and not as equal citizens with a right to full participation in the social mainstream' (1996: 124). In this context, he states that early disabled people's groups such as the British Deaf Association (1890) and the National League for the Blind (1899) campaigned hard for advances such as the 1920 and 1938 Blind Persons Acts which brought some improvements for visually impaired people and adopted approaches to welfare until the 1970s, in the context of the harsh conditions facing their members. Within the history of disabled people's direct action and political protest Mike Barrett notes the 1920 march of blind people from Wales and the north of Britain culminating in a meeting in Trafalgar Square. Their motto was 'Rights not Charity' (Campbell and Oliver 1996: 82). Their understanding of what was required was based on the need to improve current aspects of people's lives, rather than tackle the reasons why disabled people needed welfare by considering the political and social context of disabled people's lives.

In assessing the self-organisation of disabled people in defence of their rights and in creating change for the better in their lives, Campbell and Oliver clearly state that the purpose of disabled people's self organisation is to promote change: 'to improve the quality of our lives and promote our full inclusion into society. It does this both through involvement in the formal political system and through the promotion of other kinds of political activity' (1996: 22). In the 1960s disabled people began organising on issues of income, employment, rights and alternatives to community living. From the 1970s there began a transformation in the understandings of disability which helped to change policies and services. Dick Leaman asserts that: 'debates around definitions and terminology had helped (some) disabled people to develop radical new perspectives on the real causes of their problems and thereby on the means and requirements of eliminating them. In the heat and excitement of discovering the tool of theory as if for the first time, "social" and "medical" models were compared and contrasted' (1996: 165). Leaman expands upon his reservations about the uses of these terms within the particular context of his local authority.

Debates on definitions

What became known as the medical model developed over time, not through the endeavours of researching various approaches and selecting this as the most suitable but rather: 'organically over a long historical period of neglect, the professionalisation of help and piecemeal legislation. In this process the medical profession gained dominance over the services administered to disabled people' (Finkelstein and Stuart 1996: 184). This medical model impinged upon the consciousness and self-identity of disabled people, as Ann MacFarlane suggests:

> Certainly those people around me who had a disability didn't perceive themselves as in any way disabled. They focused and concentrated almost entirely on operations and it was the competitiveness that was sad. Those who perceived themselves to have the best surgeon, those who perceived themselves to have the most operations and those who perceived themselves to have the more serious illnesses thought they were the most important and the whole talk focused around those sorts of issues.
>
> (Campbell and Oliver 1996: 37)

This medicalisation of disability still affects the ways in which disabled people are regarded. In noticing a white cane, guide dog or wheelchair, people tend to remember the 'hardware' that is 'fixing' things, rather than the disabled person: 'A most common misconception is that the provision of the hardware that society has developed is a solution to any ills that may derive from disability' (Hales 1996: 2). Following from this, issues of disability are not seen to be 'ours' in any wider social or political sense but are the purview of medical professionals and workers who make provision for disabled people. In this way disabled people are not recognised as full citizens in society, with autonomy and individual freedom.

It is on these latter points, that the arguments regarding disability as socially caused are centred. Just as in feminist terms 'biology is not women's destiny' so this model distinguishes between the impairment (physical) and disability (social):

> Disability: the disadvantage or restriction of activity caused by a contemporary social organisation which takes no or little account of people who have physical impairments and thus excludes them from participation in the mainstream of social activities. Physical disability is therefore a particular form of social oppression.
>
> (UPIAS 1981: 14)

This definition has been broadened over time to include psychological, emotional, intellectual and other hidden impairments. As with other political movements this shift was from individual responsibility to recognition for the need to examine the social, political and economic perspectives which influence the lives of disabled people. These arguments are seen as heralding the end of:

> the welfare oriented 'begging bowl' period, and with it the idea that the 'experts' could administer away disabled people's problems for them. This made the early Seventies the pivotal period in the development of the movement. From this point on, the emphasis was to be less on appeals to non-disabled people's better nature, polite petitions or orderly marches on Parliament Square, but more on the mobilisation of a democratically organised, politically aware movement.
>
> (Davis 1993: 288)

A large part of the practical expression of these changing ideas on the development, control, planning and delivery of services to disabled people were those organisations established by disabled people themselves such as the Centres for Independent Living (CILs).

Alliances for self-organisation

By the 1970s disability groups were aware of their need for building alliances with, and learning from, other disability groups and not focusing on attempts at allying with local voluntary groups or the statutory sector. The first issue of the journal of the Union of Physically Impaired Against Segregation (UPIAS) emphasises the hopes raised:

> It is the Union's social definition of disability which has . . . raised the floodgates for a river of discontent to sweep all our oppression before us, and with it to sweep all the flotsam and jetsam of 'expertise', 'professionalism' and 'authority' which have fouled our minds for so long, into the sewers of history. *Disability Challenge* no. 1 May 1981.
>
> (Leach 1996: 88)

The legislation passed in 1973, The Chronically Sick and Disabled Persons Act, remained at the level of promise. Those sections giving more involvement to disabled people had been cut, so that rather than focusing on social causes of disability the emphasis was on individuals and their assumed needs. Disability groups recognised that reliance on legislation could not bring the changes many wanted to see, whereas self-organisation could affect policy-making processes and through disability politics develop a clear focus on civil rights, independence and autonomy for disabled people. In emphasising the significance of learning with and from other disabled people John Evans explains that:

> We wrote to the States and we got information from Berkeley and from a number of other CILs, and that definitely had an influence on us, without a doubt. There were also a number of TV programmes coming along about it, so all of a sudden we were invaded in the early 80s by all this information coming through.
>
> (Campbell and Oliver 1996: 59–60)

Recognising that these varying developments within disability politics needed some co-ordination, and not wanting to be part of either the 'establishment' or the 'disability establishment', Finkelstein and Stuart recall: 'a small group of dissatisfied disabled people began to question prevailing beliefs about the causes of their dependency on welfare and the area of voluntary and statutory services' (Campbell and Oliver 1996: 1970). These people met informally to discuss co-ordination and raise funds. Much past co-ordinated, collective action had failed as the state, in various guises, had effectively used divisive tactics and also because establishing agreement on priorities and tactics among disabled individuals and groups had proved difficult.

In struggling for political influence, disabled people had also to challenge the power of disability-related professionals. Leach notes that for the theoretical and political debates on disabled people's rights to have effect, disabled people themselves had to be involved with local authorities as major service and employment providers (1996: 89). Much important work was being carried on at various levels. In the area of protection against discrimination the publication of the Committee on Restrictions Against Disabled People (CORAD) Report in 1981 was very important. There was definite progress in self-organisation with agreement reached about the formation of an organisation, the British Council of Organisations of Disabled People (BCODP, now the British Council of Disabled People) in 1981. Further discussion ensued regarding who would or would not belong to this organisation. Issues of power, political influence and of resources were important as were those regarding representation and autonomous organisation by women, and gay and lesbian issues. Mike Barnett also recalls early disagreement and later discussions regarding the need for disabled people to be able to understand each others' impairments. Stephen Bradshaw recognises the importance of 'sticking to principles'. Many members could be seen to be politically naive, given their lack of decent education, experience and resources, so their principles were an incredibly important focus for organisation (Campbell and Oliver 1996: 78-9). This could also reflect the diversity of other social influences, as disabled people have less shared backgrounds. In this context the disability movement has similarities to the lesbian and gay liberation movements. In its formative years the organisation failed to gain recognition or adequate funding in its campaign for civil rights, yet it has built up solid grassroots bases particularly in community care, making coalitions and gaining international collaboration. Compared to charitable organisations run by non-disabled people for the welfare needs of disabled people, BCODP remains financially disadvantaged.

International organisation and exchanges of experience

Organisations operated and controlled by disabled people in the UK continued to grow so that by 1990 the BCODP had over 100 constituent organisations, mainly local coalitions of disabled people or Centres for Integrated Living. The disability movement in the UK became involved with the international organisation Disabled People's International (DPI), founded in 1990 and now recognised as the representative voice of disabled people by the UN. As with much international networking the sharing of ideas for change and tactics can be inspirational. In considering political activism towards changing legislation, Davis (1996) notes that despite 1981 being designated an International Year of Disabled People, attempts at introducing anti-discrimination legislation (ADL) in the UK during the 'Thatcher years' failed repeatedly with nine attempts between 1982 and 1991. European legislation through the EU progresses as proposals need, in many cases, to be agreed unanimously by Member States.

In the USA, after long campaigning by disabled people and their supporters, including the powerful AIDS lobby, the Americans with Disabilities Act (ADA) was passed into law in July 1990. The preamble acknowledges that: 'some 43 million disabled Americans had historically suffered and continued to suffer isolation, segregation and discrimination in critical areas such as employment, housing, public buildings, education, transportation, communication, recreation, health services, voting and access to public services'. Recognition was given to the exclusionary practices and the fewer services and opportunities which disabled people experienced (Davis 1996: 129). Such legislation is viewed as important in the British disability movement, to gain full recognition of disabled people's human and civil rights. Joe Hennessy argues that achieving the legislation is an important first step but it will still take 'a hell of an effort to get equal rights' implemented (Campbell and Oliver 1996: 140). The Disability Discrimination Act (1995) in the UK is considered to be very weak in terms of anti-discrimination legislation and in this context, Oliver and Campbell point out that: 'Statutory rights and the judicial process will guarantee neither an end to discrimination nor an inclusive society' (ibid.: 40).

In Australia the Disability Discrimination Act was passed in 1992 and in New Zealand ADL is in the Human Rights Act 1994. Davis highlights similar push and pull factors operating for politicians in each country with regard to such legislation, principally in terms of resources. He quotes the US Attorney General in 1990 giving an example of widespread job discrimination in the private sector which had left 58 per cent of disabled men and 80 per cent of disabled women jobless and was proving too costly: 'Dependency equals a $45,000 annual cost to maintain each unemployed person with a disability or $2 million over an unwillingly dependent and idle lifetime' (Davis 1996: 131; Thornburgh 1990: 2).

International exchange experiences such as that of *Independence 92* in Vancouver which brought together disabled people from all over the world to share experiences and strategies for change have had a powerful effect, generating recognition of diversity and disparity in disabled people's lack of facilities and services in many economically disadvantaged 'Third World' countries. Other international networks include those of lesbian and gay disabled people. Shared experiences can lead to mutual learning. Just as for lesbians 'coming out' is an important personal experience and political expression, so 'coming out' as disabled, with similar fears and rewards, can mean: 'our coming to terms and acceptance of our impairments – including our rights as equal citizens – makes us proud of our abilities and loving of our bodies . . . Owning your difference and joining with others can be a most empowering experience and watching the boundaries change makes it all worthwhile' (Gillespie-Sells and Ruebain 1992: 6). Certainly for marginalised communities whose lives are often judged 'unworthy' in some way, either through misplaced pity, ignorance or prejudice, coming together as lesbian/gay *and* disabled can lead to gains on many levels. Health issues connecting HIV, AIDS and disability are considered in terms of social oppression. It is generally not the illness which prevents people with AIDS from gaining or keeping jobs but people's attitudes and incorrect assumptions about the person that results in barriers being raised. In the booklet 'Definition of Disability' (DL60 1996) issued on behalf of the British Minister for Disabled People, progressive conditions include cancer, HIV infection, multiple sclerosis and muscular dystrophy. Many disabilities are not visible, and some incur a lot of pain whilst others are relatively pain free. Similarities between people's responses to HIV and mental health problems can be noted in terms of avoidance and rejection. As HIV is: 'largely sexually transmitted and in certain countries is endemic in the male gay community, blame, hostility and rejection have been callously added to this already intolerable situation' (ibid: 17). Coalitions between people with HIV and AIDS and disabled people generally can lead to gains in sharing of ideas and strategies in dealing with prejudice, agencies providing benefits, voluntary helpers, campaigning and mutual support. I turn now to examine some disabled feminist critiques.

Disabled feminist analyses

Exceptions and exclusions

Given past experience of 'divide and rule' from state authorities, the campaigners involved in the development of the disability liberation network faced the dilemma of how much compromise was required for a 'united front'. Patricia Rock recalls that for her, issues of representation and women's autonomous organisation were such that: 'we felt that the group was unrepresentative of women and unrepresentative of people with learning difficulties . . . The Liberation Network was very, very strong then. They used to have enormous meetings and I refused to go to them on the grounds of the argument which said that women's politics were divisive' (Campbell and Oliver 1996: 73). There are comparisons here back to nineteenth-century political organisation, and to that of women's experience in liberation politics of the 1960s, in terms of the focus of liberation being male, and in the resistance to women's autonomous organisation. The issue of autonomous organisation of women is now generally regarded as necessary for women's full involvement and integration into largely male-dominated political environments. The focus is on the historical disadvantages which women have suffered and continue to be exposed to, so that self organisation and self-education, *as women*, is something significant in disabled women's involvement in whatever political coalitions they choose. This is sometimes not recognised by disabled men.

Issues of the personal and political have been raised earlier in terms of the social model of disability. Rather than viewing conceptions of impairment as 'personal tragedy' with the associated oppression this entails, the social model raises the political issue of social barriers as dis-abling. However, feminist thinkers, among others, are now wishing to examine this general social model in terms of acknowledging the personal human experiences of disabled people in order to recognise the implications of impairment. Liz Crow (1996: 223) argues that: 'A renewed approach to the social model is vital, both individually and collectively, if we are to develop truly effective strategies to manage our impairments and to confront disability.' Key arguments are raised here in terms of disability pride, which is not in terms of pride at 'being disabled' or 'having an impairment' but of disabled people's response to that, and the strength of character gained by surmounting the barriers faced. Women's personal experience of disability and their political experience of women's oppression are viewed in disabled feminist analyses as part of a wider framework. Disabled women argue that it is not possible to separate the oppression arising from being a woman from that of being a disabled person, therefore it is vital that disabled women have the opportunity to examine their own human experiences in a political context. In discussing strategies for changing discrimination against disabled people, Anne Finger (1992: 8) has noted that it is often easier to discuss changes in services or employment than to consider sexuality and reproduction but: 'Sexuality is often the source of our deepest oppression; it is also often the source of our deepest pain'. Intersections of oppression including those based on race, class, gender and disability need to be integrated in feminist research and activism.

Feminist exclusions

Jenny Morris argues that the exclusion of disabled women's experience from 'women's experience' in feminist accounts of work, sexuality, racism and a whole plethora of issues from which theories have been built, makes these analyses incomplete as whole groups of women are missing from the picture. One set of analyses involves issues of the male gaze and the construction of 'ideal women'. On this aspect, of definition by others, Lois Keith argues that:

> being defined by others in a way you don't choose to define yourself is not, of course, a problem exclusive to disabled people. Women have for many years been writing about our need to reject being defined exclusively by our bodies and the way we look, but it is different for disabled people because some of us deviate so significantly from what is considered to be within the range of 'normal' appearance.
>
> (Keith 1996: 71)

For disabled women male norms of 'ideal womanhood' and social norms of 'ideal physicality' can impose dual pressures. In much gendered analysis, for example regarding notions of 'the family' as oppressive to all women, no account is taken of the barriers for some disabled women in gaining access to family lives, so that the feminist analyses remain partial.

In her work Julie McNamara tackles the constructed norms of mental health, making connections between professional evaluation of mental distress within a male norm and deep cultural imperatives:

> The idea that women have a propensity for madness goes far beyond the well-researched evidence that women are over-represented in mental institutions and other mental health services. It is an idea that disempowers women who deviate from their expected social role. It isn't sufficient to suggest that large numbers of women referred to the psychiatric services, or identified as presenting to their GPs with mental distress, are in the grip of their biology. Neither can it be adequately accounted for by focusing on the social conditions of women. The equation is deeply embedded in the cultural archetypes of the Western psyche: to be a woman in our society is to be at risk of being labelled as mad.
>
> (McNamara 1996: 194)

Feminist psychologists have demonstrated the means by which professionals evaluate and diagnose mental distress against a norm or stereotype of adult males (Broverman *et al.* 1970; Chesler 1972; Millet 1991; Ussher 1994). It is not a coincidence that in societies priding themselves on *rationality*, with rational the preserve of men, that some professional men choose to define women as mad with regard to *male standards*. McNamara also notes the genre of 'Madwomen' movies which has become popular with *Fatal Attraction, The Hand that Rocks the Cradle* and *Misery* (1996: 195).

Morris maintains that the lack of reflection on disabled women's experiences means also that feminist theories remain incomplete, without a full understanding of the interactions between the social construction of gender and that of disability (1996: 5). By considering the standpoints of disabled women, feminist analysis will be able to view women's experiences in a new light. Many issues are raised by disabled feminist thought (amongst others, Begum 1992; 1996; Finger 1991, 1992; Keith 1992, 1994; Lorde 1985; Morris 1989, 1991, 1993b, 1996; Tremain 1996). I focus on two aspects, motherhood and racism, which although intermeshed are separated for ease of focus. The Case Study integrates some of the connections.

Motherhood

In Chapter 4 various issues were raised regarding women's reproductive rights and questions raised by technology. That some non-disabled feminists regard prenatal testing as another means through which women can gain control over their reproduction is shown to be questionable from many perspectives and feminist writers have noted that such control has a price (Farrant 1985; Hubbard 1986; Oakley 1986; Rothman 1989). Part of that price, Ruth Bailey argues: 'includes the anxiety which now dominates early pregnancy – deciding whether to undergo testing, awaiting results – and the difficult decision to be made about continuing that pregnancy or electing for abortion if an impairment is diagnosed (Bailey 1996: 143). Arguments regarding impairment as determining can be seen to have been tackled by the political analyses of disabled people, yet with regard to selective abortion in feminist accounts, issues regarding 'ideal' babies and disabled children's rights have not been adequately examined.

Anne Finger's (1991) account, as a disabled woman, choosing a home birth during which her son developed meconium aspiration (breathing in his own faeces) which could lead to brain damage, brings together many of the interwoven complexities of motherhood and disability. That it was her right as a woman to choose a home birth was challenged by the professional establishment and non-disabled friends. When the birth was complicated, judgements were made regarding the 'danger' in which she had placed the child. Such complications can affect children in hospital births. Her account of the personal dilemmas faced, in coming to terms with the possibilities of her son's continuing ill health, highlights crucial intersections of the personal and political aspects of the medicalisation and experience of motherhood and the rights of disabled infants.

For disabled women, involvement in developing future policy in areas which affect disabled people is important. In her consideration of prenatal testing and genetic knowledge, Ruth Bailey proposes four recommendations:

- Any decision to undergo testing or to opt for abortion should rest with the woman; more research on provision of information about impairments following a positive diagnosis.
- Greater discussion at all stages of the research and implementation of prenatal testing with disabled people involved in debates. The views of disabled people and parents may conflict and it is vital that both are separately represented.
- The new findings of genetic research must not lead to abandonment of fundamental political and moral principles. The upper limit for abortion on grounds of 'serious handicap' should be lowered to 24 weeks.
- Confirmation that disabled people, whatever their impairment, are an integral part of society and should be afforded the same respect and dignity as other human beings (Bailey 1996: 163–4).

There are many other aspects for reflection regarding the experiences of disabled women becoming mothers, those of non-disabled mothers giving birth to disabled children, and how feminist research can articulate these complexities within ethical and political frameworks, recognising areas of conflicting interest. Disabled people would like positive life examples given to prospective parents to demonstrate that impairment is not all negative. In this context, Morris stresses the need for the recognition of disability in wider perspectives:

> Black people's experience of racism cannot be compartmentalised and studied separately from the underlying social structure; women's experience of sexism cannot be separated from the society in which it takes place; and neither can disabled people's experience of disablism and inequality be divorced from the society in which we live. That society is characterized by fundamental inequalities and by ideologies which divide people against each other – the experience of disability is an integral part of this.
>
> (Morris 1993b: 69)

In considering disabled women's analyses of racism specific inequalities and ideologies are highlighted in assessing the affects in their lives.

Racism

As has been considered in Chapter 5, Black feminist thinkers have developed research and insights regarding the intersections of oppressive forces in women's lives. Racism has been structured into White Anglo–American thinking and institutionalised within educational systems. Mistaken ideas on universalism in much feminist thought have fed into the racist oppression of Black women and women of Colour. Disabled Black women examine the interrelated and overlapping issues in the context of their experiences of intolerance against disabled people, racial prejudice and sexism.

In describing her education in a special school as being crucial to her liberation from the tyrannical rule of her father, Ayesha Vernon is clear that this education itself was not liberatory: 'My experience of racism started when I went to my first residential school . . . There I experienced physical and verbal abuse from the children and less favourable treatment from some of the staff' (Vernon 1996: 50). With little English, wearing Indian clothes and following a Muslim vegetarian diet, Vernon was gradually persuaded to wear English clothes and even to eat English food. Studying social policy and race relations at college she learnt nothing of the policies and politics around disability but later: 'I rejoiced heartily at discovering a movement that expressed my experience of disability as an oppression, but I still found it lacking in that it did not acknowledge my experience as a disabled Black woman which is totally different from that of a disabled white man' (1996: 51). In her work at a charity for disabled people Vernon suffered blatant racism from her White supervisor and in her next job in a Black organisation to promote race relations, she found herself an outcast as a disabled person and also experienced sexual harassment from one individual. As there is little known of the experience of Black disabled women Ayesha Vernon carried out a research project with ten disabled Black and minority ethnic women regarding their experience in education and in paid employment. For most of the women interviewed their experience of special schooling was that their academic education was devalued in favour of concentration on work on their impairment, be this in terms of speech therapy, physiotherapy or just 'fitting in better'.

Many of the interviewees felt that they had been 'written off' because they were both disabled and Black. Racial prejudice was apparent at all levels of the educational establishment. When Jackie was tested by a psychologist the test included eating-utensils. Jackie chose a spoon, as in her culture, but a fork was the 'correct' utensil and she believes this was part of the criteria used to send her to special school. At that school Jackie states: 'There was nothing positive about black people in books or in anything else, it was all about white people and what they had done' (Vernon 1996: 58). In a similar vein, Neelam as the only Asian girl at a school for blind girls, experienced the lack of knowledge of her needs in terms of food and clothing, and her assessment as poor in English was in fact due to her strong regional (Geordie) accent. Accordingly she was given elocution lessons, and less was expected of her because she was Asian.

Frustration at the lack of thought given to disabled students' needs can mean studies are cut short and can create disillusionment. Not having sign language interpreters, accessible buildings (particularly libraries) or books on tape means that disabled students struggle to complete their studies. Coupled with the oppression of racist bigotry such situations can make disabled Black women feel they have lost out on their rightful education. Jackie explains that as her special school in no way prepared her for life when she left at the age of 16 she almost had a nervous breakdown. Unable to sit at home 'like a zombie and watch television' she motivated herself to go to four different colleges to study so that she would not have to take a 'horrible job' which was deemed all that a person with learning disabilities could expect (Vernon 1996: 62). There are now some groups in London for Black disabled people, but for those outside large urban centres, the feeling of 'being the only one' can be a lonely one.

Case study: disabled feminists' research

For disabled feminist thinkers, challenges have been made to the partial thinking of male-dominated disability politics and to the feminist thinking which has excluded or marginalised the realities of disabled women's lives. In reconsidering the social model of disability from a feminist perspective Liz Crow is not supporting any aspect of the medicalisation of disability, but wants to recognise the pride disabled people have in 'understanding the oppression we experience, of our work against discrimination and prejudice, of the way we live with our impairments' (1996: 223). Feminisms are centrally concerned with choice and control for women in housing, employment, education, equal legal status, choice and control over sexuality and reproduction and about women's self worth and value. Jenny Morris recognises these concerns as familiar to disabled people because choice and control, and the rights and means to access these, are the aims put forward by the disabled people's movement for independent living and she argues:

> Although we feel that neither feminism nor the disabled people's movement has adequately identified our concerns nor campaigned for the things that would make choice and control a real possibility for disabled women, we take our inspiration from both movements. Our insight and analysis of the oppression and injustice experienced by disabled women is informed and motivated by both feminism and disability rights.
>
> (Morris 1996: 15)

Disabled feminists have generated a large research agenda in tackling issues of disabled women's oppression. In this section I consider two areas only – sexuality and sexual abuse.

As we have seen the disability movement argues that civil rights is vital to disability politics but there has been little discussion of disabled people's sexuality to counter the apparent taboo around disability and sex. Shakespeare et al. (1996: 3) describe how the 'industry' producing work on sexuality and disability is controlled by professionals from medical, psychological and sexological backgrounds with disabled voices and experiences absent. In a consideration of social relationships arising from a research report *Disabled in Britain*

Lamb and Layzell argue that the unspoken taboo about relationships and disabled people: 'reinforced the public's attitudes and expectations towards disabled people, seeing them as "sick and sexless" rather than participating in full sexual and family relationships. It is perhaps one of the most pernicious ways in which society has blanked out disabled people from fundamental areas of social life' (1994: 21).

In writing of her negative experience with a doctor who told her that experiencing pain during sex meant that she did not love her husband, Caroline writes: 'As a result of that day, I have never mentioned my problems with sex to a doctor . . . Although people can now say 'condom' without any difficulty or embarrassment, the idea that disabled people have sex is still a taboo' (Caroline in Shakespeare *et al.* 1996: 15). There is still insufficient information available to disabled people regarding sexuality, certainly in academic and political discourses, but the *Disability Now* newspaper includes pieces on lesbian and gay couples, dating agencies and relationships generally. As we have seen, 'coming out' as disabled is often a difficult process, so for many disabled lesbians there is much to overcome in exploring a sexuality that is often regarded as 'other'. Given that homosexuality was long defined as a sickness, with the World Health Organisation still defining homosexuality as an impairment in 1980, Shakespeare *et al.* raise questions: 'we find that disabled people cannot or should not be lesbian or gay: on the other hand, it is suggested that people who are lesbian or gay are themselves suffering from an impairment' (1996: 154). Sometimes parents do not wish their protected disabled children to 'become sexual' and certainly not to express a 'deviant' sexuality. Overcoming the many-layered barriers to expressing and enjoying sexual pleasure is something that is only now becoming considered in disability studies and more widely. Yet disabled lesbians are *coming out* and the anthology produced by disabled dykes in Canada shows the unique contributions, both painful and celebratory, that are being created and developed (Tremain 1996).

Personal circumstances of living at home, a lack of social opportunities to meet people, and the need for personal assistance can also affect the development of sexual relationships. In her consideration of how the experience of hiring personal assistants as part of her care package affects her relationships Sian Vasey (1996) asserts that:

> The problem for me is centred on relationships and particularly how you have a sexual relationship when you need help getting to bed, turning over in bed, someone to come into the bedroom in the morning to get you up, and so on. Before one even starts thinking about the problems of intimacy, the issue of more

everyday privacy can also be a problem. A lot of partners and
potential partners just do not like the constant intrusion of the
third party and will therefore drift away.

(Vasey 1996: 87)

Given that disabled women's bodies are not all suited to various
types of sexual activity disabled women's experience of sexual
pleasure can challenge orthodox ideas concerning sexual satisfaction.
Kirsten Hearn maintains that: 'Different women with different
disabilities have different needs and abilities, before, during and after
sex. Some of us can only lie in certain positions or may have to use
different parts of our bodies. Some of us have more strength and
energy than others' (McEwen and O'Sullivan 1988: 50 also in Begum
1992: 79). This aspect of difference clearly is something from which
all women can gain in terms of choices about the ways in which
women can express their sexuality and gain pleasure.

Nasa Begum (1992) argues that often the negative self-image forced
upon disabled women by social prejudice centrally affects how they
experience their sexuality. This situation can lead to women viewing
themselves as 'asexual' or with no control over their bodies. Such
situations can lead to women experiencing sexual abuse from
relatives, carers and health workers. In considering issues of sexual
abuse and disabled children Margaret Kennedy (1996) writes of the
complexities which feed into the dangers of negative attitudes and
other barriers that disabled children face. Attitudes which consider
that disabled children should not have been born form a big part of
the vulnerability to abuse experienced by disabled children. If children
are regarded as 'worth-less' this could be construed by offenders as
permission to abuse. Disabled children internalise ideas about being
'defective' and are sometimes overprotected. The resulting passivity
coupled with feelings of inferiority can make it hard for children to
trust their instincts in decisions about what is appropriate adult
behaviour. Children are particularly vulnerable in residential care with
isolation, increased contact with different adults and little or no sex
education. Responses to disabled children's experience of sexual
abuse can still be discriminatory and disempowering. Table 7.1 gives
some examples of the ways in which practical issues can be presented
as barriers.

This table shows that reasons given for not offering help to
disabled children often focus on the child as the problem rather than
inadequate facilities or lack of appropriate support or skills. In this
and many other areas, disabled feminists are calling for attention to
be paid to children and adults' communication needs and for workers
to acquire knowledge and understanding about disabled children who

are abused. The various work on the feminist disability research agendas can only be undertaken by building alliances with disabled people and respecting their experiences. In setting a political research agenda that reflects their concerns, the range of work being carried out by disabled feminists is momentous and will have wide-ranging impacts on feminist thinking and activism into the next century.

Table 7.1 Presenting issues as barriers

COMMENTS	REFRAMED
The child is the problem	**The facility/work is the problem**
'He can't get into the building'	'Our building is not accessible'
'She can't get into the therapy room'	'Our therapy rooms are poorly located'
'He can't use our toilets'	'Our toilet facilities are inadequate'
'He can't talk'	'We don't know how to communicate using Bliss/Makaton/Rebus or Sign Language'
'She wouldn't have the understanding to cope with counselling'	'We do not have the commitment, time knowledge or confidence to work with disabled children'
'He doesn't have the language skills to cope with group work'	ditto

Source: Marchant and Page 1992: 31 in Kennedy 1996: 128

Summary

In charting the political development of disability politics in the UK key issues of the failure of political structures to develop and implement necessary legislation are tied with nineteenth-century conceptions of disability as an issue which is best 'dealt with' by professionals and charitable organisations. Rather than recognising the rights of disabled persons and implementing policy to integrate their skills in the economy and society, various government initiatives were abstractly aimed at 'the problem of disability'.

- The terms of debate are vital in politics and have been important in changing attitudes in disability politics.

Impairment refers to the functional limitation which
affects a person's body, whereas disability refers to the loss
or limitations of opportunities owing to social, physical and
attitudinal barriers (Oliver 1990).

• Disability is not a 'new' issue and disabled people come
from many backgrounds and can be born with an
impairment or become disabled through illness, accident
or war at any time.

• Various welfare Acts of the 1940s failed disabled people
not least because disabled people were not consulted.
Paternal attitudes reinforced dependency and acted as
barriers for disabled people in moves to independence and
full citizenship.

• The disability movements which developed in the 1970s in
the UK and elsewhere were stimulated by disabled activists
challenging established political frameworks. Self-
organisation and social movements of disabled people
highlighted issues of civil rights and new understandings of
disability.

• Perspectives of disabled feminists challenge and impact
upon feminist politics and disability politics. Non-disabled
feminists can best work towards implementing feminist
disability research agendas by building alliances with
disabled people and enabling their experiences to be
respected.

• Changes in attitudes, beliefs, ideas, practices and
prejudices are vital in removing the negative attitudes that
act as barriers in disabled people's lives.

Further reading

Begum, Nasa (1992) 'Disabled Women and the Feminist Agenda'
    Feminist Review: 40 (Spring) 70–84

Campbell, J. and Oliver, M. (1996) *Disability Politics: Understanding Our
    Past, Changing Our Future* London and New York: Routledge

Hales, Gerald (ed.) (1996) *Beyond Disability: Towards an Enabling Society*
    London: Sage Publications in association with the Open University

French, Sally (ed.) (1994) *On Equal Terms: Working with Disabled People*
    Oxford: Butterworth–Heinemann

Morris, Jenny (ed.) (1996) *Encounters with Strangers: Feminism and
    Disability* London: The Women's Press

Chapter 8

Political participation, representation and resistance

these models of democracy, British, French, American, with their built in exclusion of women, and these partial theories of human rights and governance, were extended, carried around the world by colonialism and by example, in the nineteenth and twentieth century formation of state institutions and representative democracies.

(Ashworth 1998: 6)

Parity is the recognition that the 'demos' the people, being of two sexes, the 'cratos' being the government, must also be similar; it must be qualitative. The new parity sexual contract comes forth not only as political balance, but of a democratic ethic, that is the paradigm of a new human contract.

Antoinette Fouque, MEP (in Ashworth 1998: 24)

Chapter outline

Consideration of women's political participation at the levels of political parties, Parliamentary politics and women's movement activities form the central focus of this chapter.

- The main concerns are developments of women's participation in political parties, electoral politics and in Parliamentary situations across those countries globally that operate within party systems, plus participation in women's political networks in Nigeria and Sweden.
- Assessment is made of feminist analyses and activism aimed to develop those forces which assist women's entry and integration within political parties and electoral processes which are often neither democratic nor inclusive.
- Differing interpretations of participation are raised in feminist criticisms of 'malestream' political participation and perceptions.

Introduction

In this chapter, I assess the development of women's participation across those countries globally that operate within party systems, and consider different sites of political participation in women's networks in Nigeria and Sweden. In Chapter 9 ideas of *transnational feminism* and issues of international activism are assessed. At the outset it is important to stress that global overviews such as this are by their nature partial and particular. Although the material, much of it derived from the Inter-Parliamentary Union study of 115 countries, is used to emphasise trends in diversity it is not possible to give detail and depth in such a short summary. Large collections such as *Women and Politics Worldwide* (Nelson and Chowdhury 1994) and UN and other yearbooks on women's situations attempt to add flesh to the bones of such overviews. As we have seen, it is in the specific locations of women's lives and in the global connections that we can begin to understand feminist perspectives on politics.

There are many different ways of assessing **participation, activism** and **representation** in politics. Being a member of a political party or to be 'counted' numerically as participating in a voting system does not necessarily amount to participation. Often, the structures and procedures of political parties and other forms of policy-making are neither democratic nor inclusive of all voices. Participation involves being heard and having what you say respected and taken into account. Feminist reflections have considered women's varying involvements and differing interpretations of participation, and critiqued 'malestream' thinking about women's political participation and perceptions. (Ashworth 1998; Dahlerup 1986; Githens *et al.* 1994; Lovenduski and Hills 1981; Randall 1987).

Feminist perspectives on participation

Many feminists have been wary, and/or distainful of, participating in the practices of 'formal' politics such as elections, voting, political parties, Parliament. Engaging in conventional politics without first changing its cultural and ideological context has not been deemed a rewarding use of energy for many feminists. Unlike most radical movements, other than anarchism, feminisms have never envisaged any seizure of state power, as feminists generally envision alternative goals. As we saw in Chapter 4, feminists have worked to build upon the collective power of all women, even though the 'all' started off rather exclusively. For some women, local, rather than regional or central government, has seemed more conducive and inclusive of women's demands with the policies made in areas more directly affecting women's lives: community projects, childcare, education, health, housing, planning, transport and so on. However, Western women's movements have sometimes organised very efficiently over a single issue, such as abortion rights. Yet clearly conditions differ across 'Western' countries and the political situation for women with regard to abortion in Ireland, where it has been illegal since 1861 has been one which Irish feminists have long struggled over (Smyth 1992). Overlaps between these various aspects of participation are apparent, particularly in considerations of women's involvement in national liberation struggles.

The removal of distinctions between public (important political, external world of men) and private (unimportant, apolitical, internal/domestic world of women) became crucial in understanding broader conceptions of political activity and engagement. In breaking down perceived divisions, arguments concerning different outlooks and cultural histories became highlighted, including issues of sexuality, of women's autonomy in control of their bodies, resistance to male violence and of women gaining power in living their chosen lives. It is beyond the scope of this chapter to attempt to cover all aspects of formal/informal political participation but further readings are given at the end of the chapter.

In their work on women and politics Githens *et al.* examine three approaches at the core of debates on women and politics – political behaviour, social movements and political theory:

> By simultaneously raising questions about the nature of political institutions, the requirements set for any politician entering public life, the study of women and politics provides a fresh perspective on established questions and provides insights about the role of the outsider which may be useful in the broader study of minorities.
>
> (Githens *et al.* 1994: xiii)

Within a broad theoretical context, the comparative study of '**state**' political behaviour forms the first section of this chapter, moving to feminist political movements in the second part. It is essential to bear in mind when considering 'women' and participation that studies are context specific, in terms of variations in women's situations culturally and historically.

As discussed throughout this book, feminist analyses have not developed in a social vacuum but in large measure as a response to the changing circumstances and various opportunities associated with industrialism. Within colonial rule such 'opportunities' were generally distorted by Western ideological presumptions so that legacies of 'democratic' structures and procedures from 'mother' countries included barriers to women's participation. Feminist analyses and activism aim to develop the various forces which are undermining systems of male dominance by bringing gender issues into the public political arena for further consideration. Public policies have played a part in maintaining women's oppression, certainly in terms of employment and childcare issues, yet women can and do use public politics in their own interest (see Norris 1986; Kaplan 1992; Rowbotham 1992; Corrin 1994b; Githens *et al.* 1994; Charles and Hughes-Freeland 1996).

According to Western conventional models of political participation voting in national elections is viewed as the only form of participation in which the majority of the population engages. Within this perspective, voting once every three or five years is the major act of political participation by citizens, so that 'politics' narrowly defined becomes the preserve of a very few people – a minority of political activists. In this way, analysts such as Hague *et al.* (1992: 157) divide the population into three main participation groups:

1 small number of activists who are mostly party members;
2 the voters, who are the majority;
3 the inactives who ignore politics altogether.

In this view the overwhelming number of citizens in liberal democracies only participate, if at all, in the electoral aspect of politics. When considering the *new politics* – illustrated by peace campaigners, ecological groups including organisations such as Greenpeace, animal rights groups and 'road' protesters defending common land, plus various particular feminist groups and campaigns – it is apparent that participation is considerably widened. The politics of the Black Civil Rights activities and feminist input into *new* political movements were important, especially considering 'the social/personal as political' (Brock-Utne 1989; Duchen 1986; Eyerman and Jamison 1991; Scott 1990). Such analyses extended discussion towards community politics, protest initiatives and campaigns, and sexual politics.

Women's participation in Parliamentary processes

In assessing the 'state/formal' aspects of women's political participation I make use of a world comparative study by the Inter-Parliamentary Union (IPU) published in 1997, which asks two basic questions: Does women's participation in politics make a difference? and Does it advance democracy? The IPU is the world organisation of Parliaments of sovereign states. It facilitates world-wide parliamentary dialogue supporting the efforts of the UN, whose objectives its shares, and works in close co-operation with it. As of July 1997, 138 national Parliaments were members of the IPU. In considering democracy the study asserts: 'the concept of democracy will only assume true and dynamic significance when political parties and national legislation are decided upon jointly by men and women with equitable regard for the interests and aptitudes of both halves of the population' (IPU 1997: 3). Using statistics and views provided by national Parliamentary groups, political parties and community groups, the study attempts to assess the degree of women's integration into politics and at what speed and how far this integration is proceeding. The three key areas considered are: women in political parties; women's participation in the electoral process; and women in national Parliaments. One hundred and fifteen countries sent survey replies – from women and men politicians, officials, researchers and members of non-governmental organisations (NGOs).

Political parties

In assessing women in political parties this study is not concerned with activism broadly defined but focuses on how women are incorporated into decision-making structures and what mechanisms are in place to facilitate women's integration. Clashes between party involvement and family life are considered and the meaning and relevance of women's branches in parties. In this context questions are raised about whether or not such structures serve women's direct interests or those of the parties.

As political parties play an increasing role in the running of institutions of government, and are key actors in democratic processes, it is important that women are enabled to represent their aspirations and assert their political interests. A corollary between the degree of democratisation and the extent of women's participation in formal politics is suggested in some responses and that the degree of women's integration depends upon the system of values present and on established political patterns. On this core issue the response from Panama argues that:

> In the effort to increase women's participation there is no question of moving aside a competent man to make way for an incompetent woman, but of having competent men and women address our problems together. Tomorrow's society will require a human component capable of working in a group, of forming utterly dependable teams and of operating in synergy.
>
> (IPU 1997: 12)

Arguments regarding women's competence have been used by conservative thinkers to undermine the importance of changing political perceptions and culture, considering gender factors. A response from Denmark highlights this in the context of the increasing significance of women's movement issues:

> It is thus a combination of pressure from below, especially from the social movements, and the system's comparatively high degree of responsiveness towards new groups and demands (the political opportunity structure) that are among the decisive factors with respect to the integration of women into politics.
>
> (IPU 1997: 12)

The Danish response, which shares much with the women's movements in the Swedish study, also emphasises the importance of how an understanding of the political significance of gender focuses both on changes in political culture and on specific changes in relation to gender parity.

The figures show that there is a scarcity of women in executive posts in parties: only 10.8 per cent of Party Leaders in 418 parties in 86 countries were women; Deputy Presidents included 18.7 per cent women from 402 parties in 84 countries; of 871 parties considered in 80 countries 585 (67.2 per cent) had no women in their bureaux; of 402 parties considered in 86 countries only 7.7 per cent of Parliamentary Group Leaders were women; and only 9 per cent of women were Party Spokespersons from 388 parties in 85 countries. These figures speak for themselves with the only percentage as high as one third being that of parties with at least one woman in their governing body (IPU 1997: 14–15). Often women inherit leadership positions from male relatives – as mother of the President, daughter and/or widow of a past Prime Minister. Such elections often speak more of dynastic loyalties or feudal ties than gender politics. Sheikh Hasina, Prime Minister of Bangladesh was re-elected in 1996 when her party fielded women as only 1 per cent of candidates. Yet positive role models of active women politicians are also apparent such as the election of Mary Robinson in Ireland and Vigdis Finnisbogdottir in Iceland (Ashworth 1998: 21). As leaders of various movements it can be seen that women are engaging with various levels of power. Women are actively challenging the 'formal' leadership situation in many countries as the response from Senegal shows: 'Being aware of their majority within political formations and representing over 70 per cent of the electorate, women are firmly committed to reversing the trend and are calling for equality in the distribution of posts' (IPU 1997: 17). In this context gender quotas have been introduced into many systems in various ways, from Party candidates, funding for women members and on committees. In Australia the Labour Party had a quota system on the national executive from 1986 (increased to one third in 1991) and the Greens had a 5 per cent rule from their inception in 1992. Some Parties include quotas on funding for training women party members (Costa Rican National Liberation Party in 1991/1992). Danish regulations stipulate that each sex must be represented by a minimum of 40 per cent on committees established by the Governing Body.

Women's branches, parties and coalitions

The establishment of women's branches in parties is particularly apparent in African countries and somewhat less so in the Americas and Europe. As is often the case arguments regarding separate spheres centre on the dynamic nature of such organisations. In enabling women to rapidly process their political education and aims, the role of a separate women's branch can be significant. If women are expected to operate only within those realms traditionally regarded as 'women's issues' then separate organisation can marginalise women's talents and abilities. In the case when membership of a Party automatically makes women members of a women's branch (SPD in Germany) then there can be more choice about the range of activities in which women participate and their large membership has diverse political power in various local districts and at the state level. Interim women's branches can be constituted for specific goals and suspended for various reasons. In diversifying the means of participation women have established various women's parties and coalitions. Often such parties are relatively short-lived through lack of resources or by choice, in that they were formed for specific campaigns. Women's parties have been active in Spain, Peru, the Philippines and Yugoslavia. During and after the war which broke up Yugoslavia feminists kept contact with each other across 'enemy' lines and feminist activism provided much alternative support for women, and for men who wished to desert from their national armies (see Mladjenovic and Matijasevic 1996). Women's Coalitions have proved successful in stating women's claims and raising issues of the democratic deficit. Georgina Ashworth argues that:

> Others have started Women's Coalitions, sometimes cross-party, or bringing together academic advisers with grass-roots activists, with formal women's organisations. These have been intensely successful in Sweden, where the coalition was called 'Support Stockings', and South Africa, where the multi-racial coalition demanded, and received, a place at the constitutional negotiating table.
>
> (Ashworth 1998: 17)

The Women's Coalition in Northern Ireland was successful in gaining two representatives in the peace talks in 1996 and in considerably raising the profile of women's participation throughout society and at all levels of politics.

Women in the electoral process

Various studies have been undertaken regarding the phases in the electoral process, from actions by governments, political parties and non-governmental organisations, to encourage women to participate in elections and in terms of nominating women candidates and ensuring their election (Darcy *et al.* 1994; Lovenduski 1986; Norris 1985). Appendix 1 notes the timing of women's rights to vote and stand for election globally – from 1788 when women in the USA were eligible to stand for election (to vote in 1920) up to 1998 when women's rights to vote or stand for election were not yet recognised in Kuwait.

Of the two major systems of voting – multi-member majority and proportional list voting (PR) – evidence bears out the contention that the latter is more conducive to women candidates: 'in countries

Table 8.1 Method of voting in various countries according to proportion of women elected in 1996 to lower or single Houses

Percentage of women elected +25%	Countries (12)	Voting system
40.4	Sweden	Mixed (closed lists)
39.4	Norway	Proportional (closed lists)
33.5	Finland	Mixed (preferential)
33.0	Denmark	Proportional (preferential)
31.3	Netherlands	Proportional (preferential)
27.3	Seychelles	Mixed
26.8	Austria	Proportional (closed lists)
26.2	Germany	Mixed (closed lists)
25.4	Iceland	Proportional (closed lists)
25.3	Argentina	Proportional (closed lists)
25.2	Mozambique	Proportional (closed lists)
25.0	South Africa	Proportional (closed lists)

Percentage of women elected 0%	Countries (9)	Voting system
0%	Comoros	Majority
0%	Dlibouti	Majority (closed lists)
0%	Ki ri bati	Majority
0%	Mauritania	Majority
0%	Micronesia	Majority
0%	Palau	Majority
0%	Papua New Guinea	Majority (closed lists)
0%	Saint Lucia	Majority
0%	Tonga	Majority

Source: Inter-Parliamentary Union 1997: 136

with more than 30 per cent of women MPs, only proportional and mixed systems are applied; at the other extreme, in countries with no women in Parliament, only the majority and the appointment system are used (IPU 1997: 44) (see Table 8.1). Clearly the voting system is important but the survey bears out the recognition that the electoral system as a whole is important, particularly in the encouragement of women candidates. The response data generated on this was limited in that of nearly 1,000 major parties, and a number of minor parties, only a few stated that they applied electoral mechanisms which would facilitate the election of women. Given that without party nomination there is generally no candidature,

Table 8.2 Women in national Parliaments – 10 November 1998

Both Houses combined	12.7%	
Total MPs	41,259	
Gender breakdown known	35,948	
Women	**4,560**	
Men	33,981	

Single House/lower House	13.0%	Upper House/Senate 10.5%
Total MPs	34,793	6,466
Gender breakdown known	31,341	4,607
Women	**4,078**	**482**
Men	27,263	4,125

Source: IPU Website – http://www.ipu.org/wmn-e/world.htm (please see website for up-to-date details)

there are dangers that women candidates can become token in certain systems. There are various considerations which can be applied in PR systems: including women in each list; closed lists to include women in winnable positions; the alternation of men and women candidates ('zipping'); allocating a percentage of head of lists to women and priority for women in the allocation of electoral remainders. It is clear that to be nominated is merely a first step and much strategic and financial support is required for electoral success.

It is notoriously difficult to assess progress and setbacks for women in national Parliaments. In the context of state structural change, it can be noted that between 1945 and 1995 the number of sovereign states with a Parliament has increased sevenfold (26 to 176) whilst the percentage of women MPs worldwide has increased fourfold (3 per cent to 11.6 per cent). Despite many detailed statistics it is hard to encompass change in terms of rates of renewal in Parliaments and the vast differences in how 'democratic' interventions in gender relations are made within state structures. A snapshot can be gleaned from world average situations. Of course these percentages mean less without regional breakdowns which are as shown in Table 8.3.

It is clear from Table 8.3 that the Nordic countries have achieved considerably higher numbers of women MPs and, as the study of Sweden highlights, some key areas for attention are political culture and movement 'from below' in terms of women's participation

Table 8.3 Regional averages of women in Parliaments –
10 November 1998

	Both Houses combined (%)
Nordic countries	37.6
Americas	15.5
Europe – OSCE members including Nordic countries	14.4
Asia	13.4
Europe – OSCE members excluding Nordic countries	12.5
Sub-Saharan Africa	11.6
Pacific	8.3
Arab States	3.3

Source: IPU website: http://www.ipu.org/wmn-e/world.htm (please see website for up-to-date details)

and the recognition of gender significance in politics. It is the incorporation of motivated women, across the spectrum of political affiliations and styles of participation, that creates progressive political changes in the areas of under-representation of women. This is highlighted in the consideration of Nigerian politics and in the Case Study on Sweden.

Women's movements, women's politics

In considering women's movement politics I assess women's involvement in various arenas of politics. Whilst the focus remains on gaining political voice, the vast array of women's campaigns means that only a tiny portion of women's movements can be covered here. Two areas of consideration are women's movement activities within very different contexts in Nigeria and in Sweden. As discussed in Chapter 4 the ideas and actions of feminists cover a broad spectrum across and within countries. In the 1960s feminisms developed out of a politics of resistance and at least four (often overlapping) perspectives of liberal, socialist, radical and internationalist feminisms emerged with varying outlooks and emphases. Issues of legal and political reform, equality with men and extending existing frameworks to include women, were high on liberal feminist agendas. For socialist and internationalist feminists structural changes in the nature of capitalist systems were required in order that class and gender and, over time, racialised oppression could be overcome. In radical feminist analyses the celebration of difference was a key foundation in terms of elaborating patriarchal relations of power. For feminist internationalists focal points were concerned with specific locations of women's oppression and global shifts in economic and political power. So whilst the diversity of political beliefs led to concentration on different styles of political resistance, the significant key was that all strands of feminism shared the core of challenging the existing order of male power and privilege which subjected women to second-class citizenship and oppression in a variety of forms. In this regard Marianne Githens notes that:

> In short, despite political and philosophical differences, there was some consensus about the need for change. There were common themes, such as reproduction, employment discrimination, and violence against women, around which all could mobilize. All segments of the various women's movements wanted to eliminate those conditions that perpetuated women's inferior position in the economic, social and political domains.
>
> (Githens *et al.* 1994: 173)

Working through their actions, feminist campaigns were subjected to various backlashes over time, varying from attempts at devaluing politics through media humour of women's 'libbers', politicians actively resisting pro-women initiatives, to conservative activists bombing clinics which carried out abortions.

In terms of building coalitions, it is clear that the diversity of feminist ideologies did lend opportunities for developing cross-cultural work. In considering the development of Chicana feminist discourse in the 1970s Alma M. Garcia argues:

> Although Chicana feminists continued to be critical of building coalitions with white feminists toward the end of the seventies, they acknowledged the diversity of ideologies within the white feminist movement. Chicana feminists sympathetic to radical socialist feminism because of its anticapitalist framework wrote of working-class oppression that cut across racial and ethnic lines.
>
> (Garcia 1994: 192)

In this context feminist coalitions depended upon understanding racial and class differences and above all respecting them. This ability to unite across diverse positions is the key to coalition building in terms of working towards the realisation of progressive political change.

Women's movements and national liberation

Women's movements which developed in many countries have been concerned with gaining freedom from oppressive foreign rule. From the seventeenth century with people in Mauritius struggling against the Dutch and Jamaicans against the Spanish, to the nineteenth century with Surinam resisting the Dutch, Tasmania struggling against Britain, Hawaii versus the US, Brazil against Denmark – the list is enormous – all these liberation struggles involved women. In the twentieth century there have been resistance movements involving women and men in Zimbabwe, the Gold Coast (Ghana), Malaya and India against British rule, in Namibia against German oppression, in Niger and Algeria against the French, in Nicaragua against US intervention and in South Africa against the dreaded oppression of apartheid. Again such lists could be expanded in many ways – the point being that for many millions of women the vital struggle was for freedom from external aggression. As can be seen in Chapter 9 the legacies remain in women's realities today.

Women's involvement within national liberation struggles includes both state and social aspects of what is considered political participation. For millions of women throughout the world their involvement in such struggles was a basic necessity of developing a political system that was democratic and so encompassed both state and social aspects of their political participation. Oppression by foreign powers can never be a situation within which democratic politics can develop. In her work Kumari Jayawardena (1986) shows how the early feminisms in the Middle East, South-East and East Asia grew out of the same roots, and at a similar historical time, as nationalism. The ways in which women participated in the national liberation struggles differed across countries as did the ways in which women's liberation was considered. Caution is called for by Christine Pelzer White (1989) with regard to national liberation struggles and women warriors: 'There has been a tendency among socialist feminists in the West and on the left generally to romaticize women's role in national liberation armed struggle and to see it as an index of women's liberation rather than see it either as defense of traditional values or as a sign of desperation'. Arguing for further research into the impact of militarism on gender relations in both industrialised and less industrialised countries, White concludes that: 'It is tragic, not "exciting" or "heroic", when men and women in the third world have no option but to kill other human beings dressed as soldiers in order to defend their lives and their homes' (White 1989: 352).

Amina Mama considers the contradictory constructions of women in nationalist ideology with calls for 'new women' alongside views of women as bearers of cultural traditions and customs. In some countries national leaders were very conservative about sexual politics such as female excision. Mama considers the divergence of views on women's emancipation within nationalist struggle, highlighting Oliver Tambo's radical statement in 1955, when:

> he not only declared women's emancipation to be a national priority and a precondition for victory but also went so far as to deplore 'outmoded customs' and call upon Congressmen to share in domestic work so that women could also be politically active. At the other extreme, one of the most retrograde examples was the Nigerian nationalist leader Tafawa Balewa, who opposed women being given the vote in the northern part of the country, despite the enfranchisement of women in the south.
>
> (Mama 1997: 55)

Certainly it seems that more research is needed to demonstrate the links between the terms on which women participated in these resistance struggles and the transformation of gender politics after independence was achieved. As noted in Chapter 3 in terms of revolutionary struggles for regime change and social transformation, women's participation was very much on men's terms and the ways in which the struggle was enacted determined something of the outcome as to gender relations. In military regimes, as opposed to the Parliamentary systems we have concentrated on, the ways in which feminist political struggles are enacted have enormous repercussions for women's participation. The example of women's political struggle in the group 'Women in Nigeria' is taken as a contrast, and as a reminder, that many feminist struggles are not taking place within Parliamentary democracies. The substance of these discussions is considered further in Chapter 9.

WINning women – Women in Nigeria

Considering women's politics in Nigeria involves thinking through the politics of military regimes. In assessing the organisation of

Women in Nigeria (WIN) Ayesha Imam recognises that: 'it is increasingly being recognized that there is no universal feminism, no abstract feminist theorizing but rather local feminisms that develop in particular contexts, at particular periods, and in particular ways'.
In this context, Imam provides a case history of a set of feminist practices developed in a specific historical context – 'post-oil boom, "structurally adjusting" Nigeria, which has been ruled by military regimes for over twenty of the thirty years since British colonial rule' (1997: 281).

Arising out of a seminar debate on the nature of women's oppression, WIN was formally constituted in 1983. There are many organisations in Nigeria purporting to represent women's interests some of which go back well before colonialism and certainly many have proliferated since 1960. These include women's wings of political parties, the Nigerian Women's Union and the Federation of Nigerian Women's Societies which attempted to mobilize women and push for women's rights during the nationalist struggle for independence from the British. Several features make WIN unique: its fundamental organising principle is concerned with simultaneously tranforming gender and class relations to bring about changes in women's and men's lives; it is autonomous with no state organised branches nor is it a national branch of an international organisation; its membership is voluntary; it is secular and concerned with all women in Nigeria with active branches in all parts of the country. As such WIN is the only organisation promoting all women's interests with the potential to mobilise women and men in combining the concern for gender equality with popular democratic struggles.

In terms of gender relations in WIN there have been tensions, with issues such as sexual harassment, violence against women and domestic work, emerging as points of strife as they related to different gender experiences, mediated by class. In such considerations a crucial point is raised regarding whether women have the right to define their oppression (and priorities of struggle) because of their experience of it, or whether this is essentialist. For Imam, whilst women as an oppressed group must have a right to say what it is they feel in defining their oppression (and giving priority to issues) experience is not the only tool of analysis. Reflecting upon experience from the empirical world can add to experiential knowledge and in this men can be political allies.

Other questions raised include whether or not WIN is a mass organisation or a protest and campaigning group, and whether

WIN's tactics and strategies are appropriate for the current context. As to the first, while WIN's membership is largely middle class and a small percentage of the population, their focus is consistently on the interests of working-class and peasant issues. As such it is a mass-oriented organisation which is well aware of historical precedents of small groups coming to power and not representing mass interests. WIN has rejected calls to become a party and has worked as part of a broad coalition. As to strategies and tactics, some branches concentrate on gender relations and others give priority to class struggles, so that work on 'conscientisation' is carried out to assure that WIN's aims and objectives, in the constitution, are accepted. In this process WIN's priorities may change. For example, the recommendation that 50 per cent of all seats in the legislative and executive bodies of Nigeria's government be reserved for women was not originally a WIN position, but was adopted because workshops during the political bureau debates recommended it. Some Igbo women argued this point from a traditional continuation perspective; Muslim women on the grounds that women should not be disbarred and others from aspects of their varying experiences, argued that at 50 per cent women would not be in token situations.

This study of WIN highlights women's participation in a movement for improving women's conditions and providing a platform for women to speak. Sadly, due to lack of resources, WIN finds itself in a position of either having to decrease its activities (when its mobilisation strategies show the needs for increasing them) or to rely on funding from the state. Its 'success' in working for improvement in *all* Nigerian women's conditions has led it to this impasse. Questions of whether such movements can remain autonomous and work with the state structures to improve women's situations are complex. Such questions involve reflections on the criteria that will enable judgements to be made about the usefulness of working with the state, and the dangers of co-option of WIN in support of government. Being able to remain as a critical element is vital for an organisation which is attempting to transform the social relations in Nigeria, particularly in an increasingly repressive political atmosphere. The complex debates regarding activism on gender and class issues have begun to prepare the participants in WIN for further examinations.

Case study: Sweden – Women's politics, changing power

Although the United Nations ranks Sweden as the 'best' country in the world for women to live in, Swedish women are organising more than ever. Agneta Stark argues that: 'No we have not won the war. It is still going on, and as we have touched on and challenged power, power is fighting back. There is nothing strange or surprising in that. We expected it. To some extent, we were prepared for it. However, preparation does not diminish the impact of the blows' (1997: 224). So, despite the Gender-related Development Index (GDI) ranking and the Gender Empowerment Measure (GEM) which ranks Sweden first among 116 countries, Swedish feminists are not complacent. Their gains can be seen: in the reduced gender pay differential; 'women's issues' are more apparent in 'malestream' politics; the political representation is higher than elsewhere; over 80 per cent of women are in paid work and childcare is more available, of good quality and reasonable cost; abortion is available within the National Health Service; and the proportion of poor among the elderly is smaller than in most similar countries. In the framework of Sweden as a prosperous country which has been at peace for almost 200 years it certainly seems that women's situation is an enviable one.

Three authors have carried out a study focusing on the strategies and practices within the women's movement with emphasis on three cases: the women's shelter movement, women's networks in sparsely populated areas and a foundation 'Women Can'. They argue that: 'Swedish women are now engaged in a new type of democratic practice which allows them to express their diverse demands in ways that go beyond participation and policy adjustment within the existing institutional framework' (Gustafsson, Eduards and Ronnblom 1997: 182). These authors propose that what is happening in Sweden with regard to women's organisation, in developing their own democratic practices, is challenging prevailing political institutions and parties. The strength of this challenge comes from the fact that demands are being changed into activities and this is occurring in a variety of ways. Of the three types of organisation studies, I can focus only on one, the women's shelter movement.

Male violence against women has become more apparent in most countries of the world during the 1980s and 1990s (see initially Davies 1994; Bunch 1997). In Sweden around 3,000 women each week are assaulted and every tenth day a woman is beaten to death by a male acquaintance. Charlotte Bunch has asserted in the UN Progress of Nations Report 1997 that: 'Violence against women and girls . . . is so deeply embedded in cultures around the world that it is almost invisible. Yet this brutality is not inevitable. Once recognised for what it is – a construct of power and a means of maintaining the status quo – it can be dismantled' (1997: 41). Maud Eduards outlines the development of the women's shelter movement in Sweden from 1976 when a Committee on Sex Crimes was challenged by 13 women's federations, organisations and unions who were jointly critical of its composition (with only one woman) and its conclusions. By 1982 a report, *Rape and other Sexual Assault*, was published in Eduards (1997). Gothenburg was the first municipality to grant space for the first women's centre in 1977 and the shelter for 'battered women' and victims of rape was opened in 1978. In the next 20 years the women's movement has supported women through specific projects and by pressuring those deciding the political agenda at local, regional and national levels. Shelter organisations of various scope now operate in around half of the country's municipalities and: 'Men's abuse of women has mobilised women – against men and against a male political order' (Eduards 1997: 122). The democratic order as a framework for disputes about how gender, violence and power are, and should be, constituted and interacting, is also the site for a battle for interpretation:

> The conflict between the established democratic order on the one hand, and women's demands and new collective practices concerning male violence against women, on the other, gives rise to a difference of interpretation which revolves around four factors: 1. resources; 2. competence; 3. ideology; 4. organization.
>
> (Eduards 1997: 125–6)

Eduards considers the dispute over these four dimensions in order to specify the nature and context of the challenge and its implications, as well as the character of resistance towards gender-related change in Swedish local democracy.

In order to understand the challenge, Eduards argues, the shelters' political demands concerning battered women are re/named and in different ways by politicians, civil servants, the police, the media and so on. As elsewhere, the construction of the media debate has in turn, to be responded to by the women activists (see Cosgrove 1996). Over the 20 years of feminist activism it appears that the pivot of 'democracy' has moved towards more acceptance of the feminist definition of assault as an expression of men's control of women. Figure 8.1 shows a correlation between a high level of women's political representation and the existence of women's shelters.

As can be seen, municipalities with low levels of female representation had no shelters, and increasing representation raises the likelihood of shelter provision. Yet the 'success' of feminist analysis and resistance in reshaping the terms of the debate and engagement has not been linear. Disputes between ROKS (Swedish Organisation of Shelters for Battered Women) and other groups are gleefully reported by the media which creates its own power–political discourse.

In conclusion, Eduards argues that the demand for women's bodily integrity proposed by the women's organisation, whose ideology is based on the conception of a male power order, constitutes the basis of an alternative democratic practice: 'with the *feminist analysis of violence and political action interwoven* in a new way' (Eduards 1997: 168). In this way:

> What they want is to change collective decision-making procedures in order to make it possible for women to set their own priorities both with regard to what a good society for women is like and how it can be achieved. In other words, their organizing as women means that they want to influence not only the distribution of service and welfare between men and women, but also the existing institutional framework. They demand nothing less than a democratic practice of their own.
>
> (Gustafsson *et al.* 1997: 166)

Figure 8.1 Relationship between the percentage of municipalities with women's shelters and women's political representation

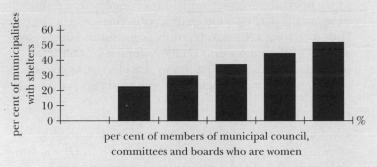

Source: Hojer and Ase, 1993: 24 in Gustafsson *et al.* (1997: 166)

This assertion seems well founded in the ways in which feminist practice, in Swedish women's organisation, is posing a direct challenge to the prevailing democratic order. However, as noted at the outset, touching power generally produces some form of 'backlash'. The authors of this study suggest that the main hope for continuing change is in developing ties to: 'the global women's solidarity movement which is slowly growing and was manifested at the 1995 Beijing Conference. If this happens then it will become obvious that women's dreams and demands are in no way destined to meet a dismal future' (Gustafsson *et al.* 1997: 183).

Summary

- Feminist analyses and activism aim to develop those forces which are undermining systems of male dominance by bringing gender issues into the public arena for further consideration.
- Orthodox studies of participation define 'politics' narrowly so that very few people are involved. Feminist definitions of politics are part of 'new' politics in which participation is considerably widened to include community activism, protest initiatives, campaigns and sexual politics.
- The structure and procedures of political parties and electoral processes are often neither democratic nor inclusive of all voices. Feminist considerations examine women's varying involvements and differing interpretations of participation in their criticisms of 'malestream' thinking of women's participation and perceptions.
- Four key areas are considered in assessing the degree of women's integration into politics: women in political parties; women's participation in the electoral process; women in national Parliaments; and women's movement politics.
- Figures show that women are under-represented in executive positions in parties, yet women are actively challenging the 'formal' leadership situation. Of the two major voting systems – multi-member majority and proportional list voting (PR) – evidence shows that PR is more conducive to women candidates.
- For millions of women their involvement with national liberation struggles was a basic necessity of developing a political system free from foreign domination. Early feminisms in some countries and regions grew out of the same roots, around the same time, as nationalism.

- Contradictory constructions of 'women' in nationalist ideology often called for 'new women' while viewing women as bearers of cultural traditions and customs.

- In revolutionary and liberation struggles for regime change and social transformation women's participation is generally on men's terms and the ways in which the struggle is enacted determines something of the outcome as to gender relations. Feminist politics within military regimes is undertaken within differing sets of constraints to those of Parliamentary politics.

Further reading

Afshar, Haleh (ed.) (1996) *Women and Politics in the Third World* London: Routledge

Inter-Parliamentary Union (1997) *Men and Women in Politics: Democracy Still in the Making, A World Comparative Survey* Geneva: IPU

Gustafsson, G., Eduards, M. and Ronnblom, M. (1997) *Towards a New Democratic Order? Women's Organising in Sweden in the 1990s* Stockholm: Publica

Nelson, B.J. and Chowdhury, N. (eds) (1994) *Women and Politics Worldwide* New Haven and London: Yale University Press

United Nations (1997) *The Progress of Nations: The Nations of the World Ranked According to Their Achievements in Child Health, Nutrition, Education, Water and Sanitation, and Progress for Women* New York: United Nations Children's Fund (UNICEF)

Chapter 9

International and transnational feminisms

'I decided, with other women, to challenge these attitudes both at home and in the community. I believe in our organisations and I feel women are reshaping them quite drastically. It's just a question of giving us a chance.'

Francisca, Brazil (Lopez 1991)

'The education and empowerment of women throughout the world cannot fail to result in a more caring, tolerant, just and peaceful life for all.'

Aung San Suu Kyi 1995

Chapter outline

In this chapter an overview is made of some of the feminist thinking concerning international feminist intervention at local and global levels and the key issues that are raised in such coalitions in various arenas.

- The necessity to reconsider, and to re-vision, new perspectives on various political issues from democracy to 'development' is argued. Consideration of differences in various guises and on the formation of varying subject positions is undertaken from the perspective of **transnational** political perspectives.
- Reconsideration is given to various political concepts from democracy to difference and '**development**'. These are radically critiqued from an international feminist viewpoint.

Introduction

Much has been written on women's self-organisation and feminist international links, from early anthologies on global sisterhood (Morgan 1984) to recent collections about women building upon and challenging various conceptions of international solidarity in sisterhood (Renne 1997; Ang-Lygate *et al.* 1997). Lack of space limits full consideration here, but I have chosen to focus on some examples to consider what is involved in working internationally and locally, and envisaging political change in a global context. Issues raised include the necessity to radically reconsider various perspectives on issues from democracy to 'development'. Re-thinking differences is something that centres this chapter. What Bernice Reagon (1983) has said about coalition work being difficult and dangerous holds true for all international feminist work because there cannot be spaces here for people who are like each other, except in terms of an identification with particular visions of change and overcoming bigotry. Audre Lorde (1984) has recognised that it is silence about the misuse of difference that bars women from generating creative politics through difference. Recognition of the silence provides a way of considering feminist solidarity work and how resistance can be reformulated in repression by a politics of culture that is redefining.

Avtar Brah's (1996) context for thinking of difference with regard to racism and feminism as about experience, social relations, subjectivity and as identity is important. Feminists have been involved in uncovering institutionalised constructions of differences that have been used to divide people and in highlighting the ongoing politics of culture which builds up images of 'dangerous or tragic others' which are contrasted to 'our' cultures. Some specific examples of feminist international work are considered to highlight the mix of issues involved in analysing women's resistance to politics of division. International work on 'development' needs reflection to tease out some of the complexities of how thinking about women affects action and vice versa. Although feminist analyses have opened up the complexities of the term 'woman', when we consider international and domestic politics, we find that politicians, aid agencies and international organisations are still producing policies aimed at blanket conceptions of 'women'. Within this, key policies such as those regarding 'overpopulation' actually centre on specific and particular conceptions (Kabeer 1994; Petchesky and Judd 1998; Wallace 1991).

Terms of debate

In asking questions about what oppresses women and shapes their lives and identities, Bhavnani argues that feminism can point to both the movement and organisation of capital across national boundaries (Mitter 1986), as well as to aspects of contemporary life: 'While these two aspects, combined together, may appear to be literally very far apart, it is the local/global, theory/practice, and experience/analysis oppositions which feminism can disrupt, interrupt and hopefully subvert' (Bhavnani 1993: 45). In the 1980s there was much discussion in Green politics about acting locally and thinking globally. This is something that many feminist groups have been working on for decades. Recognition of how global shifts in economics and politics affect women in various countries in a multitude of ways is coupled with knowledge that access to economic well-being for survival is a need shared by all humans. In Chapter 4 the legitimising of an economic order, whereby 'mother' countries exploited colonial countries, as one of 'reciprocal benefit' is part of a history of exploitation which continues in various guises. As Mitter (1986) among others, has shown, such changes have not gone unchallenged by 'Third World' women.

Since the 1980s changes have been taking place in the ways in which production is organised and new patterns of investment and wealth generation have appeared. Economic power has become more concentrated and controlled by people without political restraint. Georgina Ashworth shows that: 'the richest 368 people are wealthier than the poorest 44 countries together, but have none of the political restraints – the parliamentary checks, the judicial balances – on their use of that wealth and the influence that goes with it' (1998: 25). To work towards economic democracy is something on which some feminist groups, particularly women of the 'Third World' wherever they are living, are concentrating their political energies. Without economic democracy, political democracy is not worth a great deal.

I give an overview of some of the work being done by feminist analysts, and in feminist coalitions, which is taking account of these global changes and their impact upon women in varying ways. Work by feminists such as Audre Lorde in considering our fears and silence around difference recognises how the misnaming of differences has become structured into our lives so that some conscious unlearning has to be undertaken and some explicit demystification of official explanations for 'world shortages', 'development' and 'overpopulation'. This work is ongoing not least because while historical misuse of understandings of our differences are being uncovered and exposed, current constructions of difference are constantly being undertaken within varying cultural, economic, political and social realms.

Global sisterhood or international feminisms?

Ideas in feminist politics about sisterhood, connectivity and universal visions have been considered in various ways throughout this book. In Chapter 4 the early feminist ideas on global sisterhood were seen to have been premised on the partial analyses then prevalent regarding 'universal' aspects of women's oppression. With the critiques of Black, 'Third World', lesbian and disabled feminisms it has become possible to recognise the ways in which the category 'woman' is constructed through racialised, sexualised and embodied realities of power and prejudice. Feminist analyses of *work* have shown that women have been differently placed regarding paid work, not least by the ways in which race and class issues impact upon our lives. Women are made to suffer in many ways because their ability to have children is used to assign them particular 'roles' within most societies. Issues of maternity leave and childcare tend to make women seem more 'expensive' than men to employ. Global shifts in economic organisation show an internationally gendered division of labour.

Throughout this century many different international coalitions have been apparent in feminist politics in the growth of the antinuclear peace lobbies, ecological movements and women's resistance to violence in war and at home (Agarwahl 1986; Ashworth 1981; Brocke-Utne 1985; Bunch and Carillo 1992; Corrin 1996; Davies 1993, 1994; Enloe 1990, 1993; Mies 1986; Ridd and Calloway eds 1986; Shiva 1988). Much work has been undertaken on gendered impacts of 'development' (Dankelman and Davidson 1988; Kabeer 1994; Rowbotham and Mitter 1994; Sen and Grown 1987) and in resistance to prostitution and trafficking in women (Barry *et al.* 1984; Barry 1995; Jeffreys 1997) and fundamentalist political movements (Yuval-Davis and Saghal 1992). International collaboration work within the United Nations agencies and groups has continued since 1975 (Pietila and Vickers 1990) and one outcome of such work has been the increased focus on resistance to all forms of violence against women and women's rights as human rights (Peters and Wolper 1995). These struggles are interlinked, inevitably, in terms of a vision of freedom for all, in recognising that the oppression of one individual or group is to the detriment of all, that the earth's resources are unequally divided and are finite, and that all life on the planet is only sustainable if humankind recognises its role in destruction and does something to remedy it.

Difference revisited

Difference has been a key theme within feminisms and continues to be a central focus of concern within international politics in the ways in which the misnaming of difference is used to instil fear and justify repression, subjugation and killing of 'others'. In her work Audre Lorde argued against silence around difference, not just because we need to acknowledge our differences in order to work through conflicts but to recognise the ways in which the misuse of issues around difference can repress a politics of resistance:

> Much of Western European history conditions us to see human differences in simplistic opposition to each other: dominant/ subordinate, good/bad, up/down, superior/inferior. In a society where good is defined in terms of profit rather than in terms of human need, there must always be some group of people who, through systematized oppression can be made to feel surplus, to occupy the place of the dehumanized inferior. Within this society, that group is made up of Black and Third World people, working-class people, older people and women.
>
> (Lorde 1996 [1984]: 162)

The political dangers of these features of life in much of the world, Lorde argues, is not grounded in the actual differences between humans but in the institutionalised rejection of such difference which makes us view it with fear and to respond in three ways: ignore it; copy it if we think it is dominant and destroy it if we think it is subordinate. Such actions have resulted over time in misunderstandings about difference which have served to separate and confuse people. One result of these processes has been that we do not have any patterns for relating across our differences, as equals. As has been stressed by many feminist thinkers, people's lives differ in terms of race, age, sex, sexuality, physicality and in many other ways. What is at issue is not the fact of differences but our inability to recognise them for what they are and to work through the distortions in the way difference has been used to divide people. This is not to argue that once all people recognise structured power imbalances everyone will work towards overcoming them, or that in understanding the bases of racism everyone will become antiracists. Nor do I wish to imply that all women are working for feminist visions of change. As hooks (1989: 20) and others have pointed out, women can and do participate in the politics of domination, as perpetrators as well as victims. I want to emphasise that feminist political perspectives are committed to change by working through many of these contradictions in order to envisage how the world could look if differences were viewed creatively and what steps can be taken towards this in our politics in the short- and long-term, locally and internationally, specifically and globally.

Theorising feminist solidarity work

What are the important issues in generating theories for international feminist work? Clearly some understanding as June Jordan (1994) mentions of why we want to be in coalition is significant, as is clarity of the complexities involved in analysing changes being brought about by globalisation. In their work, Alexander and Mohanty highlight a paradigm of decolonisation which stresses power, history, memory, relational analysis, justice (not just representation) and ethics as the issues central to our analysis of globalisation (Alexander and Mohanty 1997: xix). In discussing their criticisms of much of the 'international' feminist writings, from a North American context, which has parallels with much Western European work in this area, they suggest what is missing from such strategies:

> Missing from these definitions of 'international' (what we refer to as 'transnational' from now on) are at least three elements:
>
> 1 a way of thinking about women in similar contexts across the world, in different geographical spaces, rather than as all women across the world;
> 2 an understanding of a set of unequal relationships among and between peoples, rather than a set of traits embodied in

all non-U.S. citizens (particularly because the U.S. citizenship
continues to be premised within a white, Eurocentric,
masculinist, heterosexist regime); and

3 a consideration of the term 'international' in relation to an
analysis of economic, political and ideological processes
which foreground the operations of race and capitalism (for
instance, those which would therefore require taking critical
antiracist, anti-capitalist positions that would make feminist
solidarity work possible).

(Alexander and Mohanty 1997: xix)

Here we see an agenda for change that involves not only rebal-
ancing historically structured inequalities but one that tackles
the need for unlearning prejudices regarding racism and ideas on
the politics of profit above people, in a transnational framework.
Ideas about crossing borders, such as those of Gloria Anzaldua's
(1987) inspirational work on 'borderlands' tracing the migrations
of pre-Aztec Indians from what is now part of the USA to Mexico
and back, much later, as 'mestizos' with Indian and Spanish
Conquistador blood in their veins, have been vital in generating
new ways of thinking and asking different questions about identities, 'our' place and the coming together of different cultures.
Conceptions of justice and ethics need to be radically reconsidered
if we are to move forward how we think about political organising
and mobilisation across borders. This subject of rethinking our
conceptions of politics is returned to in the Conclusion.

Global shifts

We saw in Chapter 4 the dramatic developments on the world stage,
the repercussions of which are being felt even today. In the 1990s
we have witnessed the aftermath of the Tiananmen Square killings,
the ongoing dismantling of the Apartheid regime in South Africa,
a Gulf war with ongoing consequences internationally, the 'collapse
of communism' in Central and Eastern Europe, the disintegration
of Yugoslavia in war, massacres in Rwanda, a negotiated, political
'settlement' in Ireland, nuclear testing in the Pacific, Pakistan and
India, the slide of some East Asian economies and the decimation
of the Russian rouble, starvation in Ethiopia and hurricane devastation in Nicaragua and Honduras. These processes and other major
shifts in world politics have had powerful impacts across all countries

in varying ways and have generated much feminist debate on many levels including ideas about *socialism*, 'development', *ethnic cleansing* and *human rights*. Global terrorism inciting the 'Muslim other' is a feature of late twentieth century political warfare. Such conflicts kill many people and the cultural constructions present within the battles echo strongly the ideas of Lorde on the misnaming and misuse of differences between us.

In the context of the politics of culture, Jordan and Weedon (1995: 5) argue that: 'Social inequality is legitimated through culture . . . Just as group domination has its cultural dimensions, so resistance to domination must also be rooted in culture and experience, at least, if it is to be successful . . . All revolutions . . . decentre, displace and deconstruct dominant cultural constructions, meanings and values. All seek to realize one aim: to transform human actions and being'. These authors (1995: 290) note the *Guardian* article comparing terms used in the British press in January 1991 to illustrate the ways in which perceptions can be created and manipulated.

'Mad dogs and Englishmen'

We have	They have
Army, Navy and Air Force	A war machine
Reporting guidelines	Censorship
Press briefings	Propaganda

We	They
Take out	Destroy
Suppress	Destroy
Eliminate	Kill
Neutralise or decapitate	Kill
Decapitate	Kill
Dig in	Cower in their foxholes

Here we see the politics of 'us' and 'them' used to effect. In her reflections on the war in Bosnia, Indijana Hidovic Harper writes of how readily the West bought into the Serbian nationalist message of an ethnic war between Christians and Muslims: 'Is Christian fundamentalism ever mentioned in a negative context? And why is a Muslim who adheres to the orthodox rules of Islam a fundamentalist, and his Christian counterpart just a good Christian? What good to me as a Muslim are Christian values, if they are killing me, or legitimising my victimization?' (1993: 105). In October 1995 a couple of weeks before the ceasefire, around one hundred women gathered at an international meeting in Tuzla, Bosnia to discuss women's political organising against the war. In discussing fundamentalist political projects, Bosnian women argued against the Western media strategy of invariably showing Bosnian women as 'ethnic' peasant women in headscarves – to be Bosnian was to be fundamentalist and 'backward' (see Corrin 1996). I use these examples to highlight some of the cultural constructions which feed into a politics of difference in defining ways of thinking about 'enemy others'. 'Ethnic' never applies to 'us'. Such construction is also apparent in thinking about issues of Africans as 'poor starving victims' or of 'Third World' women as having too many children and not understanding about birth control. Issues are highlighted in the above examples about ethnicity, imperialism, nation and race within international debates.

Not only is race mostly erased from conceptions of international (based on nation, without mention of race) there are ways in which the international is separated from the community- and home-life, as if the two are mutually exclusive rather than mutually constituted. Various examples have shown how slaves and indigenous peoples sometimes felt forced to choose not to have children, or to let them die, rather than have them sold into slavery or colonial systems (Davis 1982; Morrison 1988; Sharp 1993). It is clear that for many women the use of rape as an international weapon of war (highlighted in Bangladesh, Rwanda, Bosnia but part of all war) has meant that women's individual, family and community lives have been devastated. When the news media in Yugoslavia wanted 'numbers' for women who had been raped in Bosnia to feed the 'pornography of war' (Boric in Corrin 1996) feminist groups refused to feed into militaristic tactics of hate with the re-ethnicising and revising of the realities of women's abuse by saying how many *Serbs* had raped how many *Bosnian women*, or how many *Croats* or whatever. Women's experiences of rape were being used within war campaigns and feminists were able to protest against this in many ways and to show how the misuse and fears of difference were being utilised to legitimate further killing and abuse.

Feminist networking – cultural contradictions

I choose to give a few personal examples of feminist networking to highlight some of the complexities involved in working through difference and in recognising how political resistance on various scales is subverted through the processes of rewriting women's resistance. During 1984–1985 I was a student in Oxford and involved in many cross-cultural political projects. One such was helping to organise solidarity work, including a 'Mines not Missiles' march in which women from Greenham Common peace camp walked and talked with women and men from mining communities and those active in the miners' support groups. Many links were made across classes, sexualities and nationalities, with separatist lesbians discussing the depth and importance of community links for mining women and men, and many miners struggling 'manfully' to assimilate the varied images of strong women – independent wives, lesbian grannies, young women supporters and students. International aspects came to the fore when women from mining communities went, often for the first time, to speak in other countries about their struggle, the links they had chosen, and at times felt forced to make, and how this had enriched their understandings of how changes affecting their lives were being felt in various ways by communities elsewhere.

Another networking process in 1984 was through Oxfam, in which student volunteers from Anti-Apartheid groups came together with women and men from *SWAPO* and women from the *Women and Ireland Network*. One of the speakers from the cultural group 'African Dawn' gave his presentation making links around Britain's colonial presence in Ireland. For many of these students hearing a Black African man talking so passionately about the political repression through colonialism in Ireland was a shocking experience. Working on issues of colonisation of far-away people, and listening to Namibian women tell of the horrors of refugee camps was one thing. It was perhaps more challenging to consider issues such as the strip-searching of Irish Republican women prisoners in Armagh and Maghaberry prisons in Northern Ireland, and to make the connections across countries of the realities of colonialism and its impact upon our lives today. Issues of racism were brought closer to home in such considerations. It is not possible in such thumb-nail sketches to explore all of the complexities involved. An extended example of cross-cultural solidarity work perhaps gives more the flavour of mis/understandings.

In the summer of 1985 around 40 women went on a coach from Greenham Common to Moscow. This trip was organised by women who had participated in the Greenham protest for several years and were keen to exchange ideas and strategies on anti-nuclear work, environmental campaigns and the politics of peace, with women in Central and Eastern Europe, particularly peace activists in Moscow. This *women only* project, which grew out of Western feminist activism, had few parallels in the work of the peace activists that we met in Moscow who were working in small groups of women and men, some of whom were then in prison. Tatyana Mamonova's Almanac of 'underground' feminist writings (Mamonova 1984) had created an enormous resistance from Soviet authorities in the previous year and some women had to leave the country in the wake of this.

That our party of Western peace women was heralded in the Soviet press as supporting the Soviet peace initiatives (unknown to us until after these 'reports' were published) caused reflection in our joint discussions about the role of the media in 'designing news'. In the UK, Greenham activists were reported personally as disreputable, bad women (often 'dirty lesbians') whereas in the Soviet context of the time, with Gorbachev just coming to power, our activities were useful to show Western resistance to Cold War nuclear escalation. In addition, such official reports could have served to make oppositional activists in Moscow wary of us but they disdained such tactics. Our 'foreign feminism' ensured us no more than interviews with the KGB and a friendly 'tail' when we wandered around Moscow. For Soviet women at that time engaging in any form of resistance to official policy was fraught with personal danger (several 'peace' women were then in Soviet jails) and the opportunities to fundraise, gain permission to travel and freedom to undertake a project such as ours were impossible for those activists. The complexities of 'coming together' can be seen in such examples not just in terms of our different realities, of expectations and aspirations, but most particularly in the ways that our parallel work against nuclear escalation and environmental destruction, increased spending on warfare and decreased spending on everyday welfare, was used by politicians in the construction of a politics of restraint, in which our differences became viewed as barriers rather than the materials for creative work. Just five years later the Soviet Union ceased to exist in the form it had and, as noted, the changes ushered in much feminist debate about feminisms and discussions about resistance to Western feminist ideas being overlaid on to Central and Eastern European women's realities (Corrin 1992; Castle-Kanerova in Corrin 1992; Posadskaya 1994; Renne 1997; Siklova 1992; Szalai 1994).

'Development'

Often the power of language is striking. Feminists have long recognised power imbalances in communication (Spender 1980) and in naming, blaming and shaming those who misuse power (Ashworth 1998). The term 'development' can be associated with what it is to develop – to acquire, advance, evolve, grow, mature and ripen. All of these aspects of development sound 'good'. However, studies of *development thought* show a very complex picture of hierarchical divisions which reproduce much of the 'us' and 'them' thinking apparent in other areas. Naila Kabeer shows the deeply entrenched biases which underpin 'malestream' *development theory*, with women's needs being given marginal status in current policy. In identifying the household as a primary site for the construction of power relations, Kabeer compares the extent to which gender inequalities are revealed in different approaches to the concept of the *family unit*. The apparent 'difficulties' of including women are argued against:

> feminist perspectives have been either excluded from mainstream development or else included in a highly diluted or distorted form . . . women's lives across the world appear to straddle more dimensions and activities than those of men, and are consequently less easy to contain within the compartmentalised modes of thought which characterise some of the mainstream social sciences.
>
> (Kabeer 1994: ix)

In her work, and that of other feminist thinkers, issues of 'reproductive choice' are highlighted for urgent attention.

As we saw in Chapter 4, and as considered in the Case Study on native people's struggles, women have been active on issues of reproductive health for centuries across many countries of the world. Feminist arguments in the twentieth century on reproductive health have largely centred on Western White feminist concerns with abortion rights and issues of new reproductive technologies. Struggles for women to choose when and whether to have children need also to include those women who have been forcibly sterilised or denied opportunities to have children. In some senses women's movement struggles around reproductive health epitomise the varying levels of concern in terms of making priorities with regard to particular contexts. Within Western countries that have had access to cheap, safe and effective birth-control since the 1960s and within capitalist cultures which propose small, nuclear families as desirable the recognition of different needs and desires has been minimal. Consideration of native people's outlooks on our relationships with land and collective struggle can bring a wider understanding of the holistic priorities in which reproductive health is framed (Guerrero 1998).

Although there is no unanimous view on reproductive health issues within feminist analyses, it is important that feminists provide insights into the construction of population policy. In their comparison of negotiating reproductive rights across seven countries, Brazil, Egypt, Malaysia, Mexico, Nigeria, the Philippines and the USA, the contributions to the International Reproductive Rights Research Action Group (IRRAG) show how much is common in women's experiences of the power relations embedded in reproduction, despite cultural differences and geographical distance. In assessing what it is that enables women to move from entitlement to action, from strategic negotiation to demands for social justice in addressing structural conditions that structure their everyday realities, the study makes specific recommendations in keys areas:

- valuing the processes not just the outcomes of research, particularly feminist participatory action approaches, and filling in many gaps in research;
- emphasising girls' rights to protection in sex and also their rights to sexual pleasure;
- improving intergenerational communication between women particularly with regard to the role of older women as gatekeepers of traditional practices such as female genital mutilation (FGM);
- care to be taken with projects involving men that funds are not diverted from women's needs and that men and boys are educated against violence towards women and girls and to alleviating the household and childcare tasks of women and girls at all stages of life;
- encourage and support grassroots work by women and increase women's participation at all levels to expand their rights as women and citizens;
- promotion of interfaith dialogues with groups such as Catholics for a Free Choice, Sisters in Islam, Women Living Under Muslim Laws;
- governments and religious institutions should recognise the integrity of women's decisions and make abortions legal and safe;

- governments, private clinics and hospitals should ensure that caregivers respect women's dignity in the 'quality of care' offered;
- implementation of the programme of action of the Beijing conference regarding women's rights to bodily integrity and to resources to ensure livelihood for themselves and their children;
- support for the principle of indivisibility among economic, social, cultural, political and civil rights as well as the necessity of defining those rights through democratic and inclusive dialogue listening to what women say (Petchesky and Judd 1998: 318–22).

Studies such as this, that are the result of a careful process of cross-cultural collaboration and consultation, are vital to the feminist input into *development* policies and practices.

International organisations and treaties can be helpful for women in pressing demands on their national governments and resisting imposed policies. In intersections of individuals, families and the state, international law can sometimes be useful. Human Rights Watch has recognised that the Nigerian government's acquiesence in forced marriages orchestrated by parents is an example where the state could be made accountable under international law for privately perpetuated abuse. In the 'state socialist' era in Czechoslovakia, the government forced numerous Romany women to be sterilised in an effort to reduce what it considered a 'high unhealthy population' (Human Rights Watch 1995: 410–412). There are many examples where concerns over population size and its perceived relationship to state interests, be this in economic 'development', environmental conservation, national security (or whatever justification is considered useful) have been used to implement population control strategies that incorporate massive abuses of women's rights and well-being.

Work carried out by women's NGOs (non-governmental organisations) in many countries and from the follow-up after the Beijing Women's Conference in September 1995, has been useful in highlighting ways of making impact upon national governments otherwise resistant to such considerations. Yet much of the content of international agreements can go unheeded. Within feminist networking, consideration is being given to the different ways in which women are active and the differences amongst women, not least in terms of their historical situations and how knowledge has been produced, and ways of thinking about issues have developed. Careful thought is going into the various means that women use to express their resistance to perceived injustices and the ways in which campaigning, lobbying and policy development is carried out in different societies. Women in women's groups and coalitions across real and perceived boundaries are working in many ways, locally, nationally and transnationally for positive changes in the lives of women, men and children. Issues of concern are: establishing political agendas which reflect and voice women's concerns; ensuring the safety of refugees; creating good reproductive health conditions; resisting male violence against women and generally attempting to improve certain social, political and economic situations. Much resistance to such work is experienced as it challenges the orthodoxies of the powerholders.

Changing the terms of debate

Feminist thinkers have been actively considering and reshaping many of the political conceptions on issues of justice, ethics, democracy, citizenship, care and responsibility in the last ten years. Work such as Anzaldua's foregrounds some later feminist theorising concerning how diverse cultures are coming together and how this must affect how we think about and do our politics. This is not just a 'theory' for far-away countries in the 'Third World'. As the media attention to the Windrush 50th anniversary in the UK showed, in 1998 Black British people have become integrated (not assimilated) into British life, creating new identities. *Windrush* was the ship which carried many people from the Caribbean to the UK in 1948. One in five children starting school in the UK in 1999 is of 'mixed race' and has more than one cultural heritage to draw upon.

All over the world, challenging politics that seek to divide through difference is something that feminist thinkers are involved in, while recognising the importance of our specific identities and the structures that extend or delimit our possibilities. In changing ways of considering democracy and the practice of politics, Alexander and Mohanty (1997) suggest a critical application of feminist praxis:

> The practices of democracy, justice, and equality for example,
> would need to be reconceived within new definitions of justice.
> Our very understanding of democracy and its practices would

have to become cross-cultural. In place of relativism, this critical application of feminst praxis in global contexts would susbstitute responsibility, accountability, engagement and solidarity.

(Alexander and Mohanty 1997: xix)

The essays in their anthology consider feminist theories and practices concerned with imperialism, postcolonialism and the advanced capitalist nation-state questioning capitalist relations in reproducing forms of domination that are sexualised, gendered and racialised. In an intersectional and transnational framework considerations of the transformative political projects being undertaken by women in Asia, Africa, Europe and North America point to the ways in which feminist praxis in a global context can emerge within the twenty-first century. This would involve: 'shifting the unit of analysis from local, regional, and national culture to relations and processes across cultures . . . [and] a corresponding shift in the conception of political organising and mobilization across borders . . . The ideologies of "immigrants", "refugees", "guestworkers" and "citizens" would need to be reconceived with new definitions of justice' (ibid). This is not an easy project!

However, work is ongoing with feminist reconsiderations of many key political conceptions such as citizenship. Feminist theorists have developed insights into citizenship which highlight that the consistent exclusion of gendered realities is both historically contingent (Pateman 1988, 1989) and/or constitutive in the theory and practice of citizenship, with women having 'roles' as 'women' in practice and 'honorary men' in public life (Yuval-Davis *et al.* 1992; Heinen 1995). Nira Yuval-Davis (1997) argues that as the boundaries of ethnic and national groups often do not overlap those of the state, and exist within and across states, both collective identities and citizenships need consideration. Many feminist struggles contribute to deconstructing binary divisions and 'engendering citizenship' by actively recognising the 'differentiated universalism' which Ruth Lister (1997) proposes as acknowledging differences and women's differentiated positioning. These feminist reworkings of considerations around citizenship aim for an inclusive synthesis which allows for women's agency while challenging structural constraints. The distinction drawn between being a citizen and acting as a citizen is important in the context of feminist analyses and resistance to male violence. Whilst many women remain subordinate in terms of hierarchical power relations they nevertheless can, and do choose to, be agents for change, in their own lives and those of other women. Deliberations, arising from women's joint work in resisting male violence, encompass ideas of how women can fulfil their active participation in creating change in social and political domains (Boric 1997; Bunch 1995, 1997; Corrin 1996; Mama 1997; Women in Black 1996, 1997). New forms of women's economic organising and resistance in the 'Third World' are considered in the Case Study.

Case study: Political organising among women

I have chosen to focus this Case Study on economic organisation of women across 'Third' and 'First' worlds and on land rights and the erasure of cultural practice among native peoples. These are important areas of struggle for transnational feminist politics. Key issues of new technologies are affecting women's lives in various ways from the population control policies enforced upon many women in 'Third World' countries, to territorial colonisation of native lands in the USA and Australia, to the communications technology that has helped in the reorganisation of production through large corporations. I first consider a brief example of women's resistance to economic exploitation.

As we have seen in Chapter 4 a new international division of labour has emerged in which the main focus centres on the division between core, protected, male works and peripheral, vulnerable, women workers. Again, this is not 'just' a problem for women living in 'Third World' countries, as Mitter (1986) shows, it is increasingly Black women in the sweatshop economy of the West who are providing some of the most 'disposable labour'. These reorganisations, of women's livelihoods and lives, have not gone unchallenged. Much feminist research on grassroots women's organisations gives evidence of the committed strength and determination that women in many countries bring to their resistance and struggles.

As Maria Mies (1986) and others have recognised, it is hard to do away with the stereotype of the male breadwinner. This myth perpetuates the belief that women's wages do not really 'count', with ideas of 'pin money' or 'secondary wage'. Additionally, given that women's work in the home is not considered 'real work' and is unpaid, then the stereotypical ideas regarding women accepting part-time, lowly paid or home-based work abound. In her work on women's organisation in the 1980s Swasti Mitter notes that some of the new technology which supported the fragmentation of production processes also facilitated women workers in exchanging their experiences. In October 1982, women from the North and the South met in Amsterdam to consider their experiences as 'global workers' in the clothing and textiles industry: 'Of course, the experiences of these women were diverse, rooted as they were in their cultural and social specifities. But what emerged from the discussion was the striking common element in their experiences as workers, especially in the treatment they received from the transnational corporations (TNCs) and from their male colleagues' (1986: 146). Women from Hong Kong and from Tennessee experienced male tactics of collusion with management in disciplining women workers who were on strike.

At a feminist conference of women workers in the electronics, clothing and textile industries in April 1983 in London, 170 women from many countries, as far apart as Scotland and Sri Lanka, clarified the role of TNCs in creating unstable and vulnerable employment patterns for women workers. The exchange also confirmed: 'the determination of workers to resist the divisive strategies of multinationals, that set black women against white and Third World women against First' (Mitter 1986). Yet Mitter cautions against reading a seamless thread into women's lives which have experienced the realities of racism, and cites the treatment of Black workers by trade unions in the 1983 strike at Peugeot–Talbot factories in France as an example of the tarnished record of racism within the labour movement. In the UK the Imperial Typewriters strike in 1974 was organised mainly by Asian men and women against economic and racial exploitation, yet the union denied support to the strikers and attempted to assist management. One famous British strike, in the 1980s, was that of Grunwick, which was led by Asian women, yet issues of race and gender were seen as incidental in supporting 'the lads' (Parmar in Mitter 1986: 119). That 'workers' are viewed as male and White was apparent in our considerations in Chapter 2. Such entrenched stereotypes regarding White men, 'real' work, family wages and male breadwinners have proved very difficult to dislodge.

Equally difficult stereotypes to remove are those which view countries such as the USA solely as an advanced capitalist state, as it is also an advanced colonial state. Territorial colonisation remains integral to the relationship between the state and native peoples. Marie Guerrero (1998: 101) argues that: 'the mainstream feminist movement has been ineffective and inconsistent when faced with the issue of land rights and sovereignty (feminism versus "indigenism")'. Solidarity politics among native women and White women is made difficult by this reluctance to wrestle with questions of indigenism: 'Any feminism that does not address land rights, sovereignty, and the state's systematic erasure of the cultural practices of native peoples, or that defines native women's participation in these struggles as non-feminist, is limited in vision and exclusionary in practice' (ibid). Here 'land rights' needs to be understood in terms of culture and territory. 'Tribal' is viewed in its cultural context, reflecting a self-determination and self-sufficiency based on reciprocity rather than individual ownership. In this understanding, fundamental differences are apparent from Eurocentric constructions of sovereignty.

In her study, Guerrero outlines the specific ways in which the US government plays a crucial role in defining questions regarding liberation struggles for gender equality at the same time as charting an agenda for the rights of tribal peoples and their communities. Here 'civil rights versus sovereignty' and 'feminism versus indigenism' gain importance. Several examples are given of how women have lost their rights to return to tribal land because of the US government's agenda to undermine tribal sovereignty under the guise of granting 'civil rights'. Acts on Indian Citizenship, Indian Reorganisation and Indian Civil Rights have very much reduced tribal sovereignty for all native peoples. The problems of dual citizenry: 'fall disproportionately on native women, denying them legal autonomy within their own tribes as well as within federal context' (Guerrero 1997: 107). The construction of terms such as 'American Indian' and 'Native American' have served both to divide tribal peoples and to clump them together in some form of 'Pan-Indianism'. The indigenous worldview, which underpins Guerrero's arguments is one in which the meaning of indigenous conservation includes taking from the land or from animals enough for survival needs but *not* for commercial profit or gain. As such, this is very different from the preservation ideas of 'environmental fundamentalists' whose views loom large in contemporary environmental movements. Guerrero concludes that in the transformative and visionary spirit of their resistance, native American women in North America: 'engage indigenous liberation movements against colonization. We seek to build alliances and coalitions with other colonized groups, including third-world feminists, ecofeminists, gays and lesbians, and all other disenfranchised and dispossessed peoples, regardless of gender' (1997: 121).

I turn now to consider the historical and ongoing struggles of native people in Australia, where the British colonisers carried out inhuman practices and cruelty to Aboriginal peoples which were continued through processes of 'assimilation'. The importance of recognising the links between culture, identity, political expression and the historical exercise of power in attempts to kill off certain peoples and their cultures, is vital in understanding the situations in which indigenous people are now forced to live. Saundra Sharp describes one of the ways in which the historical paths of peoples were distorted by imperial rule with a key focus on women's reproductive health and family life:

In 1830 the Tasmanian Sistuh WALLOA led a five-day uprising against the internment of her tribe. Under British imperialism Tasmanian women were raped, stolen, forced into hard labor in the whaling industry and had their children taken from them. Their strongest weapon became refusing to procreate within the tribe.

(Sharp 1993: 117)

Not being able to bear children, see them grow to adulthood, is the denial of the right to existence. Over the centuries Australian and Tasmanian Aboriginal peoples, Black slaves from African countries, Black people in South Africa, native people in the USA and First Nation people in Canada have been either militarily defeated or exterminated. Survivors were herded into 'native reserves' of varying types where often the genocide continued.

The consequences for native peoples of being denied an existence on the earth, of brutal attempts at 'assimilation' and of the denial and misrepresentations of their cultures through Western racism and constructed imagery, are only recently becoming recognised within academic analysis. As Jordan and Weedon show in their consideration of Australian Aboriginal writing:

These people, who constitute the overwhelming majority of the Australian Aboriginal population, are not the exotic natives of the White Western imagination. They are not a people who live 'in harmony with nature' but an uprooted, demoralized people living in the urban slums, shanty towns and remote reserves of contemporary Australia . . . They are not some 'pure race' who have lived in isolation from other peoples and cultures for thousands of years, but a people who are overwhelmingly of 'mixed' racial and cultural background. They are a people whose everyday lives necessarily involved negotiation with structures of White power.

(Jordan and Weedon 1995: 490)

In such negotiations many 'mixed race' Aboriginal people have to undergo both processes of unlearning the lies told to them about their families and the understanding of what it is to live within a history of persecution and victimisation.

My Place, an autobiography and life history by Sally Morgan (1987), a woman of Aboriginal descent, shows many of the difficult contradictions faced by Aboriginal children who were taken away from their parents. The policy of assimilation was such that from the turn of the century until the early 1970s children of Aboriginal mothers and White fathers were taken from Aboriginal families, and their mothers had no 'rights' to their children. These children were placed in orphanages where contact with anyone, or anything, Aboriginal was banned. Twin themes in this work are of being 'taken away' from her Aboriginal community and heritage and the 'taking away' of Aboriginal land by White power. One passage quoted in Jordan and Weedon shows the depth of sorrow that the forcible division and destruction cause:

> Sally recounts how, when they visited the reserve, 'An old full-blood lady whispered to me "You don't know what it means, no one comes back. You don't know what it means that you with lights skins want to own us".'
>
> (Morgan in Jordan and Weedon 1995: 514–515)

The significance of this 'gratitude' is heavy, given all that this old woman must have suffered. It is humbling that she is 'grateful' to be recognised, remembered and respected. Jordan and Weedon conclude that Australian Aboriginal writing centres respect for difference as the basis for positive social change and: 'It suggests that there can be no alleviation of human suffering without the restoration of human dignity' (1995: 539). Here once more, issues of respecting difference and recognising the historical circumstance and constructions of certain differences, are vital to any transnational feminist ethic and politics.

Summary

As the quotations at the head of this chapter show, this section is concerned with women challenging attitudes, reshaping organisations and illustrating the importance of giving power to women's knowledge, whether from theories or daily life. Feminist perspectives have been challenging the 'terms of debate' in many areas of politics.

- Feminists have considered women's self-organisation and feminist international links with early anthologies of 'global sisterhood' and later collections concerned with various conceptions of international solidarity.

- Feminist theorising on difference (Lorde 1996 [1984]) shows that it is silence around the misuse of difference that generates continued oppression.

- Recognition of how global shifts in economic organisation and politics affect women across many countries is coupled with feminist resistance and research on issues of access to economic well being and centring dialogue on women's knowledge; feminist active research and resistance show the necessity for radical rethinking of issues from democracy to 'development'.

- Feminist coalition work involves cultural dimensions and aims to 'decentre, displace and deconstruct dominant cultural constructions, meanings and values' (Jordan and Weedon 1995).

- Official discourses often contrast perceptions of 'us' and 'them' which attempt to justify killing or legitimise victimisation.

- Constructions of 'Muslim others' as dangerous feed into images of Muslim versus Christian ethnic wars (Harper 1993). Such 'othering' is implicit in constructions around the politics of international terrorism at the close of this century.

- Terms such as 'development' involve many different perceptions of ways of working and of the goals of collaborative work. Feminist analysts have argued against the 'difficulties' of including women's knowledge and feminist practice into 'malestream' development policies and practices (Kabeer 1995).

- Reproductive health and reproductive choice are highlighted for urgent attention, and groups such as IRRAG (1998) assess how women move from entitlement to action, from strategic negotiation to demands for social justice, in addressing the conditions which structure their everyday realities. Specific recommendations are made in key areas which would help to create conditions in which women's subordination can be overcome.

Further reading

Alexander, M.J. and Mohanty, C.T. (eds) (1997) *Feminist Genealogies, Colonial Legacies, Democratic Futures* New York and London: Routledge

Jordan, G. and Weedon, C. (1995) *Cultural Politics: Class, Gender, Race and the Postmodern World* Oxford: Blackwell Publishers

Kabeer, N. (1995) *Reversed Realities: Gender Hierarchies in Development Thought* London and New York: Verso

Mitter, S. (1986) *Common Fate, Common Bond: Women in the Global Economy* London, New South Wales and New Hampshire: Pluto Press

Morgan, S. (1988) *My Place* London: Virago

Petchesky, R. and Judd, K. (eds) (1998) *Negotiating Reproductive Rights: Women's Perspectives Across Countries and Cultures* London and New York: Zed Books

Rowbotham, S. and Mitter, S. (eds) (1994) *Dignity and Daily Bread: New Forms of Economic Organising Among Poor Women in the Third World and the First* London and New York: Routledge

Chapter 10

Conclusion

In the development of feminist perspectives, the aftermath of the French Revolution can be seen as a turning point, with the publication by Mary Wollstonecraft of *A Vindication of the Rights of Woman* in 1792. This provided a feminist perspective on women's condition and criticised prevailing prejudice. The experience of the French Revolution and the discourse on democratic rights plus the Enlightenment emphasis on the language of reason, attacking prejudice, were clear influences on early feminist thinking. In the nineteenth century in Europe and North America the significance of evangelical Protestantism was apparent in encouraging many women into involvement with social and political issues. The impact of the early Utopian Socialists was important as various strands attacked the institution of marriage, the bourgeois nuclear family and promoted female equality, advocating freer sexual relations and communal childcare. In their writings Marx and Engels criticised women's positions as 'slaves' of the workers under capitalist conditions and Engels (*Origin* 1884 in Rossi 1974) can be seen as the first materialist analysis of women's oppression. Their writings were to assume greater significance with the Russian Revolution of 1917.

Up to the nineteenth century women globally were involved in struggles against slavery, although it is mainly White women's experiences that have been preserved. Many women in Europe and North America were involved in campaigning for women's suffrage, political parties, charity work, moral reforms and social works. Some links were made between gender difference and sexual and social violence against women. Resistance was apparent, for example in Britain, in campaigns against the 1860s Contagious Diseases Acts and in the actions of suffragettes from the 1890s. In the later twentieth century, feminists resisted these linked oppressions by creating alternative forms of politics such as consciousness-raising groups and women's safe houses with campaigns against abusive representations of women in pornography.

The movement of women into the workforce in the early twentieth century signalled their involvement in trade union movements and workplace struggles. Women's political struggles within growing socialist movements led to collaboration in revolutionary politics, particularly in Russia and Germany. In countries where votes for women were gained in the 1920s most feminist movements became involved in struggling for immediate, practical welfare concerns apparent during the time of the Great Depression in the 1930s. In many 'Third World' countries in the twentieth century, involvement with national liberation struggles and with feminist politics developed alongside each other. From the post-war era of the 1950s the economic growth in the USA and later in Western Europe saw an increase in affluence for much of the population. The growing numbers of educated women in Europe and the USA from the 1940s and women's entrance into previously male-dominated professions, connected in the 1960s with changes in legislation regarding abortion, equal rights and pay and the introduction of the contraceptive pill, all of which facilitated women's independent thinking in various arenas. The literature of de Beauvoir (in paperback in English from 1953) and other feminist thinkers, was developing alongside an interest in feminist politics. Many women active in civil rights campaigns moved into feminist political campaigns as they had become disillusioned with the sexism of many Left groups. In the USA the liberal strands were important very early in the feminist movements, and in the UK links with the political Left were significant.

Theories concerned with reproduction and difference in nineteenth- and twentieth-century thinking highlighted ideas concerning women's oppression being closely linked to sexuality. As we have seen, writings by sexologists, psychoanalysts and other 'experts' were popularised in the 1920s and 1930s and were used to legitimate the alliance of women's bodies to heterosexual nuclear families and to motherhood. From the medical constructions of women's abilities in the nineteenth century, to the institutionalisation of reproduction in the twentieth century, women's opportunities to gain independence through education and employment have been limited. Feminist theories provided socially based accounts of women's situations and emphasised the flaws and dangers in biological accounts. The stripping away of male-directed ideologies regarding women's biological destiny still left the dangers apparent in the medicalisation of motherhood (see Rich 1986). Links between analyses of women's reproductive power and, often male-dominated, reproductive technologies are of paramount significance because such power to control women's lives can still determine many women's present and future choices.

Difference and diversity

While feminisms have had different historical and national characteristics, key aims have remained relatively constant towards a more broad understanding of the effects of living within the range of 'being women'. As has been considered, one major reason why the category 'women' became disputed within feminist circles was because it was often used to minimise or ignore differences among women. As Henrietta Moore argues: 'Difference is, of course, a relational concept, and it is always experienced relatively in terms of political discrimination, inequalities of power and forms of domination' (1994: 26). Until the 1970s, much feminist analysis had been developed from partial and centralising perspectives – of White, Western, middle-class, non-disabled heterosexual women. Black feminists, feminist lesbians and disabled feminists have challenged these partial, dominating views of 'women' by sharing their own experiences and political priorities and thereby enriching our understanding of our individual selves and our interconnectedness. The responses of Black feminist writers such as Audre Lorde and Kum-Kum Bhavnani provide particularly clear examples of the problems posed by this lack of recognition of diversity among women. Moving from critiques of constructs of 'women' which ignored their experiences, Black feminists and women of Colour generated crucial debates on ideas: which 'women'; issues of 'whiteness'; the centrality of, and opportunities to recognise and celebrate, differences; as well as the need for women's political solidarity to acknowledge the richness of diversity. Spaces for debate have been created by lesbian politics and feminist disability politics within which our manifold identities can find expression.

Identity processes can be, among other things, creative, cumulative and coercive. By acknowledging the power of the erotic,

Lorde affirmed the creative processs of identification with being women, for ourselves and with others. In deconstructing whiteness, Black and White feminists were involved in a cumulative process of recognition of the power and privileging that whiteness afforded people, individually and collectively. The feminist resistance to the coercive aspects of identity processes which label 'women' in various ways, has sharpened powers of analysis and recognition of manipulation and misrepresentation practised through global telecommunications by government authorities and capitalist business interests. While we may now consider histories rather than History, it is clear that not all histories are equal. Certainly, in the institutionalisation of certain discourses concerned with *othering*, the power of global media resources cannot be under-estimated. The old adage 'divide and conquer' is as relevant today as it was in the eighteenth century, with images of women being seen as a prime site for engagement. Bosnian women were displayed in the Western media in headscarves in the fields during the war in Bosnia for particular reasons, mainly concerned with distancing them as 'Fundamentalist' or 'backward Others' whose plight was something very different from the concerns of 'modern European' societies, and the conflict taking place was therefore very 'difficult to understand' (see Corrin 1996).

Recognition of how our identities are shaping and forming in various ways highlights the many ways in which difference can be considered: thinking of ourselves and of others; of making our own choices; of being 'labelled' and labelling – as Black refugees, White heterosexuals, disabled lesbians, feminist activists and so on. It was pointed out with regard to race and racism that various writers have placed the term race in quotations marks – 'race' – to show that this term is a construction. However, as we have seen, it is also a lived reality for many people. Like gender, race is both a social construct and a reality in people's lives.

Certainly a sense of belonging is something which is apparent within feminist movements. Henrietta Moore points out that: 'Belonging invokes desire, and it is in this desire that much of the passion for difference resides' (1994: 2). In this way Moore emphasises that identity and difference are not so much concerned with categories as with processes, of identification and differentiation, and these processes are engaged with the desire to belong as part of some community. In considering ourselves as part of a whole, Sarah Lucia Hoagland has argued with respect to lesbian community that: 'In perceiving ourselves as one among many, we realise we are not destroyed (nor created) by another's reflection but we also realise that we are not the whole picture' (Hoagland 1988: 90). In the Case Study in Chapter 5 it was apparent that the women involved in working with Southall Black Sisters were able to sustain their own identities as feminists within their communities, in opposition to the identification of 'women' by community leaders. At the same time, as Black feminists, they were able to collaborate with some White feminists during the 1980s only with much negotiation, but with a clear identification of their political goals of challenging male violence against women.

In the context of partial perspectives, Adrienne Rich (1986) has spoken of a 'politics of location' which looks to different groups of women to recognise their own interests and those of other people, not claiming to speak for all women. This requires feminists to consider where they are *speaking from* with a consciousness of exclusions that can be recreated. In thinking through diversity, from such positions, it can then be seen as a strength and not as something necessarily divisive. The changes brought about in feminist theorising ask questions about how to express the ways in which institutional, economic and cultural oppression differentially affect women, and change over time, all the time. Our identities are generated by many aspects of our lives, which are constantly changing.

Discourses about who we are expected to be and how we are to consider 'Others' are apparent within much political writing. As was considered in Chapter 5, official uses of the media to essentialise 'enemy Others' is apparent in the reporting on sanctions, arms inspection issues and air strikes in Iraq, with the generation of 'us' and 'them' differences. Thinking through issues of identity and difference in the international sphere, William Connolly has argued that as we live in a time of *global* danger, this may provide a: 'cultural impetus to rethink strategies of identity and difference through which contemporary states define and cope with otherness' (1991: 45). Still, such global danger could push in the opposite direction, as it seems to at the end of this century, towards creating 'enemy others' to fight against.

As has been emphasised throughout, the new ideas and ways of thinking generated by feminist debates have altered conventional views of 'politics'. Crucial feminist politics of ecological and peace activism focused on non-hierarchical forms of organisation and on feminist spirituality and generated rich areas of thinking in many spheres. This book has only scratched the surface of the rich veins of women's knowledge which has been created over the past century of feminist *praxis*. This aim, of uniting feminist theory and practice through action, is developing in many, varied ways.

In drawing together the threads of changes in politics over time, and how challenges to oppression have been affected by women's activism, I want to give a glimpse of a calendar of change to highlight women's efforts in various struggles (see Table 10.1).

Table 10.1 Women's activism towards challenging oppression

600 BC	Sappho and her lesbian sisters resist imposed heterosexuality.
1300s–	Between 5–30 million Black women were taken from Africa and New Guinea and enslaved in many parts of the world. They resisted.
	Native American women assisted escaped slaves.
1600s–	Women in Africa, Ireland, Jamaica, Tasmania, Hawaii, Virgin Islands and Brazil active in resisting foreign occupation by British, Danish, Dutch, Spanish and Portuguese.
1800s–	Boa Morte in Brazil founded (originally an anti-slavery society) now one of the oldest Black Women's organisations in the western hemisphere.
1848	Seneca Falls Feminist Convention in New York, USA.
1850s–	Black women's voices recorded in speaking out against racism.
1890s–1900s	Women active in resistance to British in Zimbabwe and Gold Coast (Ghana); to Germans in Namibia and to French in Niger and Dahoney.
1890s–1930s	Campaigns for 'Votes for Women' (see Appendix 1).
1905–1917	Women active within Russian revolutionary politics.
1905	League for the Protection of Colored Women formed in USA.
1940s–	Chinese women active in campaigns on Mao's 'long march to Communism' (1949) and in building conditions for change in China.
1940s	Women active in resisting world war.
1945	Women's Wing of FRELIMO organised in Mozambique.
1945–	Women active in Thailand, the Philippines, Burma and Malaysia in independence struggles.
1948–	Women in Central and Eastern Europe take up challenges of Soviet socialism and intervene in changes.
1956	2,000 women march in Pretoria against the South African 'pass laws'.
	Hungarian women resist in Hungarian Revolution.
1956–1990	South West African women active in resisting apartheid regime Women internationally involved in anti-apartheid politics.

Table 10.1 Continued

1960s–	Women in Cuba active in resisting US aggression.
1964–1969	Women active in protesting US war in Vietnam and against imperialist aggression globally.
1968	Young women active globally in youth resistance and uprisings from France to Afghanistan.
	Feminists active in the widespread resistance to: nuclear arms and military escalation, institutionalised educational barriers, conservative political structures and inequalities.
	Feminist protest at an American 'beauty' contest in USA.
1970s	Feminist campaigns; protests and publications across many areas including women's health, women's freedom from male violence; founding of Green parties and environmental and peace movements.
1975–1985 to date	Declared UN Decade for Women – feminists involved in UN Conferences in Nairobi, Rio, Vienna, Cairo, Copenhagen and Beijing developing, documenting and demanding action on the decisions and promises being made in international fora.
1980s–	Women freedom fighters active in South Africa and Nicaragua.
	Oppositional activism by women in Central and Eastern Europe.
	Feminists active against nuclear weapons and environmental degradation; the economic downturn and conservative political retrenchment of previous feminist gains, generating changes in ways of thinking as well as in welfare programmes, equal opportunity gains and 'development' issues.
1990–to date	Women in South Africa and Namibia active in the development of new systems of government and generating changed social relations.
	Women in Central and Eastern Europe intervene in the changing social and political conditions in their countries. Women in Bosnia Herzegovina, Croatia and The F.R. Yugoslavia, Chechnya, Northern Ireland, Palestine and Israel, Rwanda, and many sites of war and conflict actively intervene to create peaceful political paths. Women in all corners of the world active in changing the terms of debates and arguing for imaginative roads toward freedom for all.

Sources: Humm, M. 1992 and Sharpe, S. 1993

This cannot be comprehensive but it can signal the massive force for change that many, diverse groups of women across the world have been and continue to become.

This table is just a partial glimpse of some aspects of women's political activities over the centuries. In the last two centuries women's activism has been informed by feminist critiques of power, politics and participation. Feminist thinking has considered women's exclusion and oppression within politics. In the nineteenth century professional 'definitions' of White women's condition as governed by their wombs, so close to 'nature' as to be unable to express civic virtues, were considered acceptable. At the same time racist notions, arguing that Black people were inferior to White people were being structured into systems of thought and dictating policies of oppression. In challenging these, and other constructed prejudices, from feminist perspectives, much research has been undertaken and new knowledge generated. The importance of historical links in understanding how women's oppression is structured is recognised by Avtar Brah: 'Structures of class, racism, gender and sexuality cannot be treated as "independent variables" because the oppression in each is inscribed within the other – is constituted by and is constitutive of the other' (Brah 1996: 109).

Audre Lorde's work in emphasising the creative aspect of difference, *once power imbalances are recognised and respected*, has caused a major shift in ways of considering alliances and coalitions for change. Reagon's significant recognition that intervention in creating political change is not something that one can enter lightly, or expect to be nourished within, is something that feminist activists are understanding more and more in terms of the changing terms of engagement at the close of this century. The kind of energy required for coalition work can only be recharged outside the site of engagement, which can be brutal within the coalition, and against whatever force is being challenged. The realisation by Lorde, noted in the Preface, is that we can create our own safehouses in which to nurture our ideas and develop strengths to contemplate change in order to imagine how best to act.

Throughout this book examples are considered of the various coalitions women have entered into to change perceived injustices and to challenge orthodox views and practices which oppress people in various ways. In Chapter 5 the politics of Black women throughout the industrialised countries and in the 'Third World' are placed in the context of an overarching racial theorising in which 'whiteness' is the silent obsession. It is relatively recently that feminist recognition has been given to the implicit and explicit powers and privileges which are bound up in whiteness. In turn, considerations of the ways in which from slavery, imperialism and colonisation, the lives of those who did not have the power of whiteness, have been inhumanly and dramatically altered *affects our lives today*. By this I mean that social relations of domination are a part of the cultures in which we live and that issues of race and racism, arising from the historical structural conditions of White racial dominance, are part of our everyday realities.

As Marx said long ago, rather than just interpreting the world, the point is to *change it*. In order to be able to set about thinking through our ideas for change we need to know something of what is happening in the world and why. For this, our historical insights are vital. Without understanding why something became what it is, such as the arbitrary nature of the construction of 'races' and how such constructions become part of political processes and movements, internalised within ourselves, we cannot effectively challenge them or conceive alternative visions. The materialist conception, that we can act upon the world to change it, is therefore contingent on many factors, not least our knowledge of how it is possible to make strategic interventions at a variety of levels.

The first level of formulating any general goals for change is our selves. In thinking about how our ideas have been developed, within what kind of educational system, social and family relations and under what kind of political regime we live. The feminist definition of what is political does not separate certain aspects of life from the social whole. In this way feminist thinking unites theory and experience and avoids many of the binaries of public/private and active/passive, yet social and political divisions remain in all societies. It is in recognising where we can best intervene for change that is our *strategic choice*. For me, education in its many forms, is one site of engagement in changing injustices by recognising new ways of viewing how power is mediated and how inequalities can be tackled.

We have seen the importance of power within political debates: from the eighteenth-century thinkers such as Wollstonecraft, considering the power of men to determine women's realities by defining her 'nature', to Sojourner Truth questioning the power of White men to deny the realities of Black women's lives; in this century, since the 1960s women's liberation activists have defined the power of sexual politics (Millett 1970) and have engaged with the concept of the power of the erotic (Lorde 1996 [1984]) from which we can pursue genuine change in our lives. Lorde untangles arguments about women's eroticism from its cultural misuse in pornography and sexual oppression and explores the realisation of the erotic as the most self-responsible source of power from which women gain energy to pursue genuine change within our world. Here the erotic can be read as passion, *we can be passionate about our politics.*

Feminists of all persuasions view power relations as something in which we are all implicated. Within this, the source of legitimacy in the exercise of power can often be contained within cultural values such as that of public politics rather than interpersonal relations. Separations based on the stereotypical myths of a family wage, male breadwinners and women as mothers, still do much damage in women's lives. Other cultural constructions such as that of the 'Muslim other' can be seen as dangerous in world politics today feeding dominant representations of Christian and Muslim wars, within which killing and victimisation is justified.

In this context feminist coalition work aims to 'decentre, displace and deconstruct dominant cultural constructions, meanings and values' (Jordan and Weedon 1995). Certainly the imaginative outpourings from the 1960s have seen feminists combine to create enormous changes in the world around us. Just as some of the slogans used underline the importance of language in voicing our ideas of change: *Black Women's Tradition: Struggle not Submission; Disabled Feminists: Pride not Prejudice; We Cannot Live Without Our Lives; Our Bodies Our Selves.* An old favourite of mine is: *Wicked Witches were invented by Frightened Men.* Underlying this phrase is the reality of millions of women who were killed as witches over the centuries because frightened men had the power to kill those women whom they could not control and could not understand.

Education for liberation

Going 'back to the sixties' has become fashionable in popular culture recently with musical re-mixes of sixties songs, 'recreational' drugs, and even some clothing fashions (bellbottoms?). The 1960s and 1970s witnessed a new kind of political participation with young radicals reacting against orthodox styles of politics and against politicians who prepared to make war in various parts of the world, particularly Vietnam and Cambodia. Of course many young people were having to fight in those wars and in national liberation strug-gles in many parts of the world (see Chapter 4). Some youngsters were growing up in a situation in which tanks could crush their peaceful revolutions, as in Prague in 1968.

At the turn of this century, the world in many ways seems very interconnected across different social and political systems. Ideas about local impacts of 'globalisation' are much discussed. Economic instability in South East Asia and the rocketing rouble affected the markets in much of the Western World and Japan, and also impacted on the ways in which debts are restructured, so imping-ing upon the lives of millions of people in the 'Third World'. 'Nat-ural' disasters such a *Hurricane Mitch* killing thousands of people in Nicaragua and Honduras highlight the frailty of our ecological systems, our interconnectedness in the use and misuse of finite resources and our power to pollute. Use of the internet and e-mail have become means of political response for activists in many parts of the globe now. Yet access is limited for many reasons and this medium has meant easy exchange for materials of pornographers. What this global telecommunication can mean for education remains unclear.

As we have seen, important links were made in the 'new' pol-itics of women's liberation concerning 'the social/personal as political'. These analyses extended discussion beyond the 'peak' of governmental systems and participation by voting, to *sexual politics* and towards community politics, protest initiatives and campaigns. Debates were raised across a range of practical issues to do with the legitimacy of governments to undertake and continue war and of issues concerning sex and gender, ranging from sexual expression to economic inequality, male violence against women and police violence against citizens. In this context, Bob Connell argues that:

> sexual politics brought to light patterns of power, interest and conflict which made little sense in terms of socialist class analysis, conventional economics, political science pluralism or sociological functionalism. A theoretical revolution in the social sciences was called for.
>
> (Connell 1987: ix)

However, such a revolution has not been fully witnessed yet. Some of the ideas present in transnational coalition politics, passionate politics and the acceptance and working through differences, allow us to learn more about our selves and how our possibilities of creating changes enable us to see the 'Others' in our selves.

I have argued that for feminist research to have an impact beyond interpreting the world, consideration of issues about generating ideas for intervention and engagement is required. An example of such intervention in population policy measures is given in Chapter 9 with regard to the IRRAG proposals for effective reproductive health measures for women in 'Third World' countries. Other examples include the many, varied, coalitions generated by feminists in the politics of peace and conflict resolution pursued by many women's groups in the face of nationalist and ethnic conflict, and the opportunities created in organising women's political strategies through the various UN Conferences for Women and the lobbying of government authorities. Despite the fact that many decisions are taken before these international conferences take place, many women in attendance at both governmental and non-governmental meetings are able to influence some aspects of decision-making. The presence of lesbians at the Beijing Conference in 1995 was influential in swaying opinion regarding the inclusion of sexual orientation in the *thinking* of those who will be drafting national laws and implementing policies (Reinfelder 1996). The coming together of thousands of women from all over the world at gatherings concerned with women's politics, in which information and experiences can be shared is of immeasurable value, as Aung San Suu Kyi (1995) has pointed out. That feminist campaigns to eradicate male violence against women were highlighted in the UN Progress of Nations Report is significant and can be viewed as 'one step forward', yet campaigners from the nineteenth century may well have believed that such violence against women would have been eradicated in less than 100 years. It remains the case that feminist politics have shifted after reflection upon the consequences of the 'swings and roundabouts' of changing political climates.

'Teaching to Transgress'

This phrase, 'teaching to transgress', is taken from a book by bell hooks (1994) subtitled *Education as the Practice of Freedom*, in which hooks argues for teaching students to 'transgress' against sexual, racial and class boundaries as a way of educating the practice of freedom. I write this as a teacher and researcher at a university in Scotland. Being passionate about learning and teaching, about my politics, is often something which I attempt to share with students. In her work, hooks sums up some of the drawbacks of our current educational environments:

> My commitment to engaged pedagogy is an expression of political activism. Given that our educational institutions are so deeply invested in a banking system, teachers are more rewarded when we do not teach against the grain. The choice to work against the grain, to challenge the status quo, often has negative consequences. And that is part of what makes the choice one that is not politically neutral. In colleges and universities teaching is often the least valued of our many professional tasks.
>
> (hooks 1994: 203)

In her work Louise Morley (1998) considers the contradictory roles of feminist teachers and authority in dominant institutions of knowledge production. Morley considers whether feminist pedagogy fulfils a micropolitical function in the academy.

In putting this work together I have been reminded of my privileged position, in having access to books and information from various sources and the time to write. Only a very small elite have access to higher education in the UK. With changes in educational policy over the years and student fees now in place, previous ideas of education as a right not a privilege are seriously undermined. Girls in some parts of the world are not even going to school as they are deemed not to 'need' any education at all. It is such imbalances that internationalist feminist analyses address at various levels, not least in terms of 'telling it like it is'. In her work, bell hooks encourages an expansive perspective on 'the theorising process'. Given its ongoing critique of theorising and how knowledge is gained, feminist work can act as a powerful catalyst for change.

It is here that the *praxis* of feminism is important in terms of feeding back knowledge which is useful to communities but also in resisting impositions of what is 'relevant' or 'suitable' knowledge both in terms of content and form. For example, no subject can be deemed 'unsuitable' without debate, nor should written testimony be privileged over oral. As we have seen, in her work Patricia Hill Collins (1990) argues that theory can be presented in such a way as to exclude, deliberately or otherwise. In the 1950s, C. Wright Mills was writing about 'the sociological imagination' with the promise of a 'way of knowing that enables individuals to grasp the relations between history and biography within society'

(Mills 1959 in Collins 1990: 230). In this context, the words of Lorde regarding all the parts of ourselves being integrated, without restrictions of imposed definitions, are significant. So too, her reminder about recognising our own prejudices is a key starting point:

> As Paulo Freire shows so well in *The Pedagogy of the Oppressed* [1970] the true focus of revolutionary change is never merely the oppressive situations which we seek to escape, but that piece of the oppressor which is planted deep within each of us, and which knows only the oppressors' tactics, the oppressors' relationships.
>
> (Lorde 1996 [1980]: 170)

Lorde shows that for us to consider the complexities of how we think about things, can mean raising, and trying to answer, difficult questions: 'But we sharpen self-definition by exposing the self in work and struggle together with those whom we define as different from ourselves, although sharing the same goals' (Lorde 1996 [1980]). We have to be able to ask the questions that others would not imagine asking and to do what we need, to be centred within our knowledge, of our selves and what opportunities are open to us, how we learn, what we choose to study and how we choose to apply our knowledge. In this way we can choose to grow together and such learning knows no bounds.

As there are always gaps in knowledge and time lags between what some women and groups are doing and what others are thinking and writing about, in many ways some women's experiences and histories still remain very much hidden. There are also gaps in the wider educational environment, especially regarding what is deemed 'suitable knowledge'. Dorothy Smith has argued that: 'feminist research practice should never lose sight of women as actively *constructing*, as well as interpreting, the social processes and social relations which constitute their everyday realities' (in Stanley and Wise 1990: 34). This is true of us as teachers and students in our learning processes. The old adage of 'knowledge is power' is still being taken up by many feminists, and in creating new knowledge, we are also involved in the processes of transforming it. It remains very much an aim worth working towards.

Appendix 1: Women's suffrage

Chronology of the recognition of women's rights to vote and to stand for election.

1788	United States of America (to stand for election)
1893	New Zealand (to vote)
1902	Australia*
1906	Finland
1907	Norway (to stand for election)*
1913	Norway**
1915	Denmark, Iceland
1917	Canada (to vote)*, Netherlands (to stand for election)
1918	Austria, Canada (to vote)*, Estonia, Georgia*, Germany, Ireland*, Kyrgyzstan, Latvia, Poland, Russian Federation, United Kingdom*
1919	Belarus, Belgium (to vote)*, Luxembourg, New Zealand (to stand for election), Netherlands (to vote), Sweden*, Ukraine
1920	Albania, Canada (to stand for election)*, Czech Republic, Slovakia, United States of America (to vote)
1921	Armenia, Azerbaijan, Belgium (to stand for election)*, Georgia**, Lithuania, Sweden**
1924	Kazakhstan*, Mongolia, Saint Lucia, Tajikistan
1927	Turkmenistan, Turkman SSR
1928	Ireland**, United Kingdom**
1929	Ecuador*, Romania*
1930	South Africa (Whites), Turkey (to vote)
1931	Chile*, Portugal*, Spain, Sri Lanka
1932	Maldives, Thailand, Uruguay
1934	Brazil, Cuba, Portugal*, Turkey (to stand for election)
1935	Myanmar (to vote)
1937	Philippines
1938	Bolivia*, Uzbekistan
1939	El Salvador (to vote)
1941	Panama*

1942   Dominican Republic
1944   Bulgaria, France, Jamaica
1945   Croatia, Guyana (to stand for election), Indonesia, Italy, Japan*, Senegal, Slovenia, Togo
1946   Cameroon, D.P.R. of Korea, Djibouti (to vote), Guatemala, Liberia, Myanmar (to stand for election), Panama**, Romania**, The F.Y.R. of Macedonia, Trinidad and Tobago, Venezuela, Viet Nam, Yugoslavia
1947   Argentina, Japan**, Malta, Mexico (to vote), Pakistan, Singapore
1948   Belgium**, Israel, Niger, Republic of Korea, Seychelles, Surinam
1949   Bosnia and Herzegovina, Chile**, China, Costa Rica, Syrian Arab Republic (to vote)*
1950   Barbados, Canada (to vote)**, Haiti, India
1951   Antigua and Barbuda, Dominica, Grenada, Nepal, Saint Kitts and Nevis, Saint Vincent and The Grenadines
1952   Bolivia**, Cote d'Ivoire, Greece, Lebanon
1953   Bhutan, Guyana (to vote), Hungary (to vote), Mexico (to stand for election), Syrian Arab Republic**
1954   Belize, Colombia, Ghana
1955   Cambodia, Eritrea (?), Ethiopia, Honduras, Nicaragua, Peru
1956   Benin, Comoros, Egypt, Gabon, Mali, Mauritius, Somalia
1957   Malaysia, Zimbabwe (to vote)**
1958   Burkina Faso, Chad, Guinea, Hungary (to stand for election), Lao P.D.R., Nigeria (?)

1959   Madagascar, San Marino (to vote), Tunisia, United Republic of Tanzania
1960   Canada (to stand for election)**, Cyprus, Gambia, Tonga
1961   Bahamas*, Burundi, El Salvador (to stand for election), Malawi, Mauritania, Paraguay, Rwanda, Sierra Leone
1962   Algeria, Australia**, Monaco, Uganda, Zambia
1963   Congo, Equatorial Guinea, Fiji, Iran (Islamic Republic of), Kenya, Morocco, Papua New Guinea (to stand for election) (?)
1964   Bahamas**, Libyan Arab Jamahiriya, Papua New Guinea (to vote), Sudan
1965   Afghanistan, Botswana, Lesotho
1967   Ecuador**, Kiribati, Tuvalu, Yemen (D.P.R.), Zaire (to vote)
1968   Nauru, Swaziland
1970   Andorra (to vote), Yemen (Arab Republic), Zaire (to stand for election)
1971   Switzerland
1972   Bangladesh
1973   Andorra (to stand for election), Bahrain (right recoginized ?), San Marino (to stand for election)
1974   Solomon Islands (?), Jordan
1975   Angola, Cape Verde, Mozambique, Sao Tomé and Principe, Vanuatu
1976   Portugal**
1977   Guinea Bissau
1978   Republic of Moldova*, Zimbabwe (to stand for election)

1979   Marshail Islands (?), Micronesia (Fed. States), Palau
1980   Iraq, Vanuatu**
1984   Liechtenstein, South Africa (Coloureds + Indians)
1986   Djinollbouti (to stand for election), Central African Republic
1989   Namibia
1990   Samoa
1994   Kazakhstan, Republic of Moldova*, South Africa (Blacks)
1997   United Arab Emirates (?)

Notes: Rights to vote and to stand for election not yet recognised for women in Kuwait. A question mark (?) signifies that the original authors of this table did not have confirmation of material at time of going to print.
* Right subject to conditions or restrictions
** Restrictions or conditions lifted
Source: IPU 1997. This table can also be found on the IPU's website http://www.ipu.org/wmn-e/suffrage.htm

Glossary

The terms in this glossary are considered in the context of feminist perspectives of politics. Explanations are focused on the analyses assessed within the arguments of this book. Two particularly useful dictionaries used in this glossary are Maggie Humm (1989) *The Dictionary of Feminist Theory* Harvester Wheatsheaf, and Iain McLean (1996) *Oxford Concise Dictionary of Politics* Oxford University Press. Useful texts are noted in the entries and are in the main bibliography.

abolition: the anti-slavery movements began to gain recognition in the mid 1830s with campaigns and petitions. By the 1850s the focus shifted to the US Congress. The movement to eradicate slavery is seen as the catalyst for the emergence of women's rights movements in the nineteenth century. First the Slave Trade and then slavery were abolished in the British Empire and in America during the nineteenth century through principled arguments, political advantage and the Union victory in the American Civil War (1861–1865).

activism: feminist activism can take many forms of intervention in social and political change; these can range across a broad spectrum including: organising campaigns, protesting, lobbying, carrying out research, standing for Parliamentary or Presidential office.

AIDS: Acquired Immune Deficiency Syndrome is thought to be caused by a virus called human immunodeficiency virus or HIV. No one has yet been known to fully recover from AIDS. The first cases of AIDS were seen in the late 1970s. Much of the fear and panic around AIDS was caused because people did not understand how HIV is transmitted and believed it was easy to catch. The HIV virus is actually very fragile and is easily killed outside the body. Vaginal and anal intercourse transmit the virus and oral sex can be a risk if blood, semen or vaginal secretions containing the virus enter the bodies. Despite the early association of AIDS with gay men, we now know that the virus can be transmitted heterosexually. At the end of this century the majority of rising cases of HIV infection are among heterosexuals and the heaviest burden of increasing new infections is in Sub-Saharan Africa where medical resources are limited and sharing of needles in clinics can result in further infections. Education on safer sexual practices is being given a priority in many countries (see Richardson 1989), and 1 December is the day dedicated to *World Aids Day* on which remembrance and future planning to ease suffering and reduce the spread of AIDS are undertaken.

anarchism: the belief that societies can be self-organising without state enforcement. There are many forms of anarchism but no single doctrine, apart from a rejection of the state. Anarchists have proposed many forms of social organisation from individualism to collectivism and various strategies from terrorism to pacifism. Emma Goldman was a leading anarchist and her writings have seen a revival in popularity among feminists since the 1980s.

ANC (African National Congress): first African liberation movement, formed in 1912 to resist White minority rule in the South African Union. Various campaigns were undertaken and in 1955 the ANC Freedom Charter proclaimed that South Africa belonged to all those who lived in it. Most of the leadership was imprisoned in 1964 with remaining activists forced into exile. Nelson Mandela and other detainees were released in 1990, and in 1994 the ANC won the election.

Apartheid: separatist policy of racial segregation undertaken by South African government from 1948–1989. The main features were population registration, demarcation of group areas, ban on mixed marriages, suppression of communism and restructuring of 'bantu' education. The main African political movements were banned in 1960 with their leaders exiled or imprisoned. Following the new leadership of F.W. de Klerk in 1989, Mandela and other political detainees were freed, parties were unbanned and most of the Apartheid legislation was repealed by 1992. At the victory of the ANC in the 1994 election Nelson Mandela became President of South Africa.

Black: before the trans-Atlantic slave trade 'Black people' did not exist. People from specific ethnic and linguistic groups from specific locales and different religious communities, 'tribes' and nations were brought in slave ships to the New World and deliberately mixed up on plantations and collectively called names from 'African' to 'blacks' and 'niggers'. The whole basis of racial classification is arbitrary and varies considerably. In the British colonies race was viewed as ancestry 'in the blood', whereas in Spanish and Portuguese colonies, appearance and sociocultural status are considered. In ancestry, which is paramount in the USA, very fair-skinned people who look 'white' are classified as Black due to how their ancestors were classified. In Spanish America and Brazil, the key factors are looks such as skin colour, hair texture and facial features, so that two siblings with different appearances could be classed as belonging to different races. 'Black people' are not the only invention as 'The Oriental' and 'The European' are also inventions (see Said 1979).

Bolshevism: theory and practice of the Bolsheviks (majority) in Russian Social Democracy who split from the Mensheviks (minority) in 1903. The Bolshevik Party, constituted in 1912 came to power under Lenin, in the Russian Revolution of October 1917. Bolshevism was committed to revolution and the overthrow of the bourgeoisie in favour of proletarian socialism. The Bolsheviks became the Russian Communist Party and with Stalin's rule authoritarian practices became entrenched.

capitalism: system of industrial organisation with private ownership and control of the means of production. Britain is generally taken as the peak of *laissez-faire* capitalism from around the 1840s. Classical political economists such as Adam Smith and David Ricardo believed that the state should adopt a liberal form, encourage competition and develop 'self-regulating' market societies. Arguments regarding the 'globalisation' of capital are used by internationalist feminists to critique oppressive practices apparent in capitalist exploitation of 'Third World' countries and specific practices in highly developed countries, through transnational operations.

citizenship: the concept of citizenship may refer to a status conferred by law. It is also used to argue that persons have entitlements as a consequence of their position within a community or polity. Since individuals participate in a common life they have rights and duties as a consequence. It has been argued that we have moral obligations to one another because of that shared existence, whether what is shared is characterised as culture, economic activity or political obligation.

civil rights: 'civil' is sometimes used restrictively as in free speech, assembly, *habeas corpus*, in distinction to economic and social (welfare) rights. For the purposes of this book civil rights are taken as those economic, social and political rights that each citizen has by virtue of being a citizen. These rights are usually upheld by law and the stress is as much on group rights (such as minority rights) as on the rights of the individual. UK legislation bans discrimination on the grounds of disability, race, sex, and (in Northern Ireland only) religion. Often groups have had to struggle over time to gain the recognition that their civil rights are being infringed. The Black Civil Rights Movement in the USA is viewed as being a bridge between the old citizen's rights movements and those of the new social movements in which values and identities are important in the overall political perspectives.

class: there are various meanings of this term. An everyday meaning could be that class marks a division or rank of society according to status. Theorists such as Marx defined class in relation to the means of production: either one controls it or one does not. Max Weber distinguished between a class and a status-group so that a Lord of the Manor is in a different status-group to that of the local butcher, yet each are in the same class as 'owners of a factor of production'. Feminists such as Delphy (1977) argued that women's class can best be understood in terms of the institution of marriage as a labour contract. Class oppression is viewed as one of the axes of domination that affect people's lives along with racial domination and prejudices regarding sexuality and disability.

collective: term for a group operating on the basis of shared values and consensus decision-making. In women's liberation politics, consciousness-raising techniques were often used in order for women to be able to relate their personal experiences within a collective framework. Feminist collectives generally embody views about equality, with all women's voices being given equal value and all members being willing to take equal responsibility in the work being undertaken.

colonialism: political practice whereby stronger powers extend their control territorially over weaker nations. Where colonisation occurred some centuries ago there are arguments that the settlers feel equally a part of the territory as those whose ancestors they displaced (as in South Africa and Northern Ireland). The main focus has been on activities of late nineteenth-century imperialists who conquered large tracts of the world to rule. The term is also used to denote an unwarranted sense of racial superiority and the set of attitudes, beliefs, and practices that arose out of this sense. It has been argued that racism and xenophobia are colonialism brought home.

coming out: phrase used to identify the processes which people go through in their moves toward self-identification. First used in terms of sexuality, the term 'coming out' means recognition of same-sex attraction to oneself and/or, publicly, to friends, family and/or colleagues. That sexual preference is not apparent from birth means that in order to fully identify with their identities, lesbians generally have to make difficult choices and often become politicised by so doing. 'Coming out' is not undertaken as a single act but is recognised as an ongoing process which shifts with the contexts in which it occurs. In recognising new subject positions such as 'gay', lesbians and gay men have to choose to speak about their sexuality in a series of ongoing processes. The term 'lesbian' describes a range of identities and practices of women within their diverse histories and contexts. The construction of sexuality varies among and within countries and communities.

communism: communism is generally viewed as the process by which the proletariat, through class struggle, are victorious over the ruling classes. In Marxist theory communism, the classless society, is viewed as the highest stage of socialism. The belief in an egalitarian society held sway in many societies and political groupings, particularly after the success of the Russian Revolution in 1917 and the devastation following the Second World War and the collapse of imperialism in African and Asian countries. The consolidation of Stalinism in the

USSR from the 1930s implicated much of the 'Soviet internationalism' with political domination, and the collapse of Soviet Communism in 1989 called into question much of the political impetus of communist internationalism.

community: generally a group of people who come together by virtue of their shared social identity and common interests. Feminists define community as a type of relationship in which a shared sense of identity and identification with particular women is present. Separatism involved setting up specific communities from which particular political developments could be generated, for example feminist lesbians and 'Third World' feminist groups.

consciousness raising: raising consciousness has long been recognised in political thinking as a means to achieve change. In feminist politics consciousness-raising (c.r.) groups enabled women to meet to discuss things of importance to them personally and therefore politically. In this way women could recognise shared oppressions and their differences in working towards their aims.

construction: to construct something is to build it. The term 'social construction' is taken to mean the processes by which definition and redefinition take place in societies, which change over time. Social construction theory can outline which aspects of social interaction become designated as 'social problems' (see Saraga 1998). Social construction theorists have been at the forefront of challenging 'essentialist' theories which were often based on biological imperatives and unchanging. Feminist thinkers used social construction theory in viewing gender and sexuality, recognising that heterosexuality was neither inevitable nor unchangeable. Social construction ideas challenged the medical models of homosexuality and disability which viewed some people as having fixed positions at birth and as 'outside society'. Constructs such as race are also lived realities for people and affect their everyday lives.

culture: the culture of a particular society is its values and orientations and how these are communicated through the education system, the mass media, law, religious organisations, and popular cultural forms. Socialist thinkers such as Raymond Williams (1981) view culture as central to structures of change, control and democracy. Our cultures are basic aspects of our everyday lives which help to give us our sense of identity, in forming who we are and where we come from and go to. All societies contain divisions, of age, gender, kinship, which are reproduced through culture – of belief systems, social rituals and ideologies. The denial or marginalisation of cultures other than those of the dominant group leads to oppression, with implications for subjectivity and identity. Social inequality is legitimated through culture. Resistance to domination is rooted in culture and experience. The Women's Liberation and 'Third World' liberation movements struggled to displace and deconstruct dominant cultural constructions, meanings and values in order to transform human action and being (see Jordon and Weedon 1995). The term 'culture' in much feminist

theory asserts ideas concerning women's 'sisterhood' and
connectivity.

deconstruction: this method of critical analysis has been applied
particularly to literary texts. It questions the ability of language,
adequately, to represent reality. As no text can have a fixed, stable
meaning then readers must clear away all assumptions when
considering any text. The deconstruction methods can be used in
unpicking certain institutionalised discourses which have become
normalised over time so that they seem like 'common sense' rather
than something which is changeable.

'development': this term remains in quoation marks because there is
no agreement as to its definition. 'Development' is relative and
cannot be reduced to a single, universally applicable formula such
as increased economic efficiency or technological advance. Such
changes can be viewed as means to certain ends, but not as ends in
themselves. Development has been viewed as improvements in key
social indicators such as education, housing provision, life expectancy
and satisfaction of needs for food. Ways of defining women's position
in development studies have changed. In the 1950s and 1960s
women's issues were subsumed under the question of human
rights, and women were viewed as objects to protect or make
recommendations *for* but not to consult. The First Development
Decade (1961–1970) had no specific references to women. By the
1970s although women were not necessarily consulted, their key
position as useful resources in development processes was recognised
especially in connection with population and food issues. The
decision in 1972 to declare 1975 'International Women's Year' led
to the UN Decade for Women culminating in the 1985 Nairobi
conference at which the *Forward Looking Strategies* were adopted. The
main themes of these Strategies were equality, development and
peace with focus on health, education and employment. *Women in
Development* (WID) emerged in the 1970s to challenge the fact that
mainstream 'development' efforts targeted the male population with
women relegated to marginal 'welfare' sectors (Kabeer 1994). Groups
such as *Development Alternatives for Women in a New Era* (DAWN) and
The International Reproductive Rights Research Action Group (IRRAG)
work from the premise that we need to know more about local
contexts and ways of thinking in which women negotiate their
everyday lives as we cannot assume what goals women seek,
particularly with regard to reproductive and sexual rights (see
Chapter 9).

difference: all societies have differences of varying sorts. The ways in
which differences are constructed, that is the ways in which they
are made to mean something, affects how we define patterns of
difference and thereby how they are acted on. 'Normalising' or
'naturalising' discourse is often undertaken from which to 'explain'
certain social processes, and feminists have been active in challenging
restrictive ideas which view some people as abnormal or unnatural.

Avtar Brah (1996) sets a context for thinking of difference as being about social relations, subjectivity and as identity. Early feminist thinking was seen to be partial in that the central ideas were generally based on White, heterosexual, middle-class, non-disabled thinking. As such, most women were made to be 'others' and so were regarded as 'different from' an unvoiced ideal.

disabled: this remains a contested term with various interpretations of its definition. As the preferred term of the British Council of Disabled People, the umbrella organisation in the UK, this is used to identify with the social oppression faced by people with impairments. In Australia the disability movement uses the term 'people with disabilities' to place emphasis on the individual and highlight the multiple identities people have in terms of race, ethnicity, class, rather than privileging disability (see Meekosha and Dowse 1997).

disability: this is also a contested term in scope and assumptions – some stress inability and others focus on institutions disabling people; three differing definitions are:

'Any restriction or loss (resulting from impairment) of ability to perform an activity in the manner or within the range considered normal for a human being' (World Health Organisation 1985);

'Disability is a category which is central to how welfare states regulate an increasing population of their citizens. In this sense and context, it is a political and social construction used to regulate' (Fulcher 1989);

'Disability is the disadvantage or restriction of activity caused by a contemporary social organisation which takes no or little account of people who have physical impairments and thus excludes them from participation in the mainstream of social activities. Physical disability is therefore a particular form of social oppression' (UPIAS 1981).

discourse: generally this means speech or language and to reason. For social analysts discourse has come to be understood as a historically, social and institutionally specific structure of statements, terms, categories and beliefs. Foucault argues that discourse is contained or expressed in organisations and institutions as well as in words and all of these constitute texts or documents to be read (see McDowell and Pringle 1992). In feminist thinking the contexts, transformations and definitions of several discourses on sexuality need to be examined in order to understand the social construction of gender difference (Coward 1978). There is a close connection between constructions and discourses such as in the medical models of sexuality and disability (see *construction*).

dyke: first used as a term of abuse toward lesbians, it has been 'reclaimed' by many lesbians and used with pride to describe something of their identity.

Enlightenment: political analysts generally delineate the American, French and Scottish Enlightenments. Despite differences between them, Enlightenment thinkers were part of a consciously 'European' movement. The term is a short-hand for a period in European Thought from roughly 1690 to 1789. In so far as it had a common focus, it is the advocacy of science and reason to dispel ignorance and superstition. Though the leading participants were men, a number of women made significant contributions, e.g., Mme. de Chatelet, Mary Wollstonecraft.

essentialism: essential views are generally hegemonic and are not statements of fact. Essentialist ideas consider certain aspects of human behaviour as 'natural' and as permanent and unchanging. This assumed similar forms of behaviour occurring in different cultures or over time have the same personal and social meanings. There are different versions of essentialism which are linked with different political agendas. Saraga (1998) explains that for conservative thinkers natural sexuality is seen as uncontrolled and uncivilised and in need of control, while radical thinkers in the 1960s viewed sex as a powerful natural force which had been repressed and restricted within the confines of the 'nuclear family'. Essentialism is attacked by many feminists as an ideological defence of the *status quo* though some feminists have adopted it in holding that women's experience is distinct and androgyny a fake ideal (see *construction*).

ethnicity: often the terms 'race' and 'ethnicity' are used interchangeably but ethnicity generally is used to refer to cultural differences so that 'ethnic minority' communities are defined by assumed cultural difference from the majority. Logically this could be used for *all* groups but it is not. Thus the term is often used to note forms of boundary formation in which a 'normalised' population, such as White people, is constructed as the group against which difference is defined (see Saraga 1998).

ethnocentrism: makes a particular ethnic reality the centre of thinking so that all experience is universalised from this position. Ethnocentrism is apparent when models are developed which characterise and thereby deny the specificity of people's experiences.

'family': Marxists have long argued about the changing nature of 'family' and the role of nuclear family units in underpinning capitalist production and profits. Feminists consider family ideology of man as breadwinner and woman as mother and homemaker to have had very destructive influences. There are competing definitions of 'family' which change over time and dominant discourses of the family have given power to state agencies to intervene in particular forms of families. Dominant ideas and practices encouraging particularly 'suitable family arrangements' can cause many people to be excluded and othered in such processes in the same way that 'legitimate' relationships or children can characterise others as illegitimate.

feminisms: this term stresses the plurality of engagement and visions within the various strands that go to make up feminist politics which is the subject of this book.

gay: term claimed by lesbians and homosexual men as a 'chosen identity'. This term generates a new subject position – it is not an imposed label as it constructs a new kind of person.

gender: a culturally shaped group of attributes and behaviour given to the female or to the male (Humm 1989). Basic distinctions are made between sex as biological and gender behaviour as a social construct. Simone de Beauvoir was first to describe 'woman' as Other and otherness has become a significant characteristic within feminist politics.

homophobia: an irrational fear of homosexuals. Some lesbian feminist thinkers argue that it is rational for men to fear lesbians as lesbianism is a political identity in opposition to 'hetero-patriarchal' power and privilege.

ideology: bodies of concepts, symbols and values which include thinking on human nature and aim to show what is and is not possible for human interaction. Ideologies both *describe* aspects of human interaction and *prescribe* the ways in which humans could/ should live to attain certain aspirations. Ideologies can be functional and can be used to mystify or conceal what societies are like by serving to explain away inequalities, such as equality before the law hiding other inequalities. Feminist ideologies are concerned with describing sexism in societies and offering ideas concerning how societies could be organised so that such sexism would be eliminated. Feminist thinkers are concerned with the recognition that gender is one factor amongst others, the intersection with which leads to oppression.

identity: our sense of self, who we are, generally combines with the sense of self of those who are like us to form our sense of belonging to a group, our *social identity*. Feminist thinkers argue that identity is not the goal but the starting point of any processes of self-consciousness. Our understanding of identity can be multiple and self-contradictory.

identity politics: identity politics refers to discourses and movements organised around questions of ethnic, religious and national identities. Ideas concerning Woman as cultural symbol and political victim in male-dominated power struggles is considered in such politics, as is women's agency in supporting and opposing such movements.

impairment: the World Health Organisation defines impairment as: 'any loss or abnormality of psychological, physiological or anatomical structure or function'. Oliver (1990) argues that impairment refers to the functional limitations which affect a person's body, unlike disability which refers to the loss or limitations of opportunities due to social, physical and attitudinal barriers. Such impairments cover a vast range of experiences such as auditory or visual impairments and learning disabilities. Some impairments are immediately apparent, others are not, and some cause great physical pain whilst others do not. A greater understanding of the perceptions of disabled people with regard to their situations and needs aids both communication and understanding with regard to service provision and protecting civil rights.

liberalism: the general belief that the aim of politics is to preserve individual rights and to maximise freedom of choice. As with socialism and conservatism, liberalism emerged from the coincidence of the Enlightenment, the Industrial Revolution and the political revolutions of the seventeenth and eighteenth centuries. Liberalism was linked, with the doctrine of *laissez-faire*, with the minimum of state intervention in society and the economy.

liberation: commitment to opposing economic, social and political oppression and repression in societies where exploitation exists. Women's liberation is based on the realities of women's lives as in Paulo Freire's belief that liberation needs to be rooted in the concrete experiences of oppressed groups.

Marxism: generally refers to the complex and comprehensive body of writing by Marx and Engels and the works of particular thinkers based on Marxist principles. This conflict model of society sees human change from a materialist perspective in which humans have agency to create changes in their lives, but not necessarily as they would choose. Class conflict is central to this thinking, so that the poorer, working class (proletariat) who are oppressed by the richer, ruling class, (bourgeois employers) will come to consciousness of their own situation and actively resist their oppression. The inevitable crisis of capitalism would therefore lead to proletarian revolution (see *revolution*). There have been many revisions, reformulations and reinterpretations arising from debates within Marxism.

materialist: this view of history emphasises human agency. A materialist account of women's oppression was first provided by Engels. Mitchell (1971) argued that a materialist analysis of the oppression of women must deal with the historical specificity of women's situations, including considerations of both production and reproduction. Materialist feminisms have changed over recent decades from Marxism to cultural materialism and poststructuralist literary theory (see Landry and MacLean 1993).

non-disabled: this term is used rather than able-bodied because people who do not experience physical, sensory or intellectual impairments are *not disabled* by the prejudice which denies opportunities to people who experience such impairments.

oppression: various forms of exploitation and repression give rise to oppression. Feminists argue that other forms of oppression, such as racism, disability prejudice, and poverty, compound patriarchal oppression. While feminists oppose the oppression of women they differ as to its causes and the ways in which it can be eradicated.

participation: political participation means taking part in politics. As the term politics both describes an activity and the *study of* that activity, participation can be across a range of involvement at different levels.

Feminist participation can be across varying aspects of politics from campaigning, lobbying, changing attitudes, making research, to teaching, learning and talking about women's lives and the ways in which change for the better can be achieved.

patriarchy: originally meaning 'rule by the father', this term has been used by feminists to mean the use and abuse of power by men, and male-dominated ideas and institutions, over women, and feminine ideas and ways of working. As a resistance to patriarchal ways of life Adrienne Rich proposed the 'lesbian continuum'. 'Patriarchal relations' is a preferred term for feminists wishing to be able to chart the intersections of various forms of oppression (Brah 1996).

post-modernism: the term was first used by Jean-Francois Lyotard to label aspects of contemporary Western society 'after modernity'. Philosophically it shares much with poststructuralism. 'Modernity' is generally seen as a period beginning sometime in the seventeenth century and ending between 1945 and the present. Post-modernists react against the failure of science and reason during this time to achieve 'progress' (particularly after the Holocaust) and against grand theories, or *meta-narratives*, such as Marxism or utilitarianism, that seek to explain social and political behaviour based on set rationales. Post-structuralists and post-modernists give culture a central role for the appraisal of social reality. It is also argued that the *cultural* cannot be fully understood outside its relation to the *political* and the *economic*. Post-modernism is challenged variously, as *conservative*, because its relativism can preclude activism for political change, and *radical*, when applied to criticising the globalisation of capital as part of modernity, so that defences of difference can be more clearly interpreted.

power: power is often distinguished in five forms: authority, coercion, force, manipulation and persuasion with only coercion and manipulation viewed uncontroversially as forms of power. For early women's liberationists, power was seen to lie within men's control. Feminist anthropologists consider power, authority and influence and demonstrate that women are not without certain forms of power. Anna Yeatman considers the ambiguous relationship of feminism to concepts of power and distils three strands: 'power as coercion; power as protection; and power as capacity' (Shanley and Narayan 1997: 145). These aspects of power run through many streams of feminist thinking.

praxis: feminist praxis is seen in the coming together of theory and practice in action, and in the reflecting upon these processes in order to generate new ideas and ways of working.

privilege: feminists have considered what the recognition of privileges such as whiteness, heterosexuality or physical privilege, tell us about systems of *male* privilege and how various aspects of privilege thereby intersect with gender in the processes of identity formation and social interaction.

race: There is only one 'race' – the human race. The term 'race' is often put in quotation marks to show that it is a socially constructed category. The social construction of 'races' can highlight physical characteristics or can consider ways of living, 'ethnicity'. Such social constructions attempt to understand the meanings that are attached to differences and how these are often hierarchically organised, often in legislation such as that concerned with immigration, nationality and citizenship laws. Factors of race are also lived realities for people. While all groups are racialised this is made explicit for Black people and generally implicit for White people. Like the construction of other 'differences' the processes involved in constructing race and ethnicity have profound effects on people's lives in reproducing processes of racial inclusion and exclusion.

racism: prejudice and bigotry based on the belief that races are unequal and that differences between people can be classified in a hierarchical way in which some become superior to others. Racist political movements are inherently intolerant and tend towards violent and simplistic political actions and solutions, such as those of Hitler. The Nazi regime (1933–1945) attempted to exterminate Jews and other 'sub-humans' such as Gypsies, homosexuals and disabled people. The creation of Black people as White people's property during the trans-Atlantic slave trade heralded inhuman consequences for millions of people. The ongoing effects of racism are translated into cultural realms with the 'simpletons' and 'baddies' in films often being based on Black stereotypes. For racist stereotypes of Black women which remain today see Wallace (1979). 'Institutional racism' makes connections between particular policies and their consequences so that the public discourse shifts the burden of evidence away from people experiencing racism and towards those elites who make decisions, in order that they respond in some ways to expectations.

representation: this term is used in different ways but the key political use is that a representative is someone acting as a deputy or substitute, such as Members of Parliament acting to represent their constituents. Different ideas on what is entailed in fair representation shows in considerations of numbers of political representatives in Parliaments and in decision making.

resistance: the act or power of resisting, making opposition. Feminist resistance ranges from personal acts of defiance to collective movements which act to oppose injustice and oppression. Such resistance can take the form of *not acting* in particular ways and in challenging the normalising discourses which make some people *other.*

revolution: since the French Revolution of 1789 this has meant the overthrow of an established order involving the transfer of state power to a new leadership and may involve a radical restructuring of social and economic relations. The processes of revolution incorporate both elite competition and mass mobilisation. Many revolutionary situations do not result in revolutions. It is possible to distinguish between social and political revolutions. Social revolutions are less frequent than political ones and generally involve political and social transformations, class struggle and pressure from below for radical change. Political revolutions are processes which produce changes in the character of both state power and personnel. Skocpol (1979) argues that specific revolutions must be analysed in depth before any causal patterns can be identified. For feminists, particularly radical feminists, the processes involved in feminist activism were aiming to 'revolutionise society from within'.

separatism: this belief originally developed in terms of women separating from male-dominated institutions in order to realise their own strength. In such separatist debates, socialist feminists argued that, whilst questioning old institutions, women and men must work together to develop new ways of working. For radical feminists, the ideas of women's cultures emerged in considerations of withdrawal from male-dominated cultures. Lesbian feminist arguments about the need for feminists to withdraw from men, rather than give them energy and attention within patriarchal conditions, caused great debates in feminist politics. Later Black feminist thinkers argued for autonomy rather than separatism.

sex: this term is used both to distinguish between the biology of females and males and, in everyday terms, to describe physical activities involved in 'having sex'. The term *gender* is generally used to distinguish the cultural and social characteristics of being women and being men. There are difficulties, outlined by many feminist scholars, with these neat distinctions. Feminists raised issues regarding the recognition that sexual activity is not generally about reproduction and that women expect physical fulfilment which does not necessarily involve men.

sexual: sexual behaviour and practices are not fixed and there is much variation in the social meanings attached to it. The particular shared meanings of what is sexual differ in various contexts. Many people consider sexual matters to be personal and private and the associations with this aspect of human activity often arouse feelings of guilt, shame and embarrassment. Historical and cultural variations in sexual practices, identities and attitudes make the question of defining what is sexual a complex one.

sexuality: for feminist thinkers, sexuality is a social issue in that it is produced through processes of regulation and control. Ideas concerning sexuality have been important in constructing sexual identities. For some people sexuality is central to identity. Its social and personal meanings vary and there are dangers involved in using categories to label certain people or groups in various societies and during different times. Feminist discourses on sexuality considerably expanded ways of thinking with regard to deconstructing normalising discourses which serve to characterise some people as abnormal and unnatural. The personal realm of sexuality and sexual practices was shown to be politically important in changing dominant conceptions of how we 'should' live, recognising the shifting nature of discourses on sexuality rooted in political structures that change. Legacies of slavery and imperialism have helped to create specific discourses of sexuality relating to racialised women and men.

slavery: the condition in which the life and liberty of a person is held within the absolute power of another. The first challenges to slaveholding were in ancient Greece. Aristotle argued that some people were slaves 'by nature' (McLean 1996). Starting from the late 1300s people were forcibly taken from African countries. Black people from West Africa were sent to the West Indies to be 'trained' for slavery in the USA; from East Africa to Turkey and other slave centres on the Black Sea and to Jamaica and Nova Scotia and many other countries (see Sharp 1993). Millions of Black people died during the trans-Atlantic slave trade and millions of Black people lived in inhuman conditions, being 'owned' by White slavers. Even though the American Declaration of Independence states 'all men are created equal' the author of this, Jefferson, did not free his own slaves. Slavery is still alleged to exist in some countries such as Myanmar (Burma).

socialism: political and economic theories and systems of social organisation based on collective or state ownership of the means of production, distribution and exchange. This is a creed with many variations and takes many diverse forms in its continual development, but all are generally committed to ideas of equality and to policies intended to ensure this. The term 'socialism' was first used in the 1830s by followers of Robert Owen in Britain and of Saint-Simon in France. In general, socialists have rejected communist ideas about political revolution as a means of achieving socialism and are inspired by ideas of social revolutionary change and the use of parliamentary political methods. Since the collapse of Soviet state-socialism or communism in 1989, much debate has been generated as to the direction of socialist thinking and movements.

state: this concept is often viewed as one of the most central in politics. It refers to a set of political institutions which are concerned with the organisation of domination in the interests of a society within a specific territory. Due to its centrality in political thinking, its definition is open to much scholarly analysis and contestation. The mismatch between state and nation is such that generally the state undertakes a role in the creation of national identity and nationalism. Feminists have differed over the importance attached to state structures and functions, in that some (anarchists and radicals) tended to minimise the importance of engaging with state forms whilst others (socialists and internationalists) recognised state politics as the level with which they must be engaged in order to create effective, long-lasting change for the better. In recent times, feminist recognition of varying short- and long-term engagements and sites of struggle generally involve strategies and campaigns aimed at analysing and changing key state interventions in society.

subjectivity: people's subjectivities are how they see themselves and understand their own experience.

subject position: this is made up of the choices or options people believe themselves to have. New subject positions can be generated from political discourse. An example is that of gay identities being framed within changing discourses on sexuality.

'Third World': this is a problematic term given its clear 'ranking' connotations. It has come to describe regions and individual countries of Africa, Asia, the Caribbean, Latin America and the Middle East. The after-effects of colonisation were felt in these countries in various ways and the label 'Third' became embedded in the literature on 'development' and international politics. These countries vary enormously between and within regions in their cultures, experiences of colonial rule, forms and level of economic activity and political developments and alliances. For feminists: 'Third world is defined through geographical locations as well as particular sociohistorical conjunctures. It thus incorporates so-called minority peoples or people of color in the USA' (Mohanty 1991: 2).

transnational: this term has been used by feminists specifically as taking over from 'international' with three elements highlighted: 1. a way of thinking about women in similar contexts in *different* geographical spaces, rather than about *all* women; 2. an understanding of a set of unequal relationships among and between peoples, rather than of a set of traits embodied in 'non-citizens'; 3. considering the term 'international' in relation to analyses of economic, political and ideological processes which foreground operations of race and capitalism, for example, analyses which would require taking critical antiracist, anti-capitalist positions that would make feminist solidarity work possible (Alexander and Mohanty 1997: xix).

White: this term is used as a political term to describe ideas and discourses which are based on a particular ethic and viewpoint with regard to whiteness and to describe racialised discourses. When I use this term for White people it is capitalised to show that it is a political term and not just used descriptively. As with the term Black, White is a socially constructed term and also a lived reality in which whiteness is often an unrecognised privilege.

whiteness: this term is used to analyse white skin as signifying power and privilege. Language and common-sense ways of thinking have been framed with imperialist and patriarchal histories so it is necessary to ask *why* the experiences of Black women and women of Colour have been denied, distorted and erased. In utilising concepts such as 'whiteness' feminists are able to explore how both Black and White women's gender is constructed through class and racism (Brah 1996).

women of Colour: this is a political term used in the USA for all women, other than White and African–American women. This term reflects more the intellectual and political coalitions that join groups of women and it aims to foster unity (Collins 1990).

Bibliography

Abbott, S. and Love, B. (1972) *Sappho was a Right-On Woman: A Liberated View of Lesbianism* New York: Stein and Day

Abelove, H., Barale, M.A. and Halperin, D.M. (eds) (1993) *The Lesbian and Gay Studies Reader* New York and London: Routledge

Afshar, H. (ed.) (1996) *Women and Politics in the Third World* London: Routledge

Afshar, H. and Maynard, M. (1994) *The Dynamics of 'Race' and Gender: Some Feminist Interventions* London: Taylor & Francis

Agarwahl, B. (1986) *Cold Hearts and Barren Slopes: The Woodfuel Crisis in the Third World* New Delhi: Allied Publishers Private Limited and Institute of Economic Growth

Akanke (1994) 'Black in the Closet' in Epstein, D. (ed.) *Challenging Lesbian and Gay Inequalities in Education* Buckingham: Open University Press, pp. 101–114

Alexander, M.J. and Mohanty, C.T. (eds) (1997) *Feminist Genealogies, Colonial Legacies, Democratic Futures* New York and London: Routledge

Allen, L. (1998) *The Lesbian Idol: Martina, kd and the Consumption of Lesbian Masculinity* Cassell: London

Amnesty International (1995) *Human Rights are Women's Right* London: Amnesty International Publications

Anderson, S. (1995) 'We are Women who Love other Women: Lesbian Visibility at the UN Conference in Beijing' *IHRSINN Lesben International* December 1995

Ang-Lygate, M. (1995) 'Shades of Meaning' *Trouble and Strife* 31, pp. 15–20

Ang-Lygate, M. (1997) 'Charting the Spaces of (un)Location: On Theorizing Diaspora' in Mirza, H.S. (ed.) *Black British Feminism: A Reader* London and New York: Routledge, pp. 168–186

Ang-Lygate, M., Corrin, C. and Henry, M. (eds) (1997) *Desperately Seeking Sisterhood: Still Challenging and Building* London: Taylor & Francis, pp. 19–30

Anthias, F. and Yuval-Davis, N. (1992) *Racialized Boundaries: Race, Nation, Gender, Colour and Class and the Anti-Racist Struggle* London: Routledge

Anzaldua, G. (1987) *Borderlands: La Frontera, The New Mestiza* San Francisco: Aunt Lute

Ashworth, G. (1998) *Equal Rule? Women, Men, Democracy and Governance* London: Change

Ashworth, G. (ed.) (1981) *Of Conjuring and Caring: Women and Development* London: Change

Astell 1694 'A Serious Proposal . . .' in Ferguson, M. (ed.) (1985) *First Feminists: British Women Writers 1578–1799* Bloomington: Indiana University Press

Atkinson, Ti-Grace (1974) *Amazon Odyssey* New York: Link Books

Aung San Suy Kyi (1995) 'Keynote Address to the NGO Forum on Women' *United Nations Conference on Women*, Huairou, China, September

Baca-Zinn, M. and Thorton-Dill, B. (eds) (1994) *Women of Color in US Society* Philadelphia: Temple University Press

Bailey, R. (1996) 'Prenatal Testing and the Prevention of Impairment: A Woman's Right to Choose?' in Morris, J. (ed.) *Encounters with Strangers: Feminism and Disability* London: The Women's Press, pp. 143–167

Baldwin, J. (1964) *Notes of a Native Son* London: Michael Joseph

Banks, O. (1981) *Faces of Feminism: A Study of Feminism as a Social Movement* Oxford: Basil Blackwell

Barrett, M. (1980) *Women's Oppression Today: Problems in Marxist–Feminist Analysis* London: Verso

Barrett, M. and McIntosh, M. (1982) *The Anti-Social Family* London: Verso

Barrett, M. and Phillips, A. (eds) (1992) *Destabilizing Theory: Contemporary Feminist Debates* Cambridge: Polity

Barry, K. (1995) *The Prostitution of Sexuality* New York and London: New York University Press

Barry, K., Bunch, C. and Castley, C. (1984) *International Feminism: Networking Against Female Sexual Slavery* New York and London: New York University Press

Beddoe, D. (1989) *Back to Home and Duty: Women between the Wars 1918–1939* London: Pandora

Begum, N. (1992) 'Disabled Women and the Feminist Agenda' *Feminist Review* 40, 70–84

Begum, N. (1996) 'Doctor, Doctor . . . : Disabled Women's Experiences of General Practioners' in Morris, J. (ed) (1996) *Encounters with Strangers: Feminism and Disability* London: The Women's Press

Begum, N., Hill, M. and Stevens, S. (eds) (1994) *Reflections: Views of Black Disabled People on their Lives and Community Care* London: Central Council for Education and Training in Social Work

Bhavnani, K.-K. (1993) 'Talking Racism and the Editing of Women's Studies' in Richardson, D. and Robinson, V. (eds) *Introducing Women's Studies: Feminist Theory and Practice* 1st edn London: Macmillan, pp. 27–48

Bhavnani, K.-K. (1997) 'Women's Studies and its Interconnections with "Race", Ethnicity and Sexuality' in Richardson, D. and Robinson, V. (eds) *Introducing Women's Studies: Feminist Theory and Practice* 2nd edn London: Macmillan, pp. 27–53

Bhavnani, K.-K. and Coulson, M. (1986) 'Transforming Socialist Feminism: The Challenge of Racism' *Feminist Review* 23, pp. 81–92

Bhavnani, K.-K. and Phoenix, A. (1994) *Shifting Identities, Shifting Racisms* London: Sage

Boric, R. (1995) 'The Oasis' *New Internationalist* August, pp. 12–13

Boric, R. (1997) 'Women Creating Peace' in Kasic, B. (ed.) *Women and the Politics of Peace. Contributions to a Culture of Women's Resistance* Zagreb: Centre for Women's Studies

Boric, R. and Desnica, M.M. (1996) 'Croatia: Three Years After' in Corrin, C. (ed.) *Women in a Violent World: Feminist Analyses and Resistance* Edinburgh: Edinburgh University Press, pp. 133–50

Boston Women's Health Collective 1973 *Our Bodies, Ourselves* New York, Simon and Schuster

Brah, A. (1990) 'The Early Days' in Southall Black Sisters 1979–89 *Against the Grain: A Celebration of Survival and Struggle* London: Southall Black Sisters, p. 13

Brah, A. (1992) 'Questions of Difference and International Feminism' in Aaron, J. and Walby, S. (eds) *Out of the Margins: Women's Studies in the 1990s* London: Falmer Press, pp. 168–176

Brah, A. (1996) *Cartographies of Diaspora: Contesting Identities* London: Routledge

Breitenbach, E. and Gordon, E. (eds) (1992) *Out of Bounds: Women in Scottish Society 1800–1945* Edinburgh: Edinburgh University Press

Bridger, S., Kay, R. and Pinnick, K. (1996) *No More Heroines? Russia, Women and the Market* New York and London: Routledge

Bridget, J. (1993) 'Perspective on Lesbians' and Gays' Mental Health' in *Directory of Lesbian and Gay Studies in the UK* London: DOLAGS

Brocke-Utne, B. (1985) *Educating for Peace* Oxford: Pergamon Press

Brocke-Utne, B. (1989) *Feminist Perspectives on Peace and Peace Education* New York: Pergamon Press

Brody, M. (1985) *Are We There Yet? A Continuing History of 'Lavender Women': A Chicago Lesbian Newspaper 1971–1976* Iowa City: Aunt Lute Book Co. noted in Penelope, J. and Wolfe, S. (eds) *Lesbian Culture: An Anthology* Freedom, California: The Crossing Press

Broverman, K. *et al.* (1970) 'Sex-role Stereotypes and Clinical Judgements of Mental Health' *Journal of Consulting and Clinical Psychology* 34(1), pp. 1–7

Brown U. (1995) 'Women, "Race" and Class' talk at the Women and Culture Plenary, *Desperately Seeking Sisterhood Conference* Stirling University, June

Brownmiller, S. (1976) *Against Our Will* Harmondsworth: Penguin

Bryson, V. (1992) *Feminist Political Theory: An Introduction* Basingstoke: Macmillan Press

Buckley, M. (1989) *Women and Ideology in the Soviet Union* Hemel Hempstead: Harvester

Bunch, C. (1995) 'Transforming Human Rights from a Feminist Perspective' in Peters, J. and Wolper, A. *Women's Rights Human Rights: International Feminist Perspectives* London and New York: Routledge

Bunch, C. (1997) 'The Intolerable Status Quo: Violence Against Women and Girls' in *The Progress of Nations* New York: United Nations Children's Fund (UNICEF)

Bunch, C. and Carillo, R. (1992) *Gender Violence: A Development and Human Rights Issue* Dublin: Attic Press

Burke *Reflections* (1790) in Burke, E. (n.d.) *Edmund Burke: Selections from his Political Writings and Speeches* London: T. Nelson and Sons

Burton, A. (1994) 'Rules of Thumb: British History and "Imperial Culture" in Nineteenth- and Twentieth-Century Britain' *Women's History Review* 3(4), 482–500

Cain, H. and Yuval-Davis, N. (1990) 'The "Equal Opportunity Commission" and the Antiracist Struggle' *Critical Social Policy* 29(10), 2

Cameron, D. and Frazer, E. (1992) 'On the Question of Pornography and Sexual Violence: Moving Beyond Cause and Effect' in Itzin, C. (ed.) *Pornography: Women, Violence and Civil Liberties* Oxford: Oxford University Press, pp. 359–83

Campbell, J. and Oliver, M. (1996) *Disability Politics: Understanding Our Past, Changing Our Future* London and New York: Routledge

Campling, J. (1979) *Better Lives for Disabled Women* London: Virago

Carby, H.V. (1982) 'White Woman Listen! Black Feminism and the Boundaries of Sisterhood' in Centre for Contemporary Cultural Studies (eds) *The Empire Strikes Back: Race and Racism in 70s Britain* London: Hutchinson

Card, C. (1995) *Lesbian Choices* New York: Columbia University Press

Card, C. (ed.) (1994) *Adventures in Lesbian Philosophy* Bloomington and Indianapolis: Indiana University Press

Caroline in Shakespeare, T., Gillespie-Sells, K. and Davies, D. (1996) *The Sexual Politics of Disability* London: Cassell, pp. 14–15

Cavin, S. (1990) 'The Invisible Army of Women: Lesbian Social Protests, 1969–1988' in West, G. and Blumberg, R.L. (eds) *Women and Social Protest* New York and Oxford: Oxford University Press, pp. 321–332

Centre for Contemporary Cultural Studies (1982) *The Empire Strikes Back: Race and Racism in 70s Britain* Birmingham: University of Birmingham

Chadwick, A. (1996) 'Knowledge, Power and the Disability Discrimination Bill' *Disability & Society* 11(1), 25–40

(charles), H. (1992) 'Whiteness – The Relevance of Politically Colouring the "Non"' in Hinds, H. Phoenix, A. and Stacey, J. (eds) *Working Out: New Directions for Women's Studies* London: Falmer Press

Charles, N. and Hughes-Freeland, F. (eds) (1996) *Practising Feminism: Identity, Difference, Power* London: Routledge

Charlesworth, H. (1994) 'What are "Women's International Human Rights"?' in Cook, R. (ed.) *Human Rights of Women: National and International Perspectives* Pennsylvania: University of Pennsylvania Press, pp. 58–84

Chesler, P. (1972) *Women and Madness* London: Allen Lane

Clarke, C. (1983) 'Lesbianism: an Act of Resistance' in Moraga, C. and Anzaldua, G. (eds) *This Bridge Called my Back: Writings by Radical Women of Colour* New York: Kitchen Table Press

Cleaver, R. and Myers, P. (1993) *A Certain Terror: Heterosexism, Militarism, Violence and Change* Chicago: American Friends Service Committee

Collins, P. Hill (1990) *Black Feminist Thought: Knowledge, Consciousness and the Politics of Empowerment* London: Harper Collins Academic

Colon-Warren, A.E. and Alegria-Ortega, I. (1998) 'Shattering the Illusion of Development: The Changing Status of Women and Challenges for the Feminist Movement in Puerto Rico' *Feminist Review* 59, pp. 101–117

Connell, R.W. (1987) *Gender and Power* Cambridge: Polity Press

Connolly, W.E. (1991) *Identity/Difference* Ithaca and London: Cornell University Press

Connors, J. (1994) 'Government Measures to Confront Violence Against Women' in Davies, M. (ed.) *Women and Violence: Realities and Responses Worldwide* London and New Jersey: Zed Books

Coole, D. (1994 [1988]) *Women in Political Theory: From Ancient Misogyny to Contemporary Feminism* Hemel Hempstead: Harvester Wheatsheaf

Corea, G. (1985) *The Mother Machine: Reproductive Technologies from Artificial Insemination to Artificial Wombs* New York: Harper and Row

Corea, G. (ed.) (1985) *Man-Made Women* London: Hutchinson

Corrin, C. (ed.) (1992) *Superwomen and the Double Burden: Women's Experience of Change in Central and Eastern Europe and the former Soviet Union* London: Scarlet Press

Corrin, C. (1993) 'Is Liberalisation Damaging Albanian Women's Health?' *Focus on Gender: Perspectives on Women and Development* Oxford: Oxfam Publications 1(3), 35–7

Corrin, C. (1994a) *Magyar Women: Hungarian Women's Lives 1960s–1990s* London: Macmillan

Corrin, C. (1994b) 'Women's Politics in Europe in the 1990s' *Women's International Studies Forum* 17 (2/3, March–June), 289–298

Corrin, C. (ed.) (1996) *Women in a Violent World: Feminist Analyses and Resistance Across 'Europe'* Edinburgh: Edinburgh University Press

Cosgrove, K. (1996) 'No Man Has the Right' in Corrin, C. (ed.) *Women in a Violent World: Feminist Analyses and Resistance Across 'Europe'* Edinburgh: Edinburgh University Press, pp. 186–203

Cott, N. (1987) *The Grounding of Modern Feminism* New Haven and London: Yale University Press

Council of Europe (1991) *Seminar on Action Against Traffic in Women and Forced Prostitution as Violations of Human Rights and Human Dignity* European Committee for Equality Between Men and Women, Strasbourg, September

Covina, G. and Galana, L. (eds) (1975) *The Lesbian Reader* Berkeley, CA: Amazon Press

Coward, R. (1978) 'Rethinking Marxism' *M/F* 2, pp. 85–96

Crow, L. (1996) 'Including All of Our Lives: Renewing the Social Model of Disability' in Morris, J. (ed.) *Encounters with Strangers: Feminism and Disability* London: The Women's Press, pp. 206–226

Crowley, H. and Himmelweit, S. (eds) (1992) *Knowing Women: Feminism and Knowledge* Cambridge: Polity Press

Cruikshank, M. (ed.) (1982) *Lesbian Studies: Past and Future* New York: The Feminist Press

Curthoys, J. (1997) *Feminist Amnesia: The Wake of Women's Liberation* London: Routledge

Dahlerup, D. (ed.) (1986) *The New Women's Movement: Feminism and Political Power in Europe and the USA* London: Sage

Daly, M. (1978) *Gyn/Ecology: The Metaethics of Radical Feminism* London: The Women's Press

Dankelman, I. and Davidson, J. (1988) *Women and Environment in the Third World: Alliance for the Future* London: Earthscan Publications Limited in association with The International Union for Conservation of Nature and Natural Resources (IUCN)

Darcy, R., Welch, S. and Clark, J. (1994) 'Women, Elections and Representation' in Githens *et al.* (eds) (1994) *Different Roles, Different Voices: Women and Politics in the United States and Europe* New York: Harper Collins pp. 89–92

Davies M. (ed.) (1993) *Third World – Second Sex: Women's Struggles and National Liberation* London: Zed Books

Davies, M. (ed.) (1994) *Women and Violence: Realities and Responses Worldwide* London and New Jersey: Zed Books

Davis, A.Y. (1982) *If They Come in the Morning: Voices of Resistance, Women, Race and Class* London: The Women's Press

Davis, A.Y. (1990) *Women, Politics and Culture* London: The Women's Press

Davis, K. (1993) 'On the Movement' in J. Swain *et al.* (eds) *Disabled Barriers – Enabling Environments* London: Sage

Davis, K. (1996) 'Disability and Legislation: Rights and Equality' in Hales, G. (ed.) *Beyond Disability: Towards an Enabling Society* London: Sage Publications in association with the Open University, pp. 124–133

de Beauvoir, S. (1988) *The Second Sex* (first published in French 1949 and in English 1953) Harmondsworth: Penguin

De Stoop, C. (1994) 'They Are So Sweet, Sir' in International Organization for Migration (1995) *Trafficking and Prostitution: The Growing Exploitation of Migrant Women from Central and Eastern Europe* Budapest, Migration Information Programme

Delphy, C. (1977) *The Main Enemy* London: Women's Research and Resources Centre

Delphy, C. (1984) *Close to Home: A Materialist Analysis of Women's Oppression* London: Hutchinson

DL60 1996 *Definition of Disability*. Booklet about The Disability Discrimination Act on behalf of the Minister for Disabled People Issued in April 1996 Printed in the UK. HSSS JO3-6299JP

Dobash, R.E. and Dobash, R.P. (1993) *Women, Violence and Social Change* London: Routledge

Donoghue, E. (1993) *Passions Between Women: British Lesbian Culture 1668–1801* London: Scarlet Press

Dublin Lesbian and Gay Men's Collectives (1996) *Out for Ourselves: The Lives of Irish Lesbians and Gay Men* Dublin: Dublin Lesbian and Gay Men's Collectives and Women's Community Press

Dubois, E.C. (1978) *Feminism and Suffrage: The Emergence of an Independent Women's Movement in America 1848–1869* Ithaca and London: Cornell University Press

Duchen, C. (1986) *Feminism in France* London: Routledge

Dworkin, A. (1991) *Woman Hating: A Radical Look at Sexuality* Plume Books

Eduards, M. (1997) 'The Women's Shelter Movement' in Gustafsson, G., Eduards, M. and Ronnblom, M. (1997) *Towards a New Democratic Order? Women's Organising in Sweden in the 1990s* Stockholm: Publica, pp. 120–168

Einhorn, B. (1993) *Cinderella Goes to Market* London and New York: Verso

Eisenstein, H. (1984) *Contemporary Feminist Thought* London: Unwin

Ekins, P. (1993) *A New World Order: Grassroots Movements for Global Change* London: Routledge

Engels, F. (1884) *The Origin of the Family, Private Property and the State* New York: Pathfinder Press

Enloe, C. (1990) *Bananas, Beaches and Bases: Making Feminist Sense of International Politics* Berkeley: University of California Press

Enloe, C. (1993) *The Morning After: Sexual Politics at the End of the Cold War* Los Angeles and London: University of California Press

Epstein, D. (ed.) (1994) *Challenging Lesbian and Gay Inequalities in Education* Buckingham: Open University Press

Essed, P. (1990) *Everyday Racism: Reports from Women of Two Cultures* Alameda, CA: Hunter House

Evans, D. (1993) *Sexual Citizenship: The Material Construction of Sexualities* London: Routledge

Evans, M. (ed.) (1994) *The Woman Question* 2nd edn London: Sage

Evans, R.J. (1977) *The Feminists: Women's Emancipation Movements in Europe, America and Australasia 1840–1920* London: Croom Helm

Evans, R.J. (1980) 'Bourgeois Feminists and Women Socialists in Germany' *Women's Studies International Quarterly* 3.

Eyerman, R. and Jamison, A. (1991) *Social Movements: A Cognitive Approach* Oxford: Polity Press

Faderman, L. (1981) *Surpassing the Love of Men: Romantic Friendship and Love Between Women from the Renaissance to the Present* London: Junction Books

Faderman, L. (1985) *Surpassing the Love of Men: Romantic Friendship and Love between Women from the Renaissance to the Present* London: The Women's Press

Faludi, S. (1992) *Backlash: The Undeclared War Against Women* London: Chatto and Windus

Farrant, W. (1985) 'Who's for Amniocentesis? The Politics of Prenatal Screening' in Homans, H. (ed.) *The Sexual Politics of Reproduction* London: Gower

Feminist Review (1986) 'Socialist Feminism: Out of the Blue' Special Issue no. 23

Ferguson, M. (1992) 'Mary Wollstonecraft and the Problematic of Slavery' *Feminist Review* 42, 82–102

Finger, A. (1991) *Past Due: A Story of Disability, Pregnancy and Birth* London: The Women's Press

Finger, A. (1992) 'Forbidden Fruit' *New Internationalist* 233, 8–10

Finkelstein, V. and Stuart, O. (1996) 'Developing new Services' in Hales, G. (ed.) *Beyond Disability: Towards an Enabling Society* London: Sage Publications in association with the Open University, pp. 170–187

Firestone, S. (1972) *The Dialectic of Sex: The Case for Feminist Revolution* [first published 1970] London: Paladin

Flax, J. (1990) *Thinking Fragments: Psychoanalysis, Feminism and Post-modernism in the Contemporary West* Oxford: University of California Press

Foucault, M. (1972) *The Archaeology of Knowledge* London: Tavistock

Foucault, M. (1976) *The History of Sexuality: An Introduction* Harmondsworth: Penguin

Fraisse, G. and Perrot, M. (eds) (1995) *A History of Women in the West: IV Emerging Feminism from Revolution to War* Cambridge and London: Harvard University Press

Frank, L. and Khaxas, E. (1996) 'Lesbians in Namibia' in Reinfelder, M. (ed.) *Amazon to Zami: Towards a Global Lesbian Feminism* London: Cassell, pp. 109–117

Frankenberg, R. (1993) *The Social Construction of Whiteness* London: Routledge

Frazer, E., Hornsby, J. and Lovibond, S. (eds) (1992) *Ethics: A Feminist Reader* Oxford: Blackwell

French, S. (ed.) (1994) *On Equal Terms: Working with Disabled People* Oxford: Butterworth–Heinemann

French, S. (1996) 'Out of Sight, Out of Mind: The Experience and Effects of a 'Special' Residential School' in Morris, J. (ed.) *Encounters with Strangers: Feminism and Disability* London: The Women's Press, pp. 17–47

Freeman, J. (1972) 'The Tyranny of Structurelessness' *The Second Wave* 2(1) USA: Female Liberation Inc.

Friedan, B. (1963) *The Feminine Mystique* London: Gollancz (Harmondsworth: Penguin 1965)

Frye, M. (1993) 'Some Reflections on Separatism and Power' in Abelove, H., Barale, M. and Halperin, D. (eds) *The Lesbian and Gay Studies Reader* London: Routledge, pp. 91–98

Fulcher, G. (1989) *Disabling Policies? A Comparative Approach to Education, Policy and Disability* Lewes: Falmer

Funk, N. and Muella, M. (eds) (1993) *Gender Politics and Post-Communism: Reflections from Eastern Europe and the former Soviet Union* New York and London: Routledge

Fuss, D. (1990) *Essentially Speaking: Feminism, Nature and Difference* New York and London: Routledge

Garcia, A.M. (1994) 'The development of Chicana feminist discourse 1970–1980 in Githens *et al.* (eds) (1994) *Different Roles, Different Voices: Women and Politics in the United States and Europe* New York: Harper Collins, pp. 190–195

Gayatri, B.J.D. (1996) 'Indonesian Lesbians Writing Their Own Script: Issues of Feminism and Sexuality' in Reinfelder, M. (ed.) *Amazon to Zami: Towards a Global Lesbian Feminism* London: Cassell, pp. 86–97

Gilbert, K. (1978) *Living Black* Ringwood: Penguin Books Australia

Gillespie-Sells, K. and Ruebain, D. (1992) *Double the Trouble, Twice the Fun* London: Channel 4 Television Broadcasting Support Services

Githens, M., Norris, P. and Lovenduski, J. (eds) (1994) *Different Roles, Different Voices: Women and Politics in the United States and Europe* New York: Harper Collins

Gittins, D. (1980) *The Family in Question: Changing Households and Familiar Ideologies* London: Gerald Duckworth

Gordon, E. (1991) *Women and the Labour Movement in Scotland 1850–1914* Oxford: Clarendon Press

Greer, G. (1970) *The Female Eunuch* London: MacGibbon and Kee

Grewal, S., Kay, J., Landor, L., Lewis, G. and Parmar, P. (eds) (1988) *Charting the Journey: Writings by Black and Third World Women* London: Sheba Feminist Publishers

Griffin, K. and Mulholland, L. (eds) (1997) *Lesbian Motherhood in Europe* London: Cassell

Guerrero, M. (1997) 'Civil Rights versus Sovereignty: Native American Women in Life and Land Struggles' in Alexander, J. and Mohanty, C.T. (eds) (1997) *Feminist Genealogies, Colonial Legacies, Democratic Futures* New York and London: Routledge, pp. 101–121

Gustafsson, G., Eduards, M. and Ronnblom, M. (1997) *Towards a New Democratic Order? Women's Organising in Sweden in the 1990s* Stockholm: Publica

Gutman, H. (1976) *The Black Family in Slavery and Freedom 1750–1925* New York: Pantheon Books

Guy-Sheftall, B. (ed.) (1995) *Words of Fire: An Anthology of African–American Feminist Thought* New York: The New Press

Haggis, J. (1990) 'Gendering Colonisalism or Colonising Gender: Recent Women's Studies Approaches to White Women and the History of British Colonialism' in *Women's Studies International Forum* 13(1/2)

Hague, R., Harrop, M. and Breslin, S. (1992) *Comparative Government and Politics: An Introduction* Basingstoke: Macmillan

Hales, G. (ed.) (1996) *Beyond Disability: Towards an Enabling Society* London: Sage Publications in association with the Open University

Hall, C. (1992) *White, Male and Middle Class: Explorations in Feminism and History* Cambridge: Polity Press

Hall, M. (1989) 'Private Experience in the Public Domain: Lesbians in Organizations' in Hearn, J., Sheppard, D., Tancred-Sheriff, P. and Burrell, G. (eds) *The Sexuality of Organisation* London: Sage, pp. 125–138

Hall, R.E. (1985) *Ask Any Woman: A London Inquiry into Rape and Sexual Assault* Report of the Women's Safety Survey conducted by Women Against Rape, Bristol: Falling Wall Press

Hall, S. (1995) 'The Whites of Their Eyes: Racist Ideology and the Media' in Dines, G. and Humez, J.M. (eds) *Gender, Race and Class in Media: A Text Reader* London: Sage, pp. 18–22

Hamner, J. and Maynard, M. (eds) (1987) *Women, Violence and Social Control* London: Macmillan

Haniff, N.Z. (1988) *Blaze a Fire: Significant Contributions of Caribbean Women* Toronto: Sister Vision

Hansard 187 (1867) J.S. Mill's *Representation of the People Bill* (20 May)

Harper, I.H. (1993) 'Personal Reactions of a Bosnian Woman to the War in Bosnia' *Feminist Review* 45, 102–107

Hart, S. (1997) 'Zero Tolerance of Violence Against Women' in Ang-Lygate, M. Corrin, C. and Henry, M. (eds) *Desperately Seeking Sisterhood: Still Challenging and Building* London: Taylor & Francis, pp. 95–105

Hartmann, H. (1979) 'The Unhappy Marriage of Marxism and Feminism: Towards a More Progressive Union' in *Capital and Class* 8

Hartsock, N. (1981) *Money, Sex and Power: An Essay on Domination and Community* New York: Longman

Havel, V. *et al.* (1985) *The Power of the Powerless* New York: Sharpe

Hayfield, A. (1995) 'Several Faces of Discrimination' in Mason-John, V. (ed.) *Talking Black: Lesbians of African and Asian Descent Speak Out* London: Cassell, pp. 186–206

Hearn, K. (1991) 'Disabled Lesbians and Gays are Here to Stay' in Kaufmann, T. and Lincoln, P. (eds) *High Risk Lives* Bridport: Prism Press

Heinen, J. (1995) 'Public/Private: Gender, Social and Political Citizenship in Eastern Europe' paper presented at the Second ESA Conference, Budapest, August/September

Heise, Lori L. (1995) 'Freedom Close to Home: The Impact of Violence Against Women on Reproductive Rights' in Peters, J. and Wolper, A. (eds) *Women's Rights, Human Rights: International Feminist Perspectives* New York and London: Routledge

Heise, Lori L., Raikes, A., Watts, C.H. and Zwi, A.B. (1994) 'Violence Against Women: A Neglected Public Health Issue in Less Developed Countries' *Social Science Medicine* 39(9), 1165–1179

Heitlinger, A. (1979) *Women and State Socialism: Sex Inequality in the Soviet Union and Czechoslovakia* London: Macmillan

Helsinki Citizens' Assembly (1992) *Reproductive Rights in East and Central Europe* Prague: hCa publications 3

Helsinki Citizens' Assembly (1993) *Violence against women in Central and Eastern Europe* Prague: hCa publications 8

Helsinki Citizens' Assembly (1994) *Ankara Report: Where does Europe end?* Prague: hCa publications

Henderson, S. and Mackay, A. (1990) *Grit and Diamonds: Women in Scotland Making History 1980–1990* Edinburgh: Stramullion Ltd and The Cauldron Collective 1990

Henry, M. (1993) *Portraits of Black Women Popular Culture* Glasgow: Centre for Women's Studies Seminar Series

Hirschmann, N. and Di Stefano, C. (eds) (1996) *Revisioning the Political: Feminist Reconstructions of Traditional Concepts in Western Political Theory* Boulder: Westview Press

Hoagland, S.L. (1988) *Lesbian Ethics: Toward New Value* Palo Alto, CA: Institute of Lesbian Studies

Hoagland, S.L. (1994) 'Why Lesbian Ethics?' in Card, C. (ed.) *Adventures in Lesbian Philosophy* Bloomington and Indianapolis: Indiana University Press, pp. 199–209

Hoagland, S. and Penelope, J. (eds) (1988) *For Lesbians Only: A Separatist Anthology* London: Onlywomen Press

Hoff, Joan (1994) 'Comparative Analysis of Abortion in Ireland, Poland and the United States' *Women's Studies International Forum* 621–646

hooks, b. (1982) *Ain't I a Woman? Black Women and Feminism* London: Pluto Press

hooks, b. (1984) *Feminist Theory from Margin to Centre* Boston: South End Press

hooks, b. (1989) *Talking Back: Thinking Feminist, Thinking Black* London: Sheba

hooks, b. (1991) *Yearning: Race, Gender and Cultural Politics* London: Turnaround

hooks, b. (1992a) 'Sisterhood: Political Solidarity Between Women' in Kourany, J., Sterba, J. and Tong, R. (eds) *Feminist Philosophies* Hemel Hempstead: Harvester Wheatsheaf

hooks, b. (1992b) *Black Looks: Race and Representation* London: Turnaround

hooks, b. (1994) *Teaching to Transgress: Education as the Practice of Freedom* New York and London: Routledge

hooks, b. (1998) *Wounds of Passion: A Writing Life* London: The Women's Press

Hoskyns, C. (1985) 'Women's Equality and the European Community – A Feminist Perspective' *Feminist Review* 20, 71–78

Hubbard, R. (1986) 'Eugenics and Prenatal Testing' *International Journal of Health Services* 16(2), 227–242

Hull, G., Bell, Scott, P. and Smith, B. (eds) (1982) *All The Women are White, All the Blacks Are Men, But Some of us Are Brave* New York: The Feminist Press

Human Rights Watch (1995) *The Human Rights Watch Global Report on Women's Human Rights* New York: Human Rights Watch

Humm, M. (ed.) (1989) *The Dictionary of Feminist Theory* London and New York: Harvester Wheatsheaf

Humm, M. (1992) *Feminisms: A Reader* Hemel Hempstead: Harvester Wheatsheaf

Humm, M. (1997) *Feminism and Film* Edinburgh: Edinburgh University Press

Hurtado, Aida (1989) 'Relating to Privilege: Seduction and Rejection in the Subordination of White Women and Women of Color' *Signs* 14(4), 833–855

Imam, A. (1997) 'The Dynamics of WINing: An Analysis of Women in Nigeria (WIN)' in Alexander, J. and Mohanty, C.T. (eds) *Feminist Genealogies, Colonial Legacies, Democratic Futures* New York and London: Routledge, pp. 280–307

Inter-Parliamentary Union (1997) *Men and Women in Politics: Democracy Still in the Making, A World Comparative Study* Geneva: IPU

International Organization for Migration (1995) *Trafficking and Prostitution: The Growing Exploitation of Migrant Women from Central and Eastern Europe* Budapest, Migration Information Programme

Jackson, S. (ed.) (1993) *Women's Studies: A Reader* Hemel Hempstead: Harvester Wheatsheaf

Jaggar, A. (1983) *Feminist Politics and Human Nature* Brighton: Harvester Press

Jay, K. (ed.) (1995) *Dyke Life: From Growing Up to Growing Old, A Celebration of the Lesbian Experience* London: Pandora

Jayawardena, K. (1986) *Feminism and Nationalism in the Third World* London and New Jersey: Zed Books

Jeffreys, S. (1985) *The Spinster and Her Enemies: Feminism and Sexuality 1880–1930* London: Pandora

Jeffreys, S. (1994) *The Lesbian Heresy: A Feminist Perspective on the Lesbian Sexual Revolution* London: The Women's Press

Jeffreys, S. (1997) *The Idea of Prostitution* Melbourne: Spinifex

Johnston, J. (1974) *Lesbian Nation: The Feminist Solution* New York: Simon and Schuster

Jordan, G. and Weedon, C. (1995) *Cultural Politics: Class, Gender, Race and the Postmodern World* Oxford: Blackwell Publishers

Jordan, J. (1994) 'Extracts from Interview with Pratibha Parmar' in Parmar, P. 'Other Kinds of Dreams' in Githens *et al.* (eds) (1994) *Different Roles, Different Voices: Women and Politics in the United States and Europe* New York: Harper Collins, pp. 259–264

Juillard, J.R. (1976) 'Women in France' in Iglitzen, L.B. and Ross, R. *Women in the World: A Comparative Study* Oxford: Clio

Kabeer, N. (1994) *Reversed Realities: Gender Hierarchies in Development Thought* London: Verso

262 Bibliography

Kabir, S. (1998) *Daughters of Desire: Lesbian Representations in Film* London and Washington: Cassell

Kaplan, G. (1992) *Contemporary Western European Feminism* London: UCL Press

Keane, J. (ed.) (1988) *Civil Society and the State* London: Verso

Keith, L. (1992) 'Who Cares Wins?' *Disability, Handicap and Society* 7(2)

Keith, L. (1996) 'Encounters with Strangers: The Public's Responses to Disabled Women and how this Affects our Sense of Self' in Morris, J. (ed.) *Encounters with Strangers: Feminism and Disability* London: The Women's Press, pp. 69–88

Keith, L. (ed.) (1994) *Mustn't Grumble: Writing by Disabled Women* London: The Women's Press

Kelly, L. (1988) *Surviving Sexual Violence* Cambridge: Polity Press

Kemp, S. and Squires, J. (eds) (1997) *Feminisms* Oxford and New York: Oxford University Press

Kennedy, M. (1996) 'Sexual Abuse and Disabled Children' in Morris, J. (ed.) *Encounters with Strangers: Feminism and Disability* London: The Women's Press, pp. 116–134

Kilcooley, A. (1997) 'Sexism, Sisterhood and some Dynamics of Racism: A Case in Point' in Ang-Lygate, M., Corrin, C., and Henry, M. (eds) *Desperately Seeking Sisterhood: Still Challenging and Building* London: Taylor & Francis, pp. 31–41

King, E. (1992) 'The Scottish Women's Suffrage Movement' in Breitenbach, E. and Gordon, E. (eds) (1992) *Out of Bounds: Women in Scottish Society 1800–1945* Edinburgh: Edinburgh University Press, pp. 121–150

Kishwar, M. and Vanita, R. (eds) (1984) *In Search of Answers* London: Zed Books

Kitzinger, J. (1995) *Interim Evaluation of Strathclyde Regional Council's Zero Tolerance Campaign* Glasgow: Glasgow University Media Group

Kitzinger, J. and Hunt, K. (1993) *Evaluation of Edinburgh District Council's Zero Tolerance Campaign* Glasgow: Glasgow University Media Group

Kitzinger, C. and Wilkinson, S. (1993) 'The Precariousness of Heterosexual Feminist Indentities' in Kennedy, M., Lubelska, C. and Walsh, V. *Making Connections: Women's Studies, Women's Movements and Women's Lives* London: Taylor & Francis, pp. 24–36

KOLA (1994) 'A Burden of Aloneness' in Epstein, D. (ed.) *Challenging Lesbian and Gay Inequalities in Education* Buckingham: Open University Press, pp. 49–64

Kollontai, A. (1977) *Selected Writings* (translated and ed. Alix Holt) London: Allison and Busby

Konrad, Gy. (1984) *Anti-Politics: An Essay* London: Quartet

Lamb, B. and Layzell, S. (1994) *Disabled in Britain: A World Apart* London: SCOPE

Lancaster, R.N. and Leonardo, M. di (eds) (1997) *The Gender Sexuality Reader: Culture, History, Political Economy* London: Routledge

Landry, D. and MacLean, G. (1993) *Materialist Feminism* Cambridge Mass.: Blackwell

Leach, B. (1996) 'Disabled People and the Equal Opportunities Movement' in Hales, G. (ed.) *Beyond Disability: Towards an Enabling Society* London: Sage Publications in association with the Open University, pp. 88–95

Leaman, D. (1996) 'Four Camels of Disability' in Hales, G. (ed.) *Beyond Disability: Towards an Enabling Society* London: Sage Publications in association with the Open University, pp. 164–9

Leeds Revolutionary Feminist Group (1981) *Love Your Enemy? The Debate Between Heterosexual Feminism and Political Lesbianism* London: Onlywomen Press

Leneman, L. (1995) *A Guid Cause: The Women's Suffrage Movement in Scotland* Edinburgh: The Mercat Press

Lesbian History Group (1989) *Not a Passing Phase: Reclaiming Lesbians in History 1840–1985* London: The Women's Press

Levine, P. (1987) *Victorian Feminism 1850–1900* London: Hutchinson

Lister, R. (1997) 'Citizenship: Pushing the Boundaries' *Feminist Review* 57, 83–111

Lopez, E.P. (1991) 'Francisca: A Testimony from a Woman Rural Trade Union Leader in Brazil' in Wallace, T. and March, C. (eds) *Changing Perceptions: Writings on Gender and Development* Oxford: Oxfam

Lorde, A. (1985) *The Cancer Journals* London: Sheba Feminist Publishers

Lorde, A. (1993) 'There is No Hierarchy of Oppressions' in Cleaver, R. and Myers, P. (eds) *A Certain Terror: Heterosexism, Militarism, Violence and Change* Chicago: Great Lakes Region American Friends Service Committee

Lorde, A. (1996) *The Audre Lorde Compendium: Essays, Speeches and Journals – The Cancer Journals 1980, Sister Outsider 1984, A Burst of Light 1988* introduced by Alice Walker, London: Pandora

Lovenduski, J. (1986) *Women and European Politics: Contemporary Feminism and Public Policy* Brighton: Harvester Wheatsheaf

Lovenduski, J. and Hills, J. (1981) *The Politics of the Second Electorate: Women and Public Participation* Boston: Routledge and Kegan Paul

Lubelska, C. and Matthews, J. (1997) 'Disability Issues in the Politics and Processes of Feminist Studies' in Ang-Lygate, M., Corrin, C. and Henry, M. *Desperately Seeking Sisterhood: Still Challenging and Building* London: Taylor & Francis, pp. 127–37

MacKinnon, C. (1982) 'Feminism, Marxism, Method and the State: An Agenda for Theory' *Signs* 7(3), 515–44

MacLeod, M. and Saraga, E. (1988) 'Challenging the Orthodoxy: Towards a Feminist Theory and Practice' *Feminist Review* 28

Magnani, R. (1992) 'Ruth Magnani' in Neild, S. and Pearson, R. (eds) *Women Like Us* London: The Women's Press, pp. 83–90

Malos, E. (ed.) (1980) *The Politics of Housework* London: Allison and Busby

Mama, A. (1989) 'Violence against Black Women: Race, Gender and State Responses' *Feminist Review* 32, 30–48

Mama, A. (1995) *Beyond the Masks: Race, Gender and Subjectivity* London: Routledge

Mama, A. (1997) 'Sheroes and Villains: Conceptualizing Colonial and Contemporary Violence Against Women in Africa' in Alexander, M.J. and Mohanty, C.T. (eds) *Feminist Genealogies, Colonial Legacies, Democratic Futures* New York and London: Routledge, pp. 46–62

Mamonova, T. (ed.) (1984) *Women and Russia: Feminist Writings from the Soviet Union* Boston: Beacon Press

Markowe, L. (1996) *Redefining The Self: Coming out as Lesbian* Cambridge: Polity Press

Marlatt, D. (1992) 'Changing the Focus' in Warland, B. (ed.) *Inversions: Writings by Dykes, Queers and Lesbians* London: Open Letters, pp. 127–34

Marshall, B. (1994) *Engendering Modernity: Feminism, Social Theory and Social Change* Cambridge: Polity Press

Martin, D. and Lyon, P. (1972) *Lesbian Woman* New York: Bantam Books

Mason-John, V. (ed.) (1995) *Talking Black: Lesbians of African and Asian Descent Speak Out* London: Cassell

Mathurin, L. (1974) 'A Historical Study of Women in Jamaica from 1655 to 1844' Ph.D. dissertation, University of the West Indies, Mona, Kingston, Jamaica

Matthews, J. and Thompson, L. (1993) 'Disability as a Focus for Innovation in Women's Studies and Access Strategies in Higher Education' in Kennedy, M., Lubelska, C. and Walsh, V. *Making Connections: Women's Studies, Women's Movements, Women's Lives* London: Taylor & Francis, pp. 130–41

Maynard, M. (1993) 'Violence Towards Women' in Richardson, D. and Robinson, V. *Introducing Women's Studies* Basingstoke and London: Macmillan Press, pp. 99–122

McDermid, J. (1997) *Women, War and Revolution* Dorset: Blackmore Limited for The Historical Association

McDowell, L. and Pringle, R. (eds) (1972) *Defining Women* Cambridge: Polity Press

McEwan, E. and O'Sullivan, S. (1988) *Out the Other Side: Lesbian Contemporary Writing* London: Virago

McIntosh, M. (1978) 'The State and the Oppression of Women' in Kuhn, A. and Wolpe, A.M. (eds) *Feminism and Materialism* London: Routledge and Kegan Paul, pp. 254–89

McIntosh, M. (1993) 'Queer Theory and the War of the Sexes' in Bristow, J. and Wilson, A. (eds) *Activating Theory: Lesbian, Gay and Bisexual Politics* London: Lawrence and Wishart, pp. 30–52

McLean, I. (1996) *Oxford Concise Dictionary of Politics* Oxford, New York: Oxford University Press

McNamara, J. (1996) 'Out of Order: Madness is a Feminist and a Disability Issue' in Morris, J. (ed.) *Encounters with Strangers: Feminism and Disability* London: The Women's Press, pp. 194–205

McQuiston, L. (1997) *Suffragettes to She-Devils: Women's Liberation and Beyond* London: Phaidon

Meekosha, H. and Dowse, L. (1997) 'Enabling Citizenship: Gender, Disability and Citizenship in Australia *Feminist Review* 57 pp. 49–72

Melucci, A. (1988) Social Movements and the Democratization of Everyday Life in Keane, J. (ed.) *Civil Society and the State* London and New York: Verso, pp. 245–260

Mertus, J. (1995) 'State Discriminatory Family Law and Customary Abuses' in Peters, J. and Wolper, A. (eds) (1995) *Women's Rights, Human Rights: International Feminist Perspectives* New York and London: Routledge

Midgley, C. (ed.) (1998) *Gender and Imperialism* Manchester: Manchester University Press

Mies, M. (1986) *Patriarchy and Accumulation on a World Scale: Women and the International Division of Labour* London: Zed Books

Miles, R. and Phizacklea, A. (eds) (1979) *Racism and Political Action in Britain* London: Routledge and Kegan Paul

Mill, J.S. (1975) *Three Essays* Oxford: Oxford University Press

Mill, J.S. (1983 [1869]) *On the Subjection of Women* issued with Harriet Taylor *The Enfranchisement of Women* [1851] London: Virago

Mill, J.S. (1998 [1869]) *On Liberty and Other Essays* edited by J. Gray, Oxford: Oxford University Press

Millett, K. (1970) *Sexual Politics* reprinted 1977 London: Virago

Millett, K. (1991) *The Loony Bin Trip* London: Virago

Minnesota Advocates for Human Rights (1995) *Lifting the Last Curtain: A Report on Domestic Violence in Romania* Minneapolis: Minnesota Advocates for Human Rights

Minnesota Advocates for Human Rights (1996) *Domestic Violence in Bulgaria* Minneapolis: Minnesota Advocates for Human Rights

Mirza, H. (1997) *Black British Feminism: A Reader* London and New York: Routledge

Mitchell, J. (1966) 'Women: the Longest Revolution' *New Left Review* 40, 11–37

Mitchell, J. (1971) *Woman's Estate* Harmondsworth: Penguin

Mitchell, J. (1974) *Psychoanalysis and Feminism* Harmondsworth: Penguin

Mitter, S. (1986) *Common Fate, Common Bond: Women in the Global Economy* London, New South Wales and New Hampshire: Pluto Press

Mladjenovic, L. and Matijasevic, D. (1996) 'SOS Belgrade July 1993–1995: Dirty Streets' in Corrin, C. (ed.) *Women in a Violent World: Feminist Analyses and Resistance across 'Europe'* Edinburgh: Edinburgh University Press, pp. 119–132

Modleski, T. (1991) *Feminism Without Women* London: Routledge

Mohammed, P. (1998) 'Rethinking Caribbean Difference' *Feminist Review* 59, 1–5

Mohanty, C.T. (1991) 'Cartographies of Struggle: Third World Women and the Politics of Feminism' in Mohanty, C.T., Russo, A. and Torres, L. (eds) *Third World Women and the Politics of Feminism* Bloomington and Indianapolis: Indiana University Press

Mohanty, C.T., Russo, A. and Torres, L. (eds) (1991) *Third World Women and the Politics of Feminism* Bloomington and Indianapolis: Indiana University Press

Monkhouse, J. (1980) *Sight in the Dark* London: Hodder and Stoughton

Moore, H.L. (1994) *A Passion for Difference: Essays in Anthropology and Gender* Cambridge: Polity Press

Moraga, C. and Anzaldua, G. (eds) (1983) *This Bridge Called my Back: Writings by Radical Women of Color* New York: Kitchen Table Press

Morgan, R. (ed.) (1970) *Sisterhood Is Powerful: An Anthology of Writing from the Women's Movement* New York: Vintage

Morgan, R. (ed.) (1984) *Sisterhood is Global: The International Women's Movement Anthology* London: Doubleday

Morgan, R. (1989) *The Demon Lover: On the Sexuality of Terrorism* New York and London: W.W. Norton and Co.

Morgan, S. (1988) *My Place* London: Virago

Morley, L. (1998) 'All You Need is Love: Feminist Pedagogy for Empowerment and Emotional Labour in the Academy' *International Journal of Inclusive Education* 2(1), 15–27

Morris, J. (1989) *Able Lives* London: The Women's Press

Morris, J. (1991) *Pride Against Prejudice: Transforming Attitudes in Disability* London: The Women's Press

Morris, J. (1993a) *Independent Lives? Community Care and Disabled People* Basingstoke: Macmillan

Morris, J. (1993b) 'Feminism and Disability' *Feminist Review* No. 43, pp. 57–70

Morris, J. (ed.) (1996) *Encounters with Strangers: Feminism and Disability* London: The Women's Press

Morrison, T. (1988) *Beloved* London: Picador

Neild, S. and Pearson, R. (eds) (1992) *Women Like Us* London: The Women's Press

Nelson, B.J. and Chowdhury, N. (eds) (1994) *Women and Politics Worldwide* New Haven and London: Yale University Press

New Internationalist (1985) *Women: A World Report* A New Internationalist Book London: Methuen. Also published (1987) Oxford: Oxford University Press

Nicholson, L. (ed.) (1990) *Feminism/Postmodernism* London: Routledge

Nie, N. and Verba, S. (1972) *Participation in America* New York: Harper and Row

Norris, P. (1985) 'Women's Legislative Participation in Western Europe' *West European Politics* 8(4), 90–101

Norris, P. (1986) *Politics and Sexual Equality* Brighton: Wheatsheaf Books

Nur, R. and A.R. (1996) 'Queering the State: Towards a Lesbian Movement in Malaysia' in Reinfelder, M. *Amazon to Zami: Towards a Global Lesbian Feminism* London: Cassell, pp. 70–85

Nye, A. (1988) *Feminist Theory and the Philosophies of Man* Kent: Croom Helm

Nye, (1990) *Words of Power: a Feminist Reading of the History of Logic* London: Routledge

O'Brien, M. (1981) *The Politics of Reproduction* London: Routledge and Kegan Paul

Oakley, A. (1986) *The Captured Womb: A History of Medicalization of Pregnant Women* Oxford: Blackwell

Offe, C. (1985) 'New Social Movements: Challenging the Boundaries of Institutional Politics', *Social Research* 52, (4), pp. 817–68

Oliver, M. (1990) *The Politics of Disablement* London: Macmillan

Paine in *The Writings of Tom Paine* vol. 1 (collected and ed. by M.D. Conway) New York and London: Putnam

Parsons, S. (1992) 'Feminism and the Logic of Morality: A Consideration of Alternatives' in Fraser, E., Hornsby, J. and Lovibond, S. (eds) *Ethics: A Feminist Reader* Oxford: Blackwell, pp. 380–412

Patel, P. (1990) 'Southall Boys' in *Against The Grain: A Celebration of Survival and Struggle, Southall Black Sisters 1979–1989* Southall, Middlesex: Southall Black Sisters, pp. 43–54

Pateman, C. (1988) *The Sexual Contract* Cambridge: Polity Press

Pateman, C. (1989) *The Disorder of Women* Cambridge: Polity Press

Patton, C. (1993) 'From Nation to Family: Containing African AIDS' in Abelove, H., Barale, M. and Halperin, D. (eds) *The Lesbian and Gay Studies Reader* London: Routledge, pp. 127–140

Petchesky, R. and Judd, K. (eds) (1998) *Negotiating Reproductive Rights: Women's Perspectives Across Countries and Cultures* London and New York: Zed Books

Peters, J. and Wolper, A. (eds) (1995) *Women's Rights, Human Rights: International Feminist Perspectives* New York and London: Routledge

Phillips, A. (1987) *Feminism and Equality* Oxford: Basil Blackwell

Phillips, A. (1991) *Engendering Democracy* Cambridge: Polity Press

Phillips, A. (1993) *Democracy and Difference* Cambridge: Polity Press

Pietila, H. and Vickers, J. (1990) *Making Women Matter: The Role of the United Nations* London: Zed Books

Pilkington, H. (ed.) (1996) *Gender, Generation and Identity in Contemporary Russia* New York and London: Routledge

Plummer, K. (ed.) (1992) *Modern Homosexualities* London: Routledge

Polish Committee of NGOs (1995) *The Situation of women in Poland: The Report of the NGOs Committee Polish Committee of NGOs Beijing 1995,* Warsaw

Popular Education Research Group (1995) 'Talking Feminist Popular Education' in Miranda Davies (ed.) *Women and Violence* London: Zed Books, pp. 223–225

Posadskaya, A. (ed.) (1994) *Women in Russia: A New Era in Russian Feminism* New York and London: Verso

Power, L. (1995) *No Bath but Plenty of Bubbles: An Oral History of the Gay Liberation Front 1970–73* London: Cassell, pp. 167–175

Radford, J. and Russell, D.E.H. (eds) (1992) *Femicide: The Politics of Woman Killing* Buckingham: Open University Press

Ramelson, M. (1967) *The Petticoat Rebellion: A Century of Struggle for Women's Rights* London: Lawrence and Wishart

Randall, V. (1987) *Women and Politics: An International Perspective* Basingstoke: Macmillan 2nd edition 1994

Ratti, Rakesh (ed.) (1993) *A Lotus of Another Color: An Unfolding of the South Asian Gay and Lesbian Experience* Boston: Alyson Publications

Reagon, B.J. (1983) 'Coalition Politics – Turning the Century' in Barbara Smith (ed.) *Home Girls – A Black Feminist Anthology* New York: Kitchen Table Press, pp. 356–368

Reinfelder, M. (ed.) (1996) *Amazon to Zami: Towards a Global Lesbian Feminism* London, Cassell

Rendall, J. (1985) *The Origins of Modern Feminism: Women in Britain, France and the United States 1780–1860* London: Macmillan

Renne, T. (ed.) (1997) *Ana's Land: Sisterhood in Eastern Europe* New York: Westview Press

Ricardo, D. (1817) 'Problems of Political Economy and Taxation' in Ellis, W. (1984) *The Classical Theory of Economic Growth* Basingstoke: Macmillan

Rich, A. (1981) *Compulsory Heterosexuality and Lesbian Existence* London: Onlywomen Press; first published in *Signs: Journal of Women in Culture*

and Society 1980, 5(4) University of Chicago, pp. 631–660; also
published by Onlywomen Press, London (1981)

Rich, A. (1986 [1977]) *Of Woman Born: Motherhood as Experience and
Institution* London: Virago Press

Rich, A. (1986) *Blood, Bread and Poetry* New York: W.W. Norton

Rich, A. (1993) 'The Distance Between Language and Violence' in
Rich, A. *What is found there: Notebooks on Poetry and Politics* London:
Virago Press, pp. 181–189

Rich, A. (ed.) (1993) *What is found there: Notebooks on Poetry and Politics*
London: Virago Press

Richardson, D. (1989) *Women and the AIDS Crisis* London, Pandora

Richardson, D. (1992) 'Constructing Lesbian Sexualities' in Plummer,
K. (ed.) *Modern Homosexualities* London: Routledge

Richardson, D. and Robinson, V. (eds) (1993) *Introducing Women's
Studies* Basingstoke and London: Macmillan Press

Ridd, R. and Calloway, H. (eds) (1986) *Caught up in the Conflict:
Women's Responses to Political Strife* London: Macmillan

Riley, D. (1988) *Am I That Name?* London: Macmillan

Rosen, R. (1990) 'Women and Democracy in Czechoslovakia: An
Interview with Jirina Siklova' *Peace and Democracy News* Fall

Rosenbloom, R. (ed.) (1995) *Unspoken Rules: Sexual Orientation and
Women's Human Rights* New York: International Lesbian and Gay
Human Rights Commission

Rossi, A. (ed.) (1974) *The Feminist Papers: From Adams to de Beauvoir* New
York and London: Columbia University Press

Rothman, B.K. (1989) *The Tentative Pregnancy: Prenatal Diagnosis and the
Future of Motherhood* London: Unwin and Hyman

Rowbotham, S. (1972) *Women, Resistance and Revolution* Harmondsworth:
Penguin

Rowbotham, S. (1973) *Hidden from History* London: Pluto

Rowbotham, S. (1992) *Women in Movement: Feminism and Social Action*
London: Routledge

Rowbotham, S. and Mitter, S. (eds) (1994) *Dignity and Daily Bread: New
Forms of Economic Organising Among Poor Women in the Third World and
the First* London and New York: Routledge

Rowlands, J. (1997) *Questioning Empowerment: Working with Women in
Honduras* Oxford: Oxfam

Russo, A. (1991) ' "We Cannot Live Without Our Lives": White Women,
Antiracism, and Feminism' in Mohanty *et al.*, pp. 297–313

Saadawi, N. el (1980) *The Hidden Face of Eve* London: Zed Books

Saadawi, N. el (1990) Interview in *Spare Rib*, London: Spare Rib
Collective, p. 23

Said, E. (1979) *Orientalism* New York: Vintage Books

Sahgal, G. and Yuval-Davis, N. (eds) (1992) *Refusing Holy Orders: Women and Fundamentalism in Britain* London: Virago

Saraga, E. (ed.) (1998) *Embodying the Social: Constructions of Difference* London and New York: Routledge

Schneider, B. (1984) 'Peril and Promise: Lesbians' Workplace Participation' in Nardi, P. and Schneider, B. (eds) (1998) *Social Perspectives in Lesbian and Gay Studies* London: Routledge, pp. 377–389

Scott, A. (1990) *Ideology and the New Social Movements* London: Unwin Hyman

Scott, H. (1974) *Does Socialism Liberate Women?* Boston: Beacon Press

Scott, J. (1993) 'The Woman Worker' in Fraisse, G. and Perrot, M. (eds) *A History of Women in the West: IV Emerging Feminism from Revolution to War* Cambridge Mass. and London: Harvard University Press, pp. 399–426

Sen, G., and Grown, C. (1987) *Development, Crises and Alternative Visions: Third World Women's Perspectives* New York: Monthly Review Press

Shakespeare, T., Gillespie-Sells, K. and Davies, D. (1996) *The Sexual Politics of Disability: Untold Desires* London: Cassell

Shanley, M.L. and Narayan, U. (eds) (1997) *Reconstructing Political Theory: Feminist Perspectives* Cambridge: Polity Press

Sharp, S. (1993) *Black Women for Beginners* London: Airlift Book Company

Shiva, V. (1988) *Staying Alive: Women, Ecology and Development* London: Zed Press

Shulman, A.K. (1996) *Red Emma Speaks: An Emma Goldman Reader* 3rd edn, New Jersey: Humanities Press

Siddiqui, H. (1996) 'Domestic Violence in Asian Communities: The Experience of Southall Black Sisters' in Corrin, C. (ed.) *Women in a Violent World: Feminist Analyses and Resistance Across 'Europe'*, pp. 94–105

Sidney, A. and Love, B. (1972) *Saphho was a Right-On Woman: A Liberated View of Lesbianism* New York: Stein and Day Publishers

Sillard, K. (1995) 'Helping Women to Help Themselves: Counselling Against Domestic Violence in Australia' in Davies, M. (ed.) *Women and Violence* London: Zed Press, pp. 239–245

Silvera, M. (Anthologised by) (1991) *Piece of my Heart: A Lesbian of Colour Anthology* Toronto: Sister Vision Press

Simmonds, F.N. (1997) 'Who are the Sisters? Difference, Feminism and Friendship' in Ang-Lygate, M., Corrin, C., and Henry, M. (1997) *Desperately Seeking Sisterhood: Still Challenging and Building* London: Taylor & Francis, pp. 19–30

Sivanandan, A. (1982) *A Different Hunger: Writings on Black Resistance* London: Pluto Press

Skocpol, T. (1979) *States and Social Revolutions: A Comparative Analysis of France, Russia and China* Cambridge: Cambridge University Press

Smart, C. (1984) *The Ties that Bind: Law, Marriage and the Reproduction of Patriarchal Relations* London: Routledge and Kegan Paul

Smart, C. (1989) *Feminism and the Power of Law* London: Routledge

Smith, B. (1993) (first published in 1982) 'Homophobia: Why Bring it up?' in Abelove, H., Barale, M. and Halperin, D. (eds) *The Lesbian and Gay Studies Reader* London: Routledge, pp. 99–102

Smith, B. (ed.) (1983) *Home Girls: A Black Feminist Anthology* New York: Kitchen Table: Women of Color Press

Smyth, A. (ed.) (1992) *The Abortion Papers* Ireland: Dublin Attic Press

Smyth, A. (1995) 'States of Change: Reflections on Ireland in Several Uncertain Parts' in *Feminist Review*, 50

Smyth, C. (1992) *Lesbians Talk Queer Notions* London: Scarlet Press

Soper, K. and Sapiro, V. (1992)

Southall Black Sisters (1990) *Against The Grain: A Celebration of Survival and Struggle, Southall Black Sisters 1979–1989* London: Southall Black Sisters

Southall Black Sisters (1995) *A Stark Choice: Domestic Violence or Deportation? Abolish the One Year Rule!* London: Southall Black Sisters

Spelman, E. (1988) *Inessential Woman: Problems of Exclusion in Feminist Thought* Boston Mass.: Beacon Press

Spender, D. (1980) *Man Made Language* London: Routledge and Kegan Paul

Spender, D. (1983) *Women of Ideas (and What Men have Done to Them)* London: Pandora

Spender, D. (1985) *For the Record: The Making and Meaning of Feminist Knowledge* London: The Women's Press

Stacey, J. (1991) 'Promoting Normality: Section 28 and the Regulation of Sexuality' in Franklin, S., Lury, C. and Stacey, J. (eds) *Off Centre: Feminism and Cultural Studies* London: Unwin Hyman

Stacey, J. (1993) 'Untangling Feminist Theory' in Richardson, D. and Robinson V. (eds) *Introducing Women's Studies* Basingstoke and London: Macmillan Press, pp. 49–73

Stanley, L. and Wise, S. (1983) *Breaking Out: Feminist Consciousness and Feminist Research* London: Routledge and Kegan Paul

Stanley, L. and Wise, S. (1990) 'Method, Methodology and Epistomology in Feminist Research Processes', in Stanley, L. (ed.) *Feminist Praxis: Research, Theory and Research Processes* London and New York: Routledge, pp. 20–60

Stark, A. (1997) 'Combating the Backlash: How Swedish Women Won the War' in Oakley, A. and Mitchell, J. *Who's Afraid of feminism? Seeing Through the Backlash* London: Hamish Hamilton, pp. 224–244

Stein, E. (1992) *Forms of Desire: Sexual Orientation and the Social Constructionist Controversy* London and New York: Routledge

Stoler, A.L. (1997) 'Carnal Knowledge and Imperial Power' in Lancaster, R.N. and Leonardo, M. di (eds) *The Gender Sexuality Reader: Culture, History, Political Economy* London: Routledge, pp. 13–36

Stoller, N. (1998) 'Lesbian Involvement in the AIDS Epidemic: Changing Roles and Generational Differences' in Nardi, P. and Schneider, B. (eds) *Social Perspectives in Lesbian and Gay Studies* London: Routledge, pp. 366–376

Swain, J., Finkelstein, V., French, S. and Oliver, M. (1993) *Disabling Barriers – Enabling Environments* London: Sage Publications in association with the Open University

Szalai (1994) 'Women and Democratization: Some Notes on Recent Changes in Hungary' Budapest: unpublished paper

Tatchell, P. (1990) *Out in Europe: A Guide to Lesbian and Gay Rights in 30 European Countries* London and Glasgow: Broadcasting Support Services Channel 4 Television

Tatur, M. (1992) 'Why is there no Women's Movement in Eastern Europe?' in Lewis, P. (ed.) (1992) *Democracy and Civil Society in Eastern Europe* London: Macmillan

Tax, M. (1980) *The Rising of the Women* New York: Monthly Review Press

Taylor, B. (1983) *Eve and the New Jerusalem* London: Virago

Taylor, V. and Whittier, N. (1998) 'Collective Identity in Social Movement Communities: Lesbian Feminist Mobilization' in Nardi, P. and Schneider, B. (eds) *Social Perspectives in Lesbian and Gay Studies* London: Routledge, pp. 349–365

Thadani, G. (1996) 'Jami or Lesbian?' in Reinfelder, M. (ed.) *Amazon to Zami: Towards a Global Lesbian Feminism* London: Cassell, pp. 56–69

Thomis, M.I. and Grimmett, J. (1982) *Women in Protest 1800–1850* London: Croom Helm

Thompson, W. (1983 [1825]) *Appeal of One-Half of the Human Race, Women, Against the Pretensions of the Other Half, Men, to Retain Them in Political, and hence in Civil and Domestic, Slavery* London: Virago

Thornburgh, D. (1990) 'The promise of the Americans with Disabilities Act'. Speech at the Office of Personnel Management Eighth Annual Government-wide Conference on the Employment of Persons with Disabilities, Library 7, Rights and Legislation, Disabilities Forum, Compuserve.

Threlfall, M. (1985) 'The Women's Movement in Spain' *New Left Review* 151, 44–73

Torres, S. (1993) 'Television/Feminism: Heartbeat and Prime Time Lesbianism' in Abelove, H., Barale, M. and Halperin, D. (eds) *The Lesbian and Gay Studies Reader* London: Routledge, pp. 176–185

Tremain, S. (ed.) (1996) *Pushing the Limits: Disabled Dykes Produce Culture* Canada: Women's Press

Tuana, N. (1993) *The Less Noble Sex: Scientific, Religious and Philosophical Conceptions of Women's Nature* Bloomington: Indiana University Press

Tucker, R.C. (ed.) (1978) *The Marx–Engels Reader* 2nd edn New York: W.W. Norton

Tyler, A.F. (1973) 'The Rights of Women' in Welter, B. (ed.) *The Woman Question in American History* New York: Hinsdale

UNDP (1998) *Human Development Report* New York, UNDP

Union of the Physically Impaired Against Segregation (1981) *Disability Challenge* No. 1, May

United Nations (1997) *The Progress of Nations: The Nations of the World Ranked According to Their Achievements in Child Health, Nutrition, Education, Water and Sanitation, and Progress for Women* New York: United Nations Children's Fund (UNICEF)

UPIAS (1981) 'Editorial' in *Disability Challenge* 1 May

United Nations Security Council (1994) *Final Report of the Commission of Experts Established Pursuant to Security Council Resolution 780 (1992)* Geneva

Ussher, J. (1994) 'Women and Madness: A Voice in the Dark of Women's Despair' *Feminism and Psychology* 4(2), 288–292

Vasey, S. (1996) 'The Experience of Care' in Hales, G. (ed.) *Beyond Disability: Towards an Enabling Society* London: Sage Publications in association with the Open University, pp. 88–95

Vernon, A. (1996) 'A Stranger in Many Camps: The Experience of Disabled Black and Ethnic Minority Women' in Morris, J. (ed.) *Encounters with Strangers: Feminism and Disability* London: The Women's Press, pp. 48–68

Vogel, L. (1983) *Marxism and the Oppression of Women: Toward a Unitary Theory* London: Pluto Press

Wahad, D.B., Mumia, A.-J. and Assata, S. (1993) *Still Black, Still Strong: Survivors of the U.S. War Against Black Revolutionaries* New York: Semiotext(e)

Walby, S. (1990) *Theorizing Patriarchy* Oxford: Blackwell

Walkowitz, J. (1980) *Prostitution and Victorian Society: Women, Class and the State* New York: Cambridge University Press

Walkowitz, J. (1993) 'Dangerous Sexualities' in Fraisse, G. and Perrot, M. (eds) *A History of Women in the West: IV Emerging Feminism from Revolution to War* Cambridge and London: Harvard University Press, pp. 369–398

Wallace, M. (1979) *Black Macho and the Myth of the Superwoman* London: Calder

Wallace, T. (with C. March) (ed.) (1991) *Changing Perceptions: Writings on Gender and Development* Oxford: Oxfam

Waters, E. (1989) 'Restructuring the "Woman Question"' *Feminist Review* 33 (Autumn), pp. 3–19

Watkins, S.A., Rueda, M. and Rodriguez, M. (1992) *Feminism for Beginners* Cambridge: Icon Books Ltd.

Waylen, G. (1996) *Gender in Third World Politics* Buckingham: Open University Press

Weedon, C. (1987) *Feminist Practice and Poststructuralist Theory* Oxford: Blackwell

Weeks, J. (1989 [1981]) *Sex, Politics and Society: The Regulation of Sexuality since 1800* 2nd edn London and New York: Longman

Welter, B. (ed.) (1973) *The Woman Question in American History* New York: Hinsdale

White, C.P. (1989) 'On Promissory Notes' in Kruks, S., Rayna, R. and Young, M.B. (eds) *Promissory Notes: Women in the Transition to Socialism* New York: Monthly Review Press, pp. 345–353

Williams, R. (1981) *Culture* Cambridge: Fontana

Wilton, T. (1995) *Lesbian Studies: Setting An Agenda* London and New York: Routledge

Wingfield, R. (1996) 'Fundamental Questions: From Southall to Beijing' *Trouble and Strife* 32, p. 61

Wollstonecraft, Mary (1992 [1792]) *A Vindication of the Rights of Woman* (edited with an introduction by Miriam Brody) London: Penguin Books

Women in Black (1996) *Yearbook* Belgrade: Women in Black

Women in Black (1997) *Yearbook* Belgrade: Women in Black

World Health Organisation (1985) *Disability Policy Report* Geneva: WHO

Yeatman, A. (1997) 'Feminism and Power' in Shanley, M.L. and Narayan, U. (eds) (1997) *Reconstructing Political Theory: Feminist Perspectives* Oxford: Polity Press

Yuval-Davis, N. (1997) *Gender and Nation* London: Sage

Yuval-Davis, N. and Anthias, F. (1989) *Women-Nation-State* London: Macmillan Press

Yuval-Davis, N., Ward, A. and Gregory, J. (1992) *Women and Citizenship in Europe: borders, rights, duties* London: Zed Books and European Forum of Left Feminists

Zajovic, S. (1992) 'Patriarchy, language and national myth: The war and women in Serbia' *Peace News* March p. 7

Zinn, M.B. and Dill, B.T. (eds) (1994) *Women of Color in US Society* New York: Temple University Press

Index